Zulu: 1879

Beresford partly lifted, partly hustled the man into the saddle (p. 197)

Zulu: 1879

the Anglo-Zulu War of 1879
from Contemporary Sources:
First Hand Accounts, Interviews,
Letters, Despatches, Official Documents
& Newspaper Reports

Compiled by

D. C. F. Moodie
& the Leonaur Editors

LEONAUR

Zulu: 1879 the Anglo-Zulu War of 1879 from Contemporary Sources:
First Hand Accounts, Interviews, Letters, Despatches,
Official Documents & Newspaper Reports

Compiled by
D. C. F. Moodie
& the Leonaur Editors

Published by Leonaur Ltd

First Edition

Copyright © 2006 Leonaur Ltd

ISBN (10 digit): 1-84677-051-3 (hardcover)
ISBN (13 digit): 978-1-84677-051-7 (hardcover)

ISBN (10 digit): 1-84677-044-0 (softcover)
ISBN (13 digit): 978-1-84677-044-9 (softcover)

http://www.leonaur.com

Publisher's Notes

In the interests of authenticity, the spellings, grammar and place names
used have been retained from the original editions or, where appropriate,
made common for the sake of clarity.

The opinions of the authors represent a view of events in which he
was a participant related from his own perspective,
as such the text is relevant as an historical document.

The views expressed in this book are not necessarily
those of the publisher.

Contents

Introduction

The Anglo-Zulu War of 1879 was a pivotal event in the history of the expansion of the British Empire.

It was a short war as wars go, but was traumatic for the British, who, as the world's greatest military power, had become unaccustomed to setbacks and defeats, especially when dealing with an enemy they viewed as savage, uncivilized and generally inferior. As a martial race the Zulus were well versed in the art of warfare, but they should not have stood a chance against the might and technological superiority of the British Empire. Despite this, and armed with little more than tremendous courage and native weapons, the Zulus, under the leadership of their inspirational king, Cetywayo, inflicted serious defeats on the British before finally succumbing.

This was a war that caught the imagination of the reading public around the world, it was reported in depth by newspapers and journals both in Britain and the colonies.

The book you are holding, *Zulu: 1879*, has been compiled from contemporary sources including press reports, interviews, official reports and first hand accounts, all written as the war progressed. Much of the compilation is the work of D. C. F. Moodie, a 19th century journalist who was born in Cape Town in 1838. First published soon after the end of the war in 1879 as part of a larger work entitled *History of the Battles and Adventures of the British, the Boers and the Zulus* it was, in effect, an instant history, a concept which, in the 21st century, we are well accustomed to, but which in those days was pioneering.

As was frequently the case with 19th century books, little attention was given to making the presentation of Moodie's text accessible and readable. Page followed page of dense type, often without paragraph breaks or anything to indicate a change of scene or a change of voice. So it was that newspaper reports ran into first hand accounts and then into official reports, with only the briefest of hints from Moodie.

For *Zulu: 1879* the editors of Leonaur decided to revisit Moodie's work and present it in a way that is more immediate for modern readers. Where Moodie added substantial comments of his own they are presented in a slightly smaller type size between horizontal rules; individual reports and accounts have been separated with pertinent headlines drawn from Moodie's attributions. A number of pages describing the lying in state and funeral of the Prince Imperial (who was, after all, a bit player in this drama), the European reaction to his death and the general sense of grief, have been removed as irrelevant to a military history. Moodie's verbose and often impenetrable closing essay, which did little but summarise what his actual selections do so admirably, has also been removed.

We have taken the decision to add to Moodie's selections three hard to find, eye-witness accounts of noteworthy events, which although written a few years after most of the reports in this book do, we feel, add to the whole. Two of these were written by a noted British officer of the day and the other by a respected journalist; they were published originally in Pearson's Magazine in the 1890s. We reprint them here with some of the fine original illustrations by R. Caton Woodville and Stanley L. Wood. As a bonus we have also included in this volume 'Facing the Zulus' by Harry O'Clery, one of the fourteen first hand accounts by British soldiers serving during Queen Victoria's reign that can be found in the Leonaur book *Tommy Atkins' War Stories*.

In taking these liberties we believe we have created in *Zulu: 1879* a book that is exciting, informative, moving and entirely relevant to the modern reader. We hope you agree with us.

The Editors
Leonaur Ltd

The Zulu War

The Zulu War

As to the cause of the Zulu War of 1879, and our right in entering upon it, I propose (avoiding Sir Bartle Frere's long list of reasons) to give some extracts from a paper by Mr. Brownlee, the Secretary for Native Affairs in the Cape Colony, as the very best authority on the subject. Mr. Brownlee spoke various Kaffir languages like a native, and he loved the natives as much as they loved and respected him. This officer (says the Natal Mercury), it must be remembered, was here in Dingaan's time, and met that monarch. He has been identified with native affairs in South Africa for forty years, and his opinion, therefore, is sustained by an unequalled experience. He at any rate has no doubt as to the necessity of action rather than persuasion.

FROM MR BROWNLEE'S PAPER

No sooner had he (Cetywayo) obtained our formal recognition of his position, amid the thunder of artillery and the sound of trumpets, and no sooner had Mr. Shepstone turned his back upon Zululand, than the Zulu King cast his engagements to the winds, murders were committed, and the mission stations which had been befriended during his father's lifetime were so persecuted and tormented that the converts were scattered, and no missionary is now in Zululand. With such a King no promise is sacred, and no conditions binding.

While professing friendship to us, Cetywayo's support and countenance are found on the side of our enemies. Between Moshesh and Pande friendly relationships had long existed. Shortly after the surrender of Langalibalele to us by Molapo, Moshesh's second son in rank, Molapo, as in the days of his father, and the days of Cetywayo's father, sent an embassy to Cetywayo, to condole with him on the death of Pande, and to congratulate him on his succession to the Zulu sovereignty.

Molapo's messengers were not permitted to approach Cetywayo. He directed that they should be driven back with indignity from the borders of Zululand, from whence their advance commenced, and they were directed to inform Molapo that he had made himself a traitor to the colored race by surrendering Langalibalele to the white men, and that for this act Cetywayo would be avenged upon him. This was about a year after his installation by us, and while he was professing the greatest friendship towards us. The falsehood of the Zulu King with regard to the Utrecht land question, is quite on a par with his other actions.

In conclusion, I may remark that Cetywayo's hand has been clearly traced in our recent troubles on the Cape frontier as well as in the Transvaal.

In July or August, 1877, Umqikela wrote to the High Commissioner expressing his willingness to obey the decision of His Excellency in regard to the surrender of the murderers in the matter of Somfuland; at the same time Sekukuni was cheerfully paying his war indemnity to the Transvaal Government. Cetywayo, however, appears upon the scene, and matters are changed. To Umqikela a deputation is sent, and from information received it appears that the mission was for the establishment of friendly relations with the Pondos, with a promise of aid from Cetywayo in case the Pondos should come into conflict with us, and it was further reported that the Pondos had been urged to comply with none of our demands.

After the deputation had been in Pondoland for about three months, Umqikela, having reported nothing to us regarding Cetywayo's messages, I, by direction of the High Commissioner, wrote to Umqikela to inform him of what we had heard, expressing surprise that he should receive such overtures from the Zulus, who till our intervention had destroyed the Pondos, and would do so again did we permit it. Umqikela denied that Cetywayo had sent any overtures hostile to us, but that Cetywayo's messengers had simply been sent to beg for dogs and skins.

This may have been the pretext, but it is by no means likely that it was the true object of the mission, which was prolonged for three or four months. At any rate, during the stay of Cetywayo's messenger, Umqikela, notwithstanding the promise contained in his letter to the High Commissioner, absolutely refused to surrender the murderers who had fled from justice, and who were then in his country. At the same time Kreli, who had personally been opposed to taking up arms against the Government, suddenly changed his policy, and had the war paint placed upon his forehead, for it was said the Zulus were coming to aid the Kaffirs, and to within a very recent period the Gcalekas and Gaikas hoped to obtain aid from this source.

In the Transvaal at the same time the same influences were visible. As has already been remarked, Sekuktini was cheerfully paying his war indemnity, but having received a deputation from Cetywayo with the present of 100 oxen, Sekukuni suddenly changed his course of action, the payment of his war indemnity ceased, and from thence began the troubles which have led to the present position in the Transvaal, and for this Cetywayo is directly responsible.

Whether or not he may be regarded as being directly responsible for our troubles in Griqualand West is not clear, but there is no doubt that whether by Cetywayo's sanction or not, the tribes in Griqualand West counted on the support of the Zulus before they took up arms against the Government.

At present the Zulus are a standing menace to us; their influence is felt by the tribes from the Zambesi to the mouth of the Orange River; and so long as they are in a position to exercise this influence, the peace of the tribes around us and in our midst rests on a most unstable foundation.

No treaty or obligation can be binding on such a perfidious race as the Zulus, ruled by a treacherous and bloodthirsty sovereign like Cetywayo. Our future safety, as well as the voice of humanity, demand that the power of the Zulus should be broken, and that the innocent blood which is daily shed upon our borders should cease to flow.

The only guarantee which we can have for the securing of peace, short of breaking up the Zulu power, is the maintenance of so large a force on their front as the Imperial Government could not keep up, or South Africa maintain. We have now such a force at our disposal; we shall never again have it. In its presence Cetywayo may promise to abide by any conditions we may name, with the full determination of breaking through them as soon as our forces are withdrawn; and should we withdraw without breaking up the power of Cetywayo, our position in South Africa will be worse than ever it has been before. Cetywayo's high prestige will be raised still higher. It will be imagined that we have raised a large force to attack him, and then feared to do so, and the effect upon him will be to make him more overbearing than ever.

Even though the peace of South Africa were not endangered by the attitude of the Zulus, even though we ourselves were not in jeopardy, we have a right to interfere; that right has not been sought by us; the Zulus voluntarily and publicly applied for it; they acknowledged their subordination to us when they solicited the installation of their king by us; we accepted the position. To gain their ends they agreed to certain stipulations, with the determination to observe none of them. This does not alter our position; and leaving out of the question the other points at issue between us and the Zulus, we have full right to insist on the strictest fulfilment of the obligations undertaken, and which were the price paid for our support and countenance, and to enforce them, if need be, by the sword.

The time has arrived for decisive action; we shall never again have so favorable an opportunity as the present; if it is lost, sooner or later we shall be taken at a disadvantage.

These extracts are long (says the Natal Mercury), but emanating from such a source they are convincing, and may well be advanced in answer to the plea that moral means only should have been resorted to. If such methods could have reasonably been expected to be successful, then it would have been Sir Bartle Frere's bounden duty to have adopted them. But there was not the slightest ground for belief that under the altered circumstances of the time they would have been any longer efficacious. Under the bland influence of Sir Henry Bulwer's unguents, the Zulu power has become what it is, and Cetywayo's attitude has grown more menacing than ever. The Zulus' spears had to be "washed," and the king has now shown how thoroughly in earnest he was when two years ago he announced hi» determination to sanction that process.

FROM ONE OF SIR BARTLE FREER'S DESPATCHES TO THE IMPERIAL GOVERNMENT

It is no exaggeration to say that his (Cetywayo's) history from the first has been written in characters of blood. I do not refer merely to the long chronicle of his butcheries -- from the slaughter of his brothers and their followers, early in his career, down to the more recent indiscriminate and wholesale destruction of all the unmarried women who attempted to evade his orders, given in a sudden fit of caprice, that they should accept as husbands the elderly unmarried soldiers of his army, the massacre being subsequently extended to all the relatives who took away for burial the exposed corpses of the slaughtered women -- but I would take his character from his own account of himself; it was sent little more than two years ago to the Lieutenant-Governor of Natal, who, on hearing of the massacre of the girls, wrote to remind him of what had very recently passed between him and the representative of the Natal Government, Sir T. Shepstone, in the way of promises of more merciful rule, on the occasion of his installation as king, expressing a hope that the Lieutenant-Governor might learn from him that the reports which had reached him were incorrect. Cetywayo replied: 'Did I ever tell Shepstone? Did he tell the white people I made such an arrangement? Because, if he did, he has deceived them. I do kill, but do not consider yet I have done anything in the way of killing. Why do the white people start at nothing? I have not yet begun. I have yet to kill; it is the custom of our nation, and I shall not depart from it. Why does the Governor of Natal speak to me about my laws? Do I go to Natal and dictate to him about his laws? I shall not agree to any laws or rules from Natal, and by so doing throw the great kraal which I govern into the water. My people will not listen unless they are killed; and, while wishing to be friends with the English, I do not agree to give over my people to be governed by laws sent to me by them. Have I not asked the English Government to allow me to wash my spears, since the death of my father Um Pande, and they have kept playing with me all this time, and treating me like a child. I go back and tell the English that I shall now act on my own account, and if they wish me to agree to their laws I shall leave and become a wanderer; but before I go it will be seen that I shall not go without having acted. Go back and tell the white man this, and let them hear it well. The Governor of Natal and I are equal. He is Governor of Natal and I am Governor here.'

Despatch to the Earl of Carnarvon
from Sir T. Shepstone,
Administrator of the Transvaal
Utrecht, Transvaal, January 5, 1878

My Lord -- In pursuance of the intention expressed in the last paragraph of my despatch on the 2nd instant, I have the honor to transmit to your Lordship the statement made by the messengers last sent by me to the Zulu King, and to whose mission that despatch had reference.

2. There are several portions of this statement which afford considerable insight into the internal condition of Zululand, when considered in connection with surrounding circumstances, past and present, and the information that is continually reaching me of what is occurring among the Zulu people.

3. But to fully understand the subject it is necessary first to state shortly the nature of the Zulu organization, its origin and objects; and this will compel a consideration of the question, how far the existence of such an organization in such a position, under the changed circumstances of the surrounding countries, can be, or can be made to be, compatible with the maintenance of peace in South Africa.

4. This organization must be looked upon as an engine constructed and used to generate power, the accumulation of which is now kept pent up in this machine, while the process that produces that power is as actively going on as ever.

5. The Zulu constitution is essentially military; every man is a soldier, in whose eyes manual labor, except for military purposes, is degrading. He has been taught from his very childhood that the sole object of his life is fighting and war, and this faith is as strong in the Zulu soldier now, and is as strongly inculcated, as it was fifty years ago, when it was necessary to the building up and existence of his nation.

6. The Zulu tribe, originally insignificant, was raised to become the greatest native power in Africa, south of the Zambesi River, by the ability and military talent of Tshaka, one of its chiefs. The genius, instincts, and traditions of the people are all military; the nation, which is less than seventy years old, had become a compact

military engine before the years of its existence had numbered twenty, and its very life depended at that time of its history upon the perfection of its aggressive and defensive powers.

7. Before Natal became a British colony, there was plenty of work to which the ever accumulating forces of this engine could be applied, and they were extravagantly applied; after that period, and when the Transvaal became occupied by people of European descent, the area upon which these forces could be expended became more and more circumscribed, and is now cut off altogether.

8. But the engine has not ceased to exist or to generate its forces, although the reason or excuse for its existence has died away; these forces have continued to accumulate, and are daily accumulating without safety-valve or outlet.

9. War is the universal cry among the soldiers, who are anxious to live up to their traditions, and are disappointed in their early expectations. The rulers of Zululand have failed to perceive in time that some alteration in the ideas, tastes, and aspirations of the people was necessary to meet the changed circumstances which have rendered their military organization a contradiction; and the idea is gaining ground among the people that their nation has outlived the object of its existence.

10. Had Cetywayo's thirty thousand warriors been in time changed to laborers working for wages, Zululand would have been a prosperous peaceful country instead of what it now is, a source of perpetual danger to itself and its neighbors.

11. The question is, what is to be done with this pent up and still accumulating power? There are not wanting signs that this question may solve itself. It is evident from the account given by the messengers, and from other evidence, that Zululand is from some cause or other in a state of great excitement. I have already shown in my despatch of the 2nd instant that this excitement could not have been produced by any action of this Government regarding the boundary line, because had the conduct of the Zulus, which was the consequence of already existing excitement, not prevented me, I should, in my ignorance of the merits of the case at my first meeting, have surrendered to them much more than I afterwards found they were entitled to.

12. Cetywayo is evidently nervous about his personal position; he dares not, he says, resist the clamours of his regiments, or they would turn against him. This means that he dares not abate a clamour which is unreasonable, and which he knows is unreasonable, and which he also knows is daily inflicting great damage upon this country, the insisting upon which must lead to war. At the same time he asserts his belief that the loudest clamourers are those most likely to desert him; his conclusion, however, is that he will not fight.

13. On the other hand, Umnyamana and his colleagues declare that they will fight, and that the Zulu people are unanimous on that point.

14. It is thought by some that the Zulus are divided into a peace party and a war party. The impression received by me, from what I have observed and learned during the long stay which I have been forced to make on the immediate Zulu border, where I yet am, is that there is in reality no party whose desire it is to go to war with us except for the purpose of securing for themselves and their country the benefits of a revolution, which in my opinion would happen the moment any active measure to enforce the claim of this Government were taken; and that the desire to accomplish this is strong in the great majority of the Zulu people.

15. I believe that the cruelties, the indiscriminate shedding of blood, and the continued dread of being put to death for the most venial fault, or for no fault at all, have rendered the conditions of Zulu life insupportable. When the Zulu people look upon their own lot and that of their brothers and sisters in Natal, who enjoy the same security to life and property that a white man does, they cannot help drawing comparisons unfavorable to their own Government, or avoid longing for a change.

16. The diversion and even comparative personal safety that in bygone days resulted from Zulu invasion of foreign tribes, and from the victories of Zulu armies, now far away from their own home, have to be expended at home and among themselves.

17. The opinion I have above expressed to your Lordship is very far from being merely speculative, although reasoning from analogy and judging from the workings of the human mind, the conclusions would seem to be unavoidable. I have, however, much

evidence from the Zulu country itself to support my opinion; I therefore no longer hesitate to express it.

18. The abandonment of so large a portion of the. lower part of the Transvaal, forced upon the white inhabitants by Cetywayo's demands and actions, and the state of things as above described in the Zulu country, produce a tension that cannot last long unless one side gives way. For this Government to yield would not help the case in Zululand; its nature admits of no such remedy. It may he that Cetywayo will tacitly give way, but even this will be but a temporary postponement of an explosion that must come, of a difficulty which must be met. This state of things points to the necessity for the presence in this part of the country of a much more powerful military force than is here, or available at present. When the Zulu Government is so changed as to be amenable to the demands of humanity, and they are allowed by that Government to be approached by civilizing and christianizing influences, without danger to the lives of those Zulu subjects who submit to those influences, but not. until then, will the peace of South Africa rest on a surer basis than it does at present.

The Fight at
Usirayo's Kraal

The Fight at Usirayo's Kraal.

What the issue of all the foregoing was is now well known. On the 11th of Jan., 1879, the day after the expiration of the full period allowed the Zulu King to meet the whole of the demands of Her Majesty's Government, as conveyed to him in the famous ultimatum of Sir Bartle Frere, General Lord Chelmsford (Thesiger), the Commander-in-chief of H.M. forces in South Africa, took action, and accordingly No. 3 Column under the command of Col. Glyn, C.B., crossed the Buffalo River into Zululand. The next day (12th Jan.) a comparatively unimportant attack was made by our forces upon the strongholds of Usirayo (the letter "r" is, in Zulu, a guttural) whose sons had pursued some young Zulu women into Natal, and having dragged them back into Zululand with thongs round their necks, tortured and then murdered them under circumstances of unparalleled atrocity. Sixteen of Usirayo's men were killed, including Unkumbi ka Zulu (i.e., the semi-circle of the Zulus), one of his sons. The loss on our side was trifling. It was here perceived that the firing of the Zulus was very indirect.

FROM THE WAR CORRESPONDENT OF THE
NATAL MERCURY, INTALALA RIVER,
NEAR USIRAYO'S KRAAL,
JANUARY 13, 1879

You will of course have received long ere this my special message sent to you on Sunday evening, conveying the intelligence that the British Forces crossed the Buffalo River into Zululand, and commenced the Zulu campaign on Saturday, the 11th of January, 1879, and had a sharp engagement with some of the enemy, part of Usirayo's tribe, on Sunday morning. The news must have been most satisfactory to all colonists as showing that the General is determined to let the Zulu King and nation know once and for all that nothing except complete submission will now satisfy the demands which Sir Bartle Frere has seen fit to make. Before describing the engagement itself and what has since occurred I think an account of our crossing the Border, viz., the Buffalo River at Rorke's Drift, will prove of interest. The troops had all been moved down gradually from Helpmakaar to the camp on the Natal side of the Drift, and on Friday were joined by the General and his staff, who inspected the 3rd Regiment of the Natal Native Contingent, and seemed much pleased with the two battalions. He addressed the Kaffirs and gave them good advice, saying that no prisoners, women or children, were to be injured in any way. Unfortunately, owing to an accident (through being thrown from his horse) Commandant Lonsdale, the Corps Commandant, was unable to be present, but the two Battalion Commandants, G. Hamilton Browne and A. W. Cooper, were present.

I forgot to mention in my last letter that on Wednesday afternoon the camp was startled by a sentry sending in the news that several mounted men were coming down to the river from the Zulu side, and at the distance it was impossible to distinguish who or what they were. All turned out and hurried down to the drift, where the punt was working, and it was then discovered that the visitors were not Zulus at all, but that the party consisted of Capt. Barton and Lieut. Baron Von Steitencron, of the Frontier Light Horse, with an escort of one corporal and three men, who had made a most adventurous ride from Colonel Wood's column, which we learn had crossed the Blood River on the previous Monday morning, and were encamped a few miles in Zululand. Captain Barton had been out exploring roads, &c, and meeting with no opposition, had penetrated right through to our camp, a distance of over thirty miles. The Kaffirs all along the road had been friendly, and given them information and milk. The only place where they heard they were likely to be annoyed was at a kraal of some mission Kaffirs, so they kept away. As it was very late when they arrived at our camp, it was considered dangerous to try and return, and they waited with us till morning, and then left on their return journey. How they fared we know not, although we heard they reached Colonel Wood's column safely.

To return to our own camp. During Friday evening (which everyone will doubtless remember was the 10th of January, the last of the thirty days given to Cetywayo) rumours were afloat that we were to cross on the morrow, and shortly the order came in that the whole column was to move over at daybreak on Saturday. Reveille sounded at 2 p.m.; tents were struck, and the different regiments in their places to cross at 4.30. The first battalion of the 3rd regt. N.N.C. were ordered to cross the drift itself, which at present is broad and deep, and with a strong current. There was a small island in the centre, which helped to ease the crossing. The entire cavalry brigade, under Lieut.-Colonel Russell, deposited their arms, &c. on the pontoons, and then rode back to follow the 2-3rd N.N.C. at the drift. The 1-24th regt., under Captain Degacher, crossed on one of the punts, and the 2-24th, under Colonel Degacher, C.B., on the other; while the 2-3rd N.N.C. crossed at a drift higher up the river. The Artillery, six guns, under Lieut-Colonel Harness, were in position on a slight rise in the camp to protect our crossing, and did not follow over until the next day. A thick fog came on just as we were ready to cross. I had previously arranged to accompany the 3rd regt. N.N.C. throughout the campaign, and so had all along remained with them. This morning I went down to the drift with their column, and with Captain Krohn led the way over, arriving first on the other side, so that I may say, as far as our column was concerned, I was actually the first man in Zululand after war was declared, and the troops moved over.

The crossing of the drift was executed under the eye of the General, who was attended by a numerous and brilliant staff, and it was most successfully carried out; although several minor accidents occurred, neither horse nor man came to grief. The water was up to the men's necks in places, and ran at the rate of over six knots an hour; this, with a very stony bottom, will show how difficult it must have been. One accident did occur, which might have ended fatally: a man of the mounted infantry was taken off his horse, and would have been carried away by the stream had it not been for the gallant conduct of Capt. Hayes, 1-3rd N.N.C., who jumped into the river again and succeeded, at the risk of his own life, in getting the man across safely. This act was witnessed by all, and drew a highly flattering mention of the same from the General, which appeared among the column orders issued on Monday. The two line regiments crossed all right on the pontoons, and, with the 3rd N.N.C., took up a position on the opposite side, ascending the hill in skirmishing order.

The line, when opened out in skirmishing order, was quite three miles long, and was formed as follows, beginning from our right: The 1-3rd N.N.C commenced from the bend of the river, having four companies for skirmishing on the rise, in reserve, on their extreme right flank. Then some companies of the 1-24th, also with a reserve. The 2-24th followed in similar order, and the line was ended with the 2-3rd N.N.C., five of whose companies were extended, the others forming a reserve, placed on the extreme left flank. The whole force was advanced a few hundred yards, and then halted until the fog lifted. After a short time, the cavalry division came through our ranks, with His Excellency Lieutenant-General Lord Chelmsford and staff in the centre, and proceeded on at a sharp trot some way inland. I was afterwards told that they rode about fifteen to eighteen miles, in order to meet the advance guard of Colonel Wood's column, which had come on some distance to do so. They did not return until the evening, and then part of them brought in our first capture, consisting of about seventy head of cattle, some horses, sheep and goats; they were afterwards followed by the rest of the division, who had 221 head of cattle, and 121 goats. These had been taken from three different kraals, away to the north-west. The inhabitants had run away, and many guns and assegais were taken and destroyed.

In the meantime while this was being done, the greater portion of our wagons, oxen, ambulances, &c, were being got across on the pontoons, and this work tried to the utmost the powers of all concerned, and resulted most successfully and creditably to those in command. At any rate by evening enough were got over to enable us all to encamp, and then after being; all day without food you can imagine how an evening meal was enjoyed. Colonel Glynn, C,B. -- attended by Major Clery and Captains Parr and Coghill -- was present all day, riding up and down the line, and also watching the wagons, &c, being got over. The tents were put up and we all encamped in exactly the same place as we occupied during the day. Outlying pickets were sent out, strong guards for the camp and the captured cattle put on, and we all retired to rest, with the pleasant consciousness that at five the next morning a re-connaisance in strength was to be made by the whole column, carrying one day's rations. The tired men grumbled, but were pleased at the chance of meeting the enemy on the next day.

At 3.30 a.m., on Sunday morning reveille sounded; the different regiments were paraded as follows: The 1st battalion 3rd N.N.C., 850 strong, under Major Black 2-24th, and Commandant Browne. Four companies of the 1-24th under Capt. Degacher, and 100 mounted infantry under Capt. Brown, 100 Natal Mounted Police under Inspector Mansell, 50 Natal Carbineers under Capt. Shepstone, and 35 Newcastle Mounted Rifles and Buffalo Border Guard under Capt. Bradsten. The whole column was under the personal command of Colonel Glyn, C.B., and Lieut.-Col. Russell had charge of the cavalry division. There was also a reserve force formed of the 2-3rd N.N.C. under Commandant Cooper, and the 2-24th under Colonel Degacher, C.B. They only started three hours after we did, and arrived on the scene when the action was over. They were, however, of great service, thoroughly clearing the valley, burning Usirayo's great kraal and capturing about 100 head of cattle, which were escaping from our men.

We started punctually at five, and rode about six miles with the Carbineers thrown out in skirmishing order, and videttes on each flank. When we arrived on the other side of the hill, where it begins to descend into the valley where Usirayo's kraals are, we heard a war song being sung, as it seemed by a large body of men, and we could also distinguish moving forms on the top of the hills opposite, and also among the rocks up a steep and stony krantz in front. The lowing of cattle was also distinguishable, and proved to us distinctly that these men having doubtless heard of our having captured cattle on the day previous, had driven their cattle up among the rocks, and established themselves up there in caves, &c, determined upon resisting. This knowledge served to redouble both our vigilance and eagerness to get at them. At the bottom of the valley a small spruit divides it, and we were halted on this side while the General and Colonel Glynn made their observations, and consequent plan of attack. Some little time elapsed before this was done, and then the cavalry were first sent over to go round the hill on the right, and try to outflank those that might escape, and also to get up to the top for the same purpose.

The main attack, made upon the centre of the krantz itself, was conducted by the men of the 3rd N.N.C., led by Commander Browne, under the command of Major Black, 2-24th, and four companies of the 1-24th, under Captain Degacher. This force was immediately extended in line, with orders to advance straight up to that part of the ravine where the Zulus were hidden. This was done steadily, although great difficulty was found in keeping the line unbroken; owing to the rough nature of the ground, and several very awkward gullies intervening. As we approached to within about five hundred yards, a voice was heard asking "By whose order the white impi had come there, and whether they were enemies". To this no answer was given, and we again advanced.

Major Black, in the meantime, sent down for orders as to when to open fire. Permission was given to fire only after they first fired on us. Shortly after, at about 7.30, the first shot was fired from behind a large rock, and injured a Kaffir belonging to the Native Contingent. After that a constant fusilade was kept up until the cattle were taken with a rush made by No. 8 Company, under Captains Duncombe and Murry, led by Commandant Browne. The Kaffirs then got desperate and retreated to their covers, pouring in a heavy fire from behind rocks. This had the effect of breaking our line, and many of our natives turned and ran. However, owing to the magnificent exertions of the European officers leading the first four columns, and notwithstanding the fact that some of the enemy began to throw down heavy rocks on the advancing men, they succeeded, after a desperate hand-to-hand fight, in shooting nearly twenty men, taking four others prisoners, as well as many women and children. In this last hand-to-hand fight, Captains Hayes and E. Hicks greatly distinguished themselves; and Captain Harford, of the 99th Regt., who is attached to us as staff officer, performed one of the most plucky actions possible, in advancing to the mouth of a cave out of which many men had been shot, and succeeded in inducing four men to come out, deliver up their arms, and give themselves up as prisoners. His revolver was empty at the time, and he might easily have been shot by either as they came out one by one.

The loss on our side was two natives killed and eighteen wounded, including Lieut. Purvis (who was shot through the arm, but is now progressing favorably), and Corporal Meyor, who received a bad assegai wound in the leg. All the other casualties were of minor importance, and occurred exclusively among the Native Contingent. In the meantime two companies, under Captains Harber and Hulley, on the extreme left, had, with the 1-24th, under Captain Degacher, advanced along to the left, and succeeded in getting round over the point of the ravine on to the other side, so as to prevent any escape, and gradually getting higher until we reached the top. This was done well, and several fugitives were shot. In many places exchange of fire was made, with no loss on our side, but about six of the enemy were killed.

The top was reached through a tremendous defile, and just on the other side we captured three horses. When on the top several fugitives were seen on foot, and mounted, away in the distance, making round the base of another hill which rises from the top of the one they were on. The sight to be obtained is a magnificent one, looking north down a precipitous cliff, a splendid valley extends for miles, rich in verdure, covered with kraals now deserted, and bounded on each side by high mountains, while to the south the Buffalo and the Natal mountains are seen in the distance, with our camp on Rorke's Drift, looking like a miniature soldiers' camp. To the eastward, Spitzberg rises in the air with its curious-shaped top, and close by it runs our road to Ulundi. Altogether it was a sight worth seeing, and when the mounted men met the four companies of the 1-24th, and those of the 1-3rd N.N.C., such a sight was never seen before and never will be seen again.

The Cavalry Division, in getting round the right flank up the valley, were followed by several Kaffirs along the heights, in number about thirty, under a younger son of Usirayo. These men constantly taunted the cavalry, and at last fired upon them. Colonel Russell ordered Captain Shepstone to send forward eight of his men to draw their fire, and although within point-blank range, they never flinched or wasted a shot. A grand advance was then made, the men being dismounted. Major Dartnell accompanied them in a gallant way. They succeeded in shooting three, wounded others, and the rest fled, among whom there were some on horseback.

The Mounted Infantry and Natal Mounted Police had also ascended, the one on the left and the other on the right, and by a counter-flank movement, were able to cut off the retreat of the others who had fled, and obliged them to cross a flat plateau, where six more were killed outright, including the son of Usirayo. The whole division then went up to the top, and halted for a short meal. They afterwards went on the hill, accompanied by some of the native levies, and examined a large kraal on the top. The whole then returned by the way they had come, and, through heavy thunderstorms, all returned home.

Several guns were taken, also many assegais and lots of sour milk and other Kaffir produce. None of the guns were modern, but consisted of old Tower muskets and carbines. A large quantity of ammunition was found, including several hundred rounds of Westley-Richards' cartridges on a new wagon of Usirayo's. The cartridges were brought away, but it was impossible to get the wagon down. We have now moved on our camp to the scene of action, and shall be here some days road-making for the rest of the column to come on.

The Battle of
Isandhlwana

The Battle of Isandhlwana

On the 20th January a position was taken up at Isandhlwana, and the camp was pitched under the brow of the Isandhlwana Hill, which is an abrupt and precipitous termination of a mountain ridge running eastward. Lord Chelmsford was with this camp from the morning of the 20th January to the morning of the 22nd, when he proceeded further into the country in order to take up a new position. No attempt to "laager" the wagons or to entrench the Isandhlwana camp was made while the General was thus with it, and when he left he gave Colonel Pulleine, of the 1-24th Regiment, his orders, which were "to contract the line of defence, and defend the camp." The English papers have pictorially and otherwise explained what a "laager" is, but in case some of my readers have not seen such explanation, I here give a description of it. The wagons are drawn up, sometimes in a square, sometimes in a circle, in single, or when the number of wagons permit it, in double rows, the pole of one wagon being pushed in under the one just in front of it, and so on. Strong boughs, thorny if possible, are then well wattled and interlaced wherever an opening occurs, and cannons are mounted at the corners of the square. The draught and other cattle are penned up in the circle or square on one side. This form of defence has been adopted by the Boers and others from the earliest days, and in fact it is well known to every novice that it is the only sure protection against the great numbers and headlong valor of the Zulus. Sir Theophilus Shepstone, late Secretary for Native Affairs in Natal, a Kaffir scholar, and a very old and long-headed resident, accompanied Lord Chelmsford, so it seems passing strange that the Isandhlwana camp should have been left in an "unlaagered" state.

At a Court of Enquiry on the subject, the evidence taken at which will be given in its proper place, it was stated by witnesses that the General gave Colonel Pulleine the orders as above, that after the General left the camp Colonel Durnford, Colonel Pulleine's superior officer, rode into the camp, and the latter handed over to the former his command and the orders. Lieut. Cochrane, of the 32nd Regiment, who was transport officer of No. 3 Column, says in his evidence that Colonel Durnford after taking over the command "sent two troops of mounted natives to the tops of the hills to the left, and took with him two troops of Rocket Battery, with escort of one Company Native Contingent on to the front of the camp, about four or five miles off. Before leaving he asked Colonel Pulleine to give him two companies 24th Regiment. Colonel Pulleine said that with the orders he had received he could not do it, but agreed with Colonel Durnford to send him help if he got into difficulties." It may be here said that Colonel Durnford's reason for sending the two troops of Mounted Natives out was that a messenger had reported the Zulus retiring in all directions. And so in this wise were Colonel Pulleine's soldiers of the 1-24th (Warwickshire) Regiment drawn away from the camp, and led to engage in the open with the overwhelming masses of Zulus which now came rapidly on the scene. The cause of the disaster under Isandhlwana must be summed up in a couple of sentences— First and foremost the absence of a "Laager" form of defence, and secondly the unfortunate disregard of the General's orders by the gallant Colonel Durnford, and the consequent embroilment of Colonel Pulleine and his men. Anyway, if the camp had been properly "laagered" the two companies left in it to defend the baggage could have held it easier than the one company subsequently did their camp at Rorke's Drift.

A Survivor's Account:
The Battle of Isandhlwana

On the morning of the 22nd January, at about six o'clock, Colonel Durnford gave orders to march. We at once packed up the tents, and inspanned the wagons. We started about seven o'clock a.m. from our camp on the Zulu side of the Buffalo. We marched as far as the Bashee stream about ten a.m., where Capt. Russell of the Rocket Battery gave orders for D company to march on with all speed with him, and E company, with Capt. Stafford, stayed behind to escort the wagons. After staying there about a quarter of an hour, orders came for Capt. Stafford to leave part of his company as escort for the wagons, and to hurry on with the rest to the front. He left me with 16 men, and told me to hurry on the wagons, which I accordingly did, to the best of my ability. We had then heard the firing of the cannon for about a quarter of an hour (since about ten a.m.), and I continued to hear it until I arrived at the camp (about half-past ten or eleven a.m.) at Isandhlwana. There I took my escort to the front, which was then about a mile ahead of the camp. The Zulus were then about 700 yards away. I placed my men in position, and told them "to fire low," while I sat down and watched the progress of affairs. After sitting so for about five minutes, I felt I myself must have some shots, and accordingly went back to camp to get a gun, not having had one before. Capt. Stafford told me to give my gun to a Kaffir while I went back to the wagons, saying that I could get it at the camp on my arrival. My company was already at the front, so that I did not again see the Kaffirs.

When I returned, I was just mounting to the top of the hill where my Kaffirs were, when I saw the hill to the right of the camp black with Zulus. I got into my place, and began firing. I had fired only a few shots when Pakadi's men, among whom I was, began to run. When the Zulus got about 300 yards from me, I saw that the Mounted Native Contingent and the whole column to the right of the guns, were retiring (about three o'clock) and I followed, firing as I went, thinking they were falling back on the camp. When we got about 200 yards in front of the camp we all stood, except Pakadi's men, who were then in full flight.

The cannon here began to fire harder than ever, but the Zulus kept on pouring down in front and on our flank; those in front of the cannon when they saw the gunners stand clear would either fall down flat or divide in the middle, so as to leave a lane, and when the shot had passed would shout out 'Umoya !' (only wind). There was no confusion or hurry in these movements of theirs, but all was done as though they had been drilled to it. They kept on advancing till within 100 yards. The Zulus on our flank were then about 200 yards off, when the whole army made a simultaneous charge upon the camp. I had then retired as far as the wagons, when seeing the Zulus carrying everything before them, and everybody scattered and bolting, I naturally did the same on foot, about four o'clock. After running a long way I got completely blown with the weight of my gun and ammunition.

I thereupon threw my ammunition away, all except five rounds which I kept for self-defence, having no doubt that the Zulus would catch me. After running a few yards further I was dead beat, and sat down on a stone with my gun beside me. On looking round I saw the Zulus killing soldiers close behind me. I jumped up and ran on, forgetting my gun in my haste. I soon overtook Capt. Stafford, who was riding one horse and leading another. I asked him to lend me a horse, as I could not go any further. He dismounted and gave me the one he was riding, while he mounted the other. He said, 'Keep behind me,' but on looking round he had disappeared. I thereupon watched where the Contingent Kaffirs were making for, and followed them.

After riding about two miles, I was watching a soldier who was running about ten yards from me, when just as he had passed a bush a Zulu sprang out and said, 'Uya ngapi umlungu? (Where are you going, white man?), and threw a broad-bladed assegai at him with his left hand, which pierced the poor soldier between the shoulders. The poor fellow fell forward on his face, and the Zulu ran up to him and calling out 'Usutu,' stabbed him to the heart with the same assegai. He had no sooner done this than I saw him throw one at me, and bobbing on one side to avoid the assegai, it stuck in my leg. I had just shaken it out when another one came and stuck in my horse. I pulled it out and threw it down, when, on looking for the Zulu, he had disappeared.

After going about 500 yards further I saw a puff of smoke, and a bullet whizzed about an inch from my nose. I shouted out to the marksman, 'Iya wa uti u ya dubula bane na?' (Who do you think you are shooting?). After this this I came to a precipice, which I found impassable. I was going to turn back, when I saw the Zulus about twenty yards behind me. I therefore thought I had better risk my neck over the precipice, which was about twelve feet high, than the Zulus. I shut my eyes and jumped my horse over it. I landed safely at the bottom, but never looked back to see what had become of the enemy.

When I arrived at the river I could not get my horse into it on account of his being nearly exhausted. I made way for Capt. Cochrane, whose horse mine then followed. When I got into the middle of the stream, out of the horse's depth, four or five men caught hold of his tail, so that he could not move. While they were still holding on the Zulus came up and assegaied some, while others let go and were carried away by the stream, only to be murdered further down. On getting out on this side the Edendale men told me to lie flat on my horse's neck, which I did, thinking the Zulus were going to fire at me, but was surprised to hear our own men firing over my head; they killed about a dozen Zulus. While watching this little skirmish I saw one of our Kaffirs brought to bay by a Zulu. After some preliminary guarding on the part of both, the Zulu stabbed our Kaffir in the shoulder; thereupon our Kaffir jumped up into the air and stuck his assegai to the Zulu's heart. Both of them then rolled into the river. The Zulus crossing, we continued our flight to Helpmakaar, where we arrived quite safely at about half-past six. The Zulus chased us about three miles this side of the river.

An Interview with the Survivor

When you arrived at the camp what was its position? Were any wagons inspanned, and if so, for what purpose?

I did not take minute notice of the formation of the camp. Noticed the tents, and the wagons arranged behind them; some of the wagons were inspanned, for what purpose I cannot say; at other wagons I saw the oxen tied to the yokes.

How far were you from the military during the engagement?

At one time with them, but most of the time about half a mile from them.

In what order of battle were they, so far as you observed, and how far from the camp?

They appeared in double column, in line; they did not skirmish. They were about half a mile from the camp, in front, facing the high hills.

Did you hear the sound of any bugle, or was that impossible from the noise of cannon and small arms?

I heard no sound of bugle; there was too much noise.

Did you see any aide-de-camp riding and conveying orders during the day?

I did not. I never heard of any. I did hear that some one was sent to the column under the General, to request aid.

You say you were engaged from about 11 a.m. until 4 p.m. During this time was any general or particular order conveyed to you, or to your company, so far as you are aware, with reference to your plan of operations?

None to myself. I am not aware of any having been issued to my company. I saw no staff officer, nor did I see any commander.

Do you know whether the cannon fired ball, grape, or canister shot?

I think only ball was fired, from what I saw, and afterwards heard.

Did the Rocket Battery, so far as you could observe, do any execution?

I did not see the Rocket Battery fired; but I was told by a brother officer that only one rocket was fired, and he was watching it very particularly He saw the rocket pass over the heads of the Zulus without doing any execution; that is, so far as he saw.

When did you last see Colonel Durnford?

At about 11a.m., after I arrived at the camp, I saw him some distance off, on our right. After the retreat I saw his horse without a rider, near the Buffalo, the saddle hanging at its side. A soldier tried to catch it without avail; it rushed into the river, and was carried down. I do not know whether it swam out.

Did you hear the Zulus say, "Leave the black men, and attack the soldiers and the whites"?

I never heard this myself, but the Native Contingent told me they heard the Zulus say, "Leave the Kaffirs, as the white men cause them to fight."

Did you recognise any women in the field

I never saw one, or the appearance of one.

Were there any women, do you know, amongst our camp followers?

I did not see any, and I never heard of any being with the wagons.

Did you notice, or hear of any white man being with the enemy?

I never saw a white man; but I was told that a white man was engaged at Rorke's Drift, and the man who told me said he himself shot him; but the next morning, on looking for the body, it could not be found. He was very like a white man if he was not one; he wore European clothes.

When the general stampede took place, at about 4 p.m., about what number of men were still alive and engaged?

But few were then killed. Up to this time I never saw a dead white man or a dead Contingent. The Zulu shots went over our heads, and it was only when the "chest" of the Zulu army came that the contest appeared hopeless, and then the general fight and massacre took place. We all think that had the General's column appeared, the day would have been ours.

What was the Zulu war-cry?

"Usutu" and "Qoka a Amatye" (clash stones). I don't know what they meant by calling "Usutu;" but every time a white man was stabbed to death the cry was "Usutu." (*"Usutu" was the war-cry adopted by Cetywayo's soldiers in 1856, in contradistinction to that of Umbulazi, "Usixosa." "Usutu" is the name of a river in Amazwaziland.*)

Did you understand every word?

Yes; but I do not know what they intended to convey by the word "Usutu." When the cannon fired they cried out "Umoya" (wind).

How many of the contingent officers understood the Kaffir language?

Many of the captains and lieutenants, but none of the non-commissioned officers.

When you say Pakadi's men began to run, had they lost many white officers?

I saw no white officer with Pakadi's men; no commander at all. They were acting entirely on their own account. They kept up a fire against the Zulus until the latter were within three hundred yards of them; when, being without control, they bolted. Some of the indunas called out "Mani buya," meaning "Return to the fight;" but a panic had evidently seized them, and they would not obey the induna; that is if they heard him.

How did Zikali's people behave?

Well; splendidly. They were commanded by Captains Nourse and Stafford.

During the five minutes you were watching the progress of affairs did you notice anything special, and did you realise the position as critical?

I was noticing the calm, steady way the Zulu army advanced under such a heavy fire as it was receiving from us. I thought the Zulus would soon retire, long before they could reach us; but no, they never halted in their step. Once they were driven back by Captain Barton. They were the left horn of the Zulu army. After this they came steadily on, every one of us retiring for the camp.

What distance was it from the camp to the Buffalo, where you escaped?

The way we took would be about seven miles. It was away from the main road.

What distance from the Buffalo to Helpmakaar, and what the nature of the country?

I think seven or eight miles, open, flat country to within two miles of Helpmakaar, where there is a stiff rise; after that it is flat to the fort.

During the five minutes you were watching did you notice the effect of our fire upon the Zulus, and theirs upon our own people?

I did not see any of our people shot; and whether the gaps I saw in the Zulu army were from shots or from their own guarding ("vika") I cannot say.

Did you hear the Zulu commander give orders to his men not to cross the Buffalo?

I did not. I could not distinguish any induna from a common Zulu. I heard no such order. I do not dispute that such may have been given; and I cannot understand why the Zulus did not follow up their victory.

When you saw George Shepstone return to the camp, do you know what he came for?

I do not know; but I heard him rallying the people, and saying they were wanted at the front. There were soldiers and others left in charge of the baggage. The only time I saw Captain George Shepstone was when I went the second time to the wagons to get a gun, the one I had having got out of order in the breech. He was saying this— 'Why are you men not at the front? Do you not know that every man is wanted there?—to those men who had been left in charge of the baggage. Captain Barton was also there trying to get ammunition, which, however, he did not get, the man refusing, saying that all the ammunition there was for the military and not for the Contingent. Immediately after this the Zulus rushed into the camp, and Captain Shepstone must have been killed then (about 4). I forgot to mention that just as I crossed the river a Zulu shot at me, the bullet passing within an inch of my ear. I felt my head to see if I was hit; it killed a conductor by the name of Dubois who was walking up the hill in front of me; this was about 5 o'clock.

"HONOR TO THE SLAIN"
FROM THE NATAL MERCURY, MARCH 12TH, 1879

To-day will be to most a time of sad thought and bitter retrospection. The purposes for which it is set apart invest the occasion with gloom. It is the past rather than the present or the future to which we look. Our regards are fixed, not upon the brighter incidents of the campaign that is going on, but upon the dark field of Isandhlwana. The memorable hour which witnessed the slaughter of so many brave men will recur to the memory in all its ghastly vividness; and the terrible incidents which have been bit by bit disclosed will again troop across the mind. There is no need for us to recall them. There is not a heart in the country that does not feel sore with constant contemplation of the distressful theme, nor a tongue that has not spent itself in discussing it. There has been a morbid fascination in the topic that has proved irresistible to all of us, and made sustained attention to any other subject a moral impossibility.

Let us rather glance for a moment at the names and memories of those who died so nobly in their country's service. Durnford, the fearless and the impetuous; Pulleine, genial, active, and large-hearted; George Shepsrone, modest and manful, as brave in death as ever he was in life; Coghill, dashing, light-hearted, and chivalrous, one's ideal of a beau sabreur; Melville, faithful unto death in the sacred charge of his Queen's colors; Stewart-Smith, who died while spiking the guns he could no longer hold; Bradstreet, one of Newcastle's most popular townsmen; Durrant Scott, dauntless, and yet soft-hearted, the oft-applauded hero of many a merry 'sock'; Anstey, Degacher, Porteous, Hodson, Mostyn, Dyson, and all the other fine young officers of both the regular and irregular forces, better known elsewhere than here, but not the less sincerely mourned by those they came out to defend.

No less reverently must and do we think of those who in humbler capacities fought for their country's safety and honor on that fatal day. Macleroy, London, Bullock, Davis, Blaikie, Hitchcock, Grant, and the rest, familiar to us as youths and citizens, bound to us by long ties of friendship or of kin; whose missing places to-day cause voids in many homes. And what of that long list of names —the bone and sinew of the army—the obscurer but not less gallant units belonging to all branches of the service, whose arms and hearts are the mainstay of the Empire? Little known to us indeed by personal acquaintance, they nevertheless have established an indefeasible claim upon our gratitude; and so long as Natal has a history, and so long as valor is held to be a virtue, it will be remembered to their glory how unflinchingly they fought and died where they stood, in the face of an overwhelming and overpowering foe.

Nor do we forget 'those others,' men of a darker hue, and of an alien race—men divided from us by the barriers of a strange tongue and of heathen ways, though the bravest of them, be it remembered, were the mission converts of Edendale—the loyal natives who fought with us and for us on that day, and who, by their fidelity and courage, established between white and black a bond of 'blood brotherhood' which will never be forgotten or effaced.

These be the staple of our thoughts to-day. It is their swift and sudden doom that has humiliated us. It is their death that we mourn. Had they escaped that doom we should not now be grieving, and the only ray of solace that we allow ourselves just now is the hope that the blood thus shed will prove to have been the purchase price of a peace-crowned, a united, and a regenerate South Africa.

Sir Robert Peel was very severe upon Lord Chelmsford and Sir Bartle Frere in the House of Commons, with what amount of reason will be judged. He says:— "The Government had enforced caution upon Sir Bartle Frere, who had exceeded and defied their authority, while the incompetency of Lord Chelmsford had led to the miserable disaster at Isandhlwana. Upon his head (until tried by court martial) was the blood of 53 officers and 1,400 men, or a greater number of officers than had fallen at the battle of Inkermann. The conclusion that he had arrived at was that Sir Bartle Frere ought not to have been kept in his place a moment after he had been censured, and that there was no ground for supposing that the war was either just or necessary."

Sir M. Hicks-Beach in speaking on the subject of censuring a Governor while retaining him in office, says:

"But when it is said, as I have heard it said, that this is an unprecedented censure on a Governor who is retained in office, I think it will be very easy to show, without any lengthened research through the archives of the Colonial Office, that it is nothing of the kind. I do not like to reopen questions that have been settled, or to give pain to valuable servants of the Crown; but I think the House will give me credit when I say that a censure ten times exceeding in severity that which was awarded to Sir Bartle Frere, was awarded by the Colonial Office to the Governor of a Colony, for acting against directions he had received from Her Majesty's Government, and for carrying out a line of policy which they disapproved; and yet that Governor was not recalled, but was retained in his office to the great benefit of the Colony, and now holds also to the great benefit of the Service, the Governorship of one of the most important colonies of the empire."

Lord Beaconsfield denied that the resolution before the House raised either the question of the policy of Her Majesty's Government or that of the High Commissioner. The proposal really was to censure the Government because they had retained in the post of High Commissioner the man whom, on the whole, they considered to be the best qualified for that position. Had the Government, in deference to the panic of the hour, recalled Sir Bartle Frere, the world would have been delighted, as it always was, to find a victim. But they had not recalled Sir Bartle Frere because they thought it their duty in the public interest to retain him. The noble earl], amid loud cheers, concluded by saying that if their lordships placed the public advantage above party considerations, they would negative the resolution then before the House.

SIR M. HICKS-BEACH DRAWS THE ATTENTION OF THE BRITISH PARLIAMENT TO LOSSES IN ENCOUNTERS WITH THE ZULUS

Attention has been called to the fact that the losses we have sustained in our encounter with the Zulus are out of all proportion to the British forces engaged and to the average casualties in war. Our killed at Isandhlwana eclipsed the best-remembered figures of the Crimean war—twenty-six British officers and 327 men killed at the Alma, and 462 English and French, killed at Inkerman. Yet our forces at the Alma were about 26,000, and at Inkerman the allies numbered 14,000 against 40,000 Russians. The proportions at Balaklava, where 472 fell out of a total of 670 engaged in the famous charge, came nearest to those of the early results of this war with the Zulus. There is of course the improved rifle to be taken into consideration, but the numbers of breechloaders in the hands of the Zulus is not sufficient to account for the high percentage of casualties to the numbers in the field.

After the desperate combat at Isandhlwana, a scene of utter confusion seems to have occurred—horse and foot, black and white, English and Zulu, all in a struggling mass, making gradually through the camp towards the road, where the Zulus already closed the way of escape. Of what happened during that half-hour even those who lived to tell can remember but little. Every man who had a horse attempted to escape towards the river; those who had none died where they stood. One of the few saved was Lieutenant Smith-Dorrien; who was the transport officer with Colonel Glyn's column, and had been sent that morning by Lord Chelmsford with a despatch to Colonel Durnford at Rorke's Drift ordering him to join Colonel Pulleine at the Isandhlwana camp. He describes the fight and the subsequent flight to the Buffalo, of which he says:—

LIEUTENANT SMITH-DORRIEN'S ACCOUNT OF ISANDHLWANA

The ground there down to the river was so broken that the Zulus went as fast as the horses, and kept killing all the way. There were very few white men. They were nearly all mounted niggers of ours flying. This lasted till we came to a kind of precipice down to the river Buffalo. I jumped off and led my horse down. There was a poor fellow of the mounted infantry (a private) struck through the arm, who said as I passed that if I could bind up his arm and stop the bleeding he would be all right. I accordingly took out my handkerchief and tied up his arm. Just as I had done it Major Smith, of the Artillery, came down by me, wounded, saying 'For God's sake, get on, man; the Zulus are on the top of us!'

I had done all I could for the wounded man, and so turned to jump on my horse. Just as I was doing so the horse went with a bound to the bottom of the precipice, being struck with an assegai. I gave up all hope, as the Zulus were all round me finishing off the wounded, the man I had helped and Major Smith among the number. However, with the strong hope that everybody clings to that some accident would turn up, I rushed off on foot and plunged into the river, which was little better than a roaring torrent. I was being carried down the stream at a tremendous pace when a loose horse came by me and I got hold of his tail, and he landed me safely on the other bank but I was too tired to stick to him and get on his back. I got up again and rushed on, and was several times knocked over by our mounted niggers, who would not even get out of my way; then up a tremendous hill, with my wet clothes and boots full of water.

About twenty Zulus got over the water and followed us up over the hill, but I am thankful to say they had not their firearms. Crossing the river, however, the Zulus kept firing at us as we went up the hill, and killed several of the niggers all round me. I was the only white man to be seen until I came to one who had been kicked by his horse and could not mount. I put him on his horse and lent him my knife. He said he would catch me a horse. Directly he was up he went clear away I struggled into Helpmakaar, about twenty miles off, at nightfall to find a few men who had escaped (about ten or twenty), with others who had been intrenched in a wagon laager.

Lieutenant Newnham Davis' Account
of Escape from the Zulus

When we saw that the camp was gone, and that our men began to try to get away by twos and threes, I said to Henderson, 'What are we going to do? Our only chance now is to make a run for it and dash through. We started; he took to the right and I took to the left, and rode slap at the enemy. One fellow seized hold of my horse's bridle and I made a stab at him with my rifle (a foolish thing that has a 9-in. knife attachment); but the man caught hold of it and pulled it out of my hand, which at the same time made my horse rear and shy and cleared me of the man.

I then had only my revolver, and I saw a Zulu right in my course, and rode at him and shot him in the neck. My horse got a stab, and many assegais were thrown at me; but, as I was lying along my horse, they did not hit me. The ground was stony that I was going over, and I soon came to grief; but, as there was no time to think, I was soon up and away again, and took the river in front of me. Many were then escaping, but, not being accustomed to take horses across rivers, they fell and rolled over, as the current was strong. I have had a good deal of experience in swimming horses, and I kept mine from falling, and directly he was in the water I threw myself off and caught hold of the stirrup. The Zulus followed us down and fired at us crossing. Some of the Zulus took the water after us, as our natives stabbed two Zulus just as they reached the Natal side. I never saw Colonel Durnford or George Shepstone after we left the gully or water-wash, and I did not see Henderson after we began our race until I met him next day at Helpmakaar.

A Zulu Deserter Speaks
from The Witness, February 24th 1879

We are indebted to our Special War Correspondent for the following report, made by a deserter from the Zulu army, with regard to the affair at Isandhlwana:—

The Zulu army, consisting of the Undi corps, about 3,000 strong; the Nokenke regt., 2,000 strong; the Nko-bamakosi regt., including the Uve, about 5,000 strong; the Umcityu, about 4,000 strong; the Nodwengu corps, 2,000 strong; the Umbonambi, 3,000 strong; and the Udhloko, about 1,000 strong, or a total of about 20,000 men in all, left the great military kraal of Nodwengu on the afternoon of the 17th January. It was first addressed by the King, who said: "I am sending you out against the whites, who have invaded Zululand, and driven away our cattle. You are to go against the column at Rorke's Drift, and drive it back into Natal, and if the state of the river will allow, follow it up through Natal, right up to the Drakensberg. You will attack it by daylight, as there are enough of you to 'eat it up,' and you will march slowly, so as not to tire yourselves."

We accordingly left Nodwengu late in the afternoon, and marched in column to the west bank of the White Umfolosi, about six miles distant, where we bivouacked for the night. Next day we marched to the Isixepi military kraal, about nine miles off, where we slept; and on the 19th we ascended on the table land near the Isihlungu Hills, a inarch of about equal duration with that of the day previous. On this day the army, which had hitherto been marching in single column, divided into two, marching parallel to and within sight of each other. That on the left consisting of the Nokenke, Umcityu, and Nodwengu regts., under the command of Tyingwayo; the other commanded by Mavumingwana. There were a few mounted men belonging to the Chief Usirayo, who were made use of as scouts. On the 20th we moved across the open country, and slept by the Isipezi Hill. We saw a body of mounted white men on this day to our left.

On the 21st, keeping away to the eastward, we occupied a valley running north and south under the spurs of the Nqutu Hill, which concealed the Isandhlwana Hill, distant from us about four miles, and nearly due west of our encampment. We had been well fed during the. whole march, our scouts driving in herds of cattle and goats, and en this evening we lit our camp fires as usual. Our scouts also reported to us that they had seen the videttes of the English force at sunset, on some hills west-south-west of us.

It may be here explained that "Isandhlwana" is the name of the crag situated in the district or tract of country known as "Isandula".

Our order of encampment on the 21st January was as follows:—On the extreme right were the Nodwengu, Nokenke, and Umcityu; the centre was formed of the Nkobamakosi and Umbonambi; and the left of the Undi corps and the Udbloko regiments.

On the morning of the 22nd January there was no intention whatever of making any attack, on account of a superstition regarding the state of the moon, and we were sitting resting, when firing was heard to our right (the narrator was in the Nokenke regiment), which we at first imagined was the Nkobamakosi engaged, and we armed and ran forward in the direction of the sound. We were, however, soon told it was the white troops fighting with Matyana's people some ten miles away to our left front, and returned to our original position.

Just after we had sat down again a small herd of cattle came past our line from our right, being driven by some of our scouts, and just where they were opposite the Umcityu regiment a body of mounted men appeared on the hill to the west, galloping up, evidently trying to cut them off. When several hundred yards off they saw the Umcityu dismounting, and fired one volley at them and then retired. The Umcityu at once jumped up and charged, an example which was then taken up by the Nokenke and Nodwengu on their right, and the Nkobamakosi and Umbonambi on their left, while the Undi Corps and the Udhloko formed a circle (as is customary in Zulu warfare), and remained where they were.

With the latter were the two commanding officers, Mavumingwana and Tyingwayo, and several of the king's brothers, and after a short pause they bore away to the north-west, and keeping on the northern side of the Isandhlwana, performed a turning movement on the right, without any opposition from the whites, who, from the nature of the ground, could not see them. Thus the original Zulu left became their extreme right, while their right became their centre, and the centre the left. The two regiments which formed the latter, the Nkobamakosi and Mbonambi, made a turning movement along the front of the camp towards the English right, but became engaged long before they could accomplish it, and the two regiments and a battalion of the Nkobamakosi were repulsed, and had to retire until reinforced by the other battalion, while the Mbonambi suffered very severely from the artillery fire.

Meanwhile the centre, consisting of the Umcityu on the left, and the Nokenke and Nodwengu higher up to the right, under the hill, were making a direct attack on the left of the camp. The Umcityu suffered very severely both from artillery and musketry fire; the Nokenke from musketry fire alone, while the Nodwengu lost least. When we at last carried the camp our regiments became mixed up; a portion pursued the fugitives down the Buffalo, and the remainder plundered the camp, while the Undi and Udhloko regiments made the best of their way to Rorke's Drift to plunder the post there, in which they failed, and lost very heavily, after fighting all the afternoon and night.

We stripped the dead in the camp of all their clothes, and plundered everything we could find, many of the men getting drunk; and then towards sunset we moved back to our halting ground of the night before, all the more quickly that we saw another white force approaching. Next morning the greater part of the men dispersed to their homes with their plunder, a few going to the king to report, and they have not reassembled since.

A Native of the Natal Contingent Recalls
Colonel Durnford of the Royal Engineers

The Colonel rode up and down our line continually, encouraging us all, talking and even laughing with us— 'Fire away, my boys !' 'Well done, my boys !' he cried. Some of us did not like his exposing himself so much, and wanted him to keep behind, but he laughed at us and said, 'All right, nonsense.' He was very calm and cheerful all the time. Sometimes, as he passed amongst us, one or another of the men brought him his gun with the old cartridge sticking, and he dismounted, and taking the gun between his knees, because of having only one hand with strength in it, he pulled the cartridge out and gave back the gun.

There were not very many of us, but because of the way in which we were handled by our leader we were enough to stop the Zulus on that side for a long time. We could have carried him off with us safely enough at this time, only we knew him too well to try. But we now say, 'If we had known what would happen, we would have seized him and bound him, no matter if he had fought us for doing so, as he certainly would; no matter if he had killed some of us, we would have saved his life, for he was our master.'

Now we say that we shall always remember him by his commanding voice, and the way in which he gave us all some of his own spirit as he went along our line that day, and those amongst us who had not served under him before, as I have, say, 'Why did we not know him sooner?

We see also that but for him we should all have died that day. But at last our cartridges were nearly done. The Colonel had sent a messenger back to the camp for more, but none came. Then he sent Mr. Henderson and another (Mr. Cochrane?), but now our cartridges were quite done, and suddenly the Colonel, who was watching intently, told us all to come back with him into the camp. We went, but on the outskirts of the camp we met Mr. Henderson, who took us to our own wagons for more ammunition. The Colonel rode straight on to the General's tent at the upper end of the camp.

While we were getting our ammunition, the Zulu army swept down right round the upper camp, shutting us out, but our leader was within, and we saw no more of him. We were only a few, and the Zulus were too many to count. What could we do? Our leader had said that we had done well.

From the Natal Mercury

Oham's warriors that were at Isandhlwana have been examined by Colonel Wood concerning that calamity, and the events that came under their notice at the time. They say that our troops fought like lions, defending themselves fiercely until killed, and that all who were stabbed through the back were fighting with the Zulus in front, and died with their front to the enemy. When the Zulus made the attack it was the impression that there would be no fighting on our side, that the sight of their number alone would terrify the troops into running away, but to their cost they found out the contrary when too late. They say that their loss was more by the rifles than by the cannon, although the cannon mowed lines through their ranks at each discharge; and it is not true that the front ranks of the Zulus were pushed on by those in the rear. That each regiment rushed on voluntarily to the fight. This is certainly a high testimonial from our enemies to the valor and devotion of the gallant victims of Isandhlwana, every man of whom proved himself a hero by sharing in a sacrifice of life which shattered the power of the Zulu savage. Oham, his servants, and 700 of the women and children of his tribe, are in Utrecht. Some of his indunas with 150 or 200 of his warriors remain as hostages under the surveillance and orders of the officer commanding.

From a Natal Newspaper

We have received the following extract from the letter of a gentleman whose testimony may be relied upon:— 'When the loss of the camp seemed quite certain Colonel Pulleine called Lieutenant Melville and said — "Lieutenant Melville, you, as senior Lieutenant, will take the colors, and make the best of your way." He shook hands with him, and then turned round and said — "Men of the 1-24th, we are here, and here we stand to fight it out to the end," he was quite cool and collected.' The gentleman who wrote this would not pen anything for the sake of mere dramatic effect, and we are glad to be able to publish it, to show an English officer knows how to die when duty holds him to his post. The above will be a refutation of the severe remarks upon the late Lieutenant Melville by a writer in the Saturday Review, who implies that that officer rode away when his place was to remain and die with the rest.

The Isandhlwana Battlefield
by a Gentleman, January, 1879

The saddest reflection of the month has arisen from the remembrance of the unburied slain on that fatal field, where, we are told by private visitors, little else than bones now meet the eye. The flocks of vultures that hover about the spot tell their own horrible tale. The looted wagons are said to be there still, in a more or less smashed condition, though many, doubtless, were left in a workable state after the Zulus retired from the field. We are not aware whether any official inspection has been made of the locality. If it has taken place, the public has not heard of it.

From a Ceylon Newspaper

The 24th Regiment, it seems, lost at Chillianwallah about as severely as in the recent Natal affair. We quote from the Times of India of 12th February:

The unfortunate 24th Regiment was in India some years ago, the first battalion returning to England in the middle of 1861, and the second battalion in the early part of 1873. The 24th was one of the regiments which supplied detachments for the Little Andaman Island Expedition, and for his services on that occasion Captain Much, one of the officers of this regiment, who commanded the force, was thanked by the Commander-in-Chief in India, commended by the Government of India, and made the subject of a special notice in an official letter to Sir William Mansfield from the Horse Guards. It will be remembered that in the Chillianwallah affair the first regiment to reach the Sikh batteries was the 24th, which was overwhelmed by a fearful fire of grape and musketry, 459 men, with 23 officers, being at once killed and wounded.

The battle of Chillianwallah may be said to have sounded the knell of Sikh independence, and now the Sikhs are amongst the best and bravest of our Indian soldiers, and the Punjaub is at rest. Who knows if the men of our 24th, as brave and as devoted as their predecessors, may not be remembered as the pioneers who met their death in the first effort at the reduction of another Punjaub, whose inhabitants may yet be as faithful subjects of the Queen as any Sikh warrior?

Motto for the 24th from the Natal Colonist

The honor paid by the natives to the fallen at Isandhlwana we heard recently embodied in the pregnant expression, "Ba felwa ndawoyne". "They died in one place." The gallant 24th might do worse than adopt this tribute of admiration, extorted from the race of the enemy, as a motto for their regimental colors.

From the Special Correspondent of the London Times

When we had all ascended on to the ridge, it was between 8 and 9 o'clock, and it was decided to bivouac where we were, and move on at daylight in the morning. We took every precaution we could, as we knew we were followed by a large body behind, and might equally well be attacked from the front. Oh! how dreadful to all were those fearful hours which followed when all of us had to wait with what patience we could for daybreak, knowing that we were standing and lying among the bodies of our own comrades, though how many we little knew then. Many and deep were the sobs which came from the breasts of those who, may be, never sobbed before, at discovering, even in the dim morning light, the bodies of dear friends brutally massacred, stripped of all clothing, disembowelled, and in some cases with their heads cut off. How that night passed, I fancy few of us know. For my own part, I was both reckless and despairing—reckless at the chance of falling in with the enemy, and despairing because of the sad awakening I felt sure we should have in the morning. During the night, fires were constantly burning on all the adjoining hills, and one bright blaze in particular riveted our attention all night, as it seemed to be near Rorke's Drift, and we again feared for the safety of those within that small place, knowing we were utterly helpless to aid them in any way before morning.

At about an hour before daylight I arose, for I had been lying down close to the General and his staff, and went and had a quiet look around me to see for myself the state of affairs, and recognise any bodies that I could. I did this with a strong feeling of duty upon me, as otherwise I could not have got through it. I have seen many battlefields in Europe and elsewhere, and although on some I have seen thousands lying where I then saw tens, I do not think I ever saw such a sickening sight in all my life. Mixed with the debris of our commissariat wagons, the contents of which, such as flour, sugar, tea, biscuits, mealies, oats, &c, &c, were all scattered about in pure wantonness on the ground; there were also dead horses shot in every position, oxen mutilated, and mules stabbed, while lying thick upon the ground in clumps were bodies of white men with only their boots and shirts on, or perhaps an old pair of trousers or part of their coats with just enough showing to recognise to which branch they belonged. In many cases they lay with sixty to seventy rounds of empty cartridges alongside of them, showing that they had only died after doing their duty. The great wonder to me at the time was that so few men were able, in the open and with no protection or cover, to keep off for four or five hours such a large number of Kaffirs as that which must have attacked them.

How News of the Defeat was Received – from the London Times

The vicinity of Downing Street was the scene of an unusual excitement. Ministers were positively frightened out of their calm orderly bearing; Sir Michael Hicks-Beach was seen half-running and half-walking in the direction of Earl Beaconsfield's official residence; the latter, oblivious of the painful twinges of gout, rushed with the Colonial Secretary to the War Office, there consulting with the Secretary for War and the Commander-in-Chief for one hour. A Cabinet Council summoned under his own hand immediately met. with what result you already know. Would you like to know the general opinion as expressed by the London press? Most of them look upon the disaster with the same feeling, namely, that the lost ground must be retrieved at all costs.

From The Daily Telegraph, London

There is nothing except mournful glory in the behaviour of the officers and men who have fallen, however seriously the affair may reflect upon the military dispositions of their leaders; for that some one has blundered in this deplorable affair is, in truth, obvious. Yet, so far from being a blot upon the British annals, the conduct of these men and officers in their desperate strait casts new lustre upon our arms. They were not conquered, but overwhelmed; and the 24th Foot may inscribe the story of that cruel day in January upon their record not only without shame, but with sorrowful pride and satisfaction. Meanwhile, there is but one word to write as to what must be done. At any cost, with whatever necessary strength, the reverse must be effaced, the savage victors chastised, conquered, and disarmed, and these daring Zulus made as harmless as the Hottentots.

It would require more than ordinary courage to look into the columns of some papers. A rising of the whole of the black population in Cape Colony and Natal would be hailed with delight, as likely to embarrass the present Administration. It does seem a scandal that political capital should be coined out of what must surely be regarded as a military disaster.

If the Zulus had not been severely checked at Rorke's Drift, there was certainly a grave probability of their sweeping southward, gathering up the over-awed tribes as they went, and devastating South Africa from the Zambesi to Cape Town. We cannot over-estimate our debt of gratitude to the defenders of Rorke's Drift.

From a Letter Published in the Natal Mercury, February 11th

I am afraid you will think we have forgotten you up here. It is such a job to get paper, envelopes, or even a pencil; if you get hold of one you may consider yourself lucky indeed. You ask if I recognised any of our men who were killed at Isandhlwana. Well, I didn't; but some of the others did. They identified Swift, Tarboton (who had his head cut clean off), and the two Jacksons. Swift was the man who died hard. It seems they killed him with knobkerries. Moodie was not seen by anyone. Mackleroy was shot through the side while fighting with the others. He was not sick at the time. After he was wounded he managed to get on his horse and ride about half-a-mile, when he fell, and nothing more was seen of him. George Shepstone was shot dead. Only two of the Carbineers were sick that day — Moodie and Dean. Moodie turned out, and was seen to fire some shots, but Dean must have been killed in his tent. One thing is certain, that all fought well that day. If it had not been for the mismanagement, the Zulus would have been beaten off. Just fancy sending a company (70 men) out at a time to stop 20,000 Zulus; Barker, who escaped, said he saw one company which was sent on to the high hills to the left of the camp to keep the Zulus back. They shot hundreds of them, but in five minutes there was not a man left. Two other companies were served the same way. Now if the general orders had been obeyed, and had the wagons been formed into a laager, and everyone kept inside, all would have gone well; they could have kept them off until our column came to relieve them. My word! there were mistakes all round that day.

They taught the Zulus a lesson at Rorke's Drift, didn't they? We counted 351 dead bodies round the camp. One of our spies came in the other day. He says Cetywayo had the induna who led the attack at Rorke's Drift killed for attacking a place that was barricaded; but he was very angry with all his men for not following up and wiping us all out; but the beggars were afraid to attack. They did not know we were short of ammunition, lucky for us. This morning we learn the gratifying news that Major Black— hearing from a fellow officer that Lieutenant-Adjutant Melville, of the l-24th regt, was last seen on the Buffalo River, endeavoring to swim across with the colors of the regiment, in company with Lieut. Coghill—went out to the spot, and succeeded in finding the bodies of the two officers 300 yards this side of the Buffalo. In the river he found the colors much dilapidated. They were next day presented back by Major Black to Colonel Glyn, who received them on behalf of his regiment, thanking Major Black very cordially for recovering them. Major Black was assisted by two officers of the Native Contingent.

The Recovery of the Colors of
the 24th Regiment by a correspondent
on the Zulu frontier

A party went from our little camp at Rorke's Drift, consisting of Major Black, of the 2-24th Regiment; the Rev. George Smith, chaplain of the forces; Captain Harford, nineteen men, the commandant of Lonsdale's corps, Captain Charles Raw; four men of the Native Mounted Contingent, and Brickhill, the interpreter to the staff. The downward course of the Buffalo River was followed until a crossing place at an almost impassable drift was reached, where many of our brave fellows, after the carnage of Isandblwana camp, essayed to pass and perished in the attempt. The route was strewn with dead bodies, those of the natives composing the majority, these being either members of the Natal Native Contingent or loyal natives who believed in the supreme power of the Government or the magical effect of the boundary line even to the last.

When the steep path leading down the precipitous rocks to the river was reached scouts were posted. A descent was made, and half way down, nearly half-a-mile from the river, lay the bodies of Adjutant Melville and Lieutenant Coghill. These were decently interred, and service was performed by the chaplain. Lieutenant Coghill's ring, Adjutant Melville's spurs, and other articles belonging to the brave fellows being carefully taken charge of by their comrades. The path thence to the river was strewn with dead Zulus and various paraphernalia of savage warfare.

Arrived at the river, the dead horses, saddles, stirrups, spurs, leggings, charms, and articles of native dress, accidentally or purposely cast off, lying by the roaring stream, foaming over huge boulders, and passing between precipitous cliffs covered with bush and aloes, showed the spot where the rushing torrent and savage foe alike overwhelmed many brave men. About 500 yards below, at the crossing-place, Mr. Harbour, of Commandant Lonsdale's corps, succeeded in finding the Queen's colors of the 1-24th, with the pole complete, injured by the action of the rapid stream, but otherwise untouched, the gilt lion and crown surmounting the poles, and the color-case were found by two other of Lonsdale's men a few yards lower down.

These colors were borne back at the head of the little cavalcade in triumph, and when Rorke's Drift was reached the soldiers left their dinners or whatever occupation they were engaged upon, overjoyed at the sight of their lost colors regained, and gave their heartiest cheers for the old flag and for Major Black and the volunteers who had recovered them. The Major, in a few well-chosen words, then handed the colors to Colonel Glyn amidst loud huzzahs, and the Colonel, with heartfelt emotion, on behalf of himself and his regiment, thanked the little band for the noble work they had voluntarily undertaken and successfully performed."

Colonel Glyn and the Saving of the Colors of the 24th Regiment – from the London Gazette

The famous exhortation to the Spartan warrior of old to bring back his shield or to be borne back upon it finds its counterpart in the British army in the universal feeling of sanctity which attaches to the colors, and prompts to acts of heroism and sacrifice in preserving them. No more noble deed of this kind was ever done than that of Lieutenants Melville and Coghill in carrying off and preserving the Queen's color belonging to the First Battalion of the 24th Regiment in the miserable flight towards the Buffalo River on the fatal afternoon of Jan. 22. That the colors had been recovered from the river has been known for some time, but the thrilling story of the way they were carried off from Isandhlwana and saved from falling into the hands of the Zulus is now first told in its entirety in Colonel Glyn's despatch. If we lament, as, indeed we must, that the two heroes of this story perished in their gallant enterprise, there is yet no Englishman but will echo the words of Colonel Glyn, that their deaths could not have been more noble or more full of honor.

When the camp at Isandhlwana had been surrounded by the Zulus, and when it was clear that the day was lost, the Adjutant of the First Battalion of the 24th Regiment, Lieutenant Teignmouth Melville, seized the Queen's color belonging to the regiment and started off on horseback in the hope of saving it. The road between the camp and Rorke's Drift was already blocked, and Melville, therefore, took as direct a line as he could across a rugged country towards the Buffalo, pursued and almost encompassed by bands of the victorious enemy. The ground to be traversed was so rough and precipitous that only men flying for their lives, or like Lieutenant Melville, having something more precious than their own lives in their keeping, would have attempted to cross it on horseback. So slow was the progress of the fugitives that the nimble Zulus kept pace with them, harassed them at every point, kept up a constant fire on them, and at times got so close to them as to slay both men and horses with their assegais. Melville, however, encumbered as he was with his precious burden, held on his way and reached the river unscathed. Man and horse together plunged at once into the stream, but, the river being full, the rider, being more concerned for the safety of the colors than the control of his horse, got dismounted in mid-stream, and was carried down by the current, still clinging to his burden, towards a large rock in the middle of the water. To this rock Lieutenant Higginson, an officer of the Natal Native Contingent, was also clinging, and he at once came to Melville's aid. The stream, however, washed both men away, and carried them, together with the colors, into still water. Here another officer came to their assistance. Lieutenant Coghill, of the 24th Regiment, had been left in camp in the morning disabled for marching by a severe injury to his knee. He, too, had escaped on horseback, and had crossed the river in safety, but looking back and seeing Melville in difficulties, he turned round and at once rode back into the river to his comrade's assistance. By this time the pursuing Zulus had gathered in force on the further bank and opened a brisk fire on the little party, the red jacket of Melville offering a conspicuous mark. Coghill's horse was shot, and both he and Melville had great difficulty in struggling out of the water. The color was wrested out of their grasp by the force of the stream, and they reached the bank in a state of extreme exhaustion. Happily, however, their gallant task was accomplished, for the color, though lost to them, was saved from the enemy, its embroidery and heavy fringe causing it to sink in the river, from which it has since been recovered. Melville and Coghill, dismounted, exhausted, and one of them crippled, now endeavored to mount the hill on the right bank of the river, but their strength at last failed them, and they sat down to await the attack of their pursuers. Some days afterwards their bodies were found in the spot where they had last been seen alive, surrounded by parties of the enemy. Their task was accomplished, their duty was done, their strength was exhausted, and there was nothing left but to sell their lives as dearly as they could. They died, as many a gallant soldier has died before them, but the touching record of their noble death will long live in the memory of their comrades and their countrymen.

Colonels Glyn and Degacher and several officers went down the Buffalo a few days back, and erected a stone to the memory of Lieuts. Melville and Coghill. The bodies were exhumed and placed in coffins and reburied under a huge boulder. While moving the remains of Lieut. Melville Colonel Glyn found in his pocket his watch and chain.

Reaction to Melville's Heroism – from the Bendigo Advertiser

By the last mail a lady residing in Sandhurst, who is a relative by marriage of Captain Melville, the gallant young officer who sacrificed his life whilst protecting the colors of his regiment in the disastrous engagement which took place between a small force of British troops and an overwhelming number of Zulus a short time back, received a letter in which reference is made to the death of the hero of the occasion. We have been furnished with the following extract:

I am dreadfully grieved about poor young Melville, the adjutant of the 24th Regiment. He married just three years ago, at the Cape, E------'s favorite sister, and came home last year to the Staff College at Aldershott, with his wife and a little boy a year old. He had not been in England a week when he was ordered to rejoin his regiment at the Cape, as this dreadful Zulu war broke out; so he left his wife and child at home with his family in Cornwall, where she has been ever since, and now, poor girl, she is left a widow, and has another little son only two months old. She is not yet twenty-one. One consolation to her will be the noble way in which he died, as he was fortunate enough to escape the battle of Isandhlwana, but was last seen cutting his way through over 100 natives, cutting them down like grass with his sword, as he was determined to save the colors of the regiment, which had fallen into the hands of the enemy. After being mortally wounded in seven places he rescued the colors, which he had tied around him, and swam the river in time to lie down and die, knowing, as the papers say, that he had saved the honor of his country and regiment. A more noble or glorious death, of course, no soldier could possibly die. He is quite the hero of the day; the papers are full of his wonderful bravery, and he was mentioned in Parliament. The Queen is to present his two little boys with the Victoria Cross in admiration of their father's singular bravery in saving her colors at the cost of his own life, and is also going to give them a commission in the army when they grow up.

KNIGHTHOODS FOR STRICKLAND, WOOD AND PEARSON? – FROM A CAPE PAPER

It is rumored that the honor of knighthood is to be conferred on Commissary-General Strickland and Brigadiers-General Wood and Pearson, in recognition of their services during the war. The Times says that, in consequence of the large number of medical officers who have been sent to the Cape, the various home stations have been almost drained, and the sick at Fort Pitt Hospital, Chatham, are now partly under the care of civilian doctors. Large quantities of military stores continue to be sent out by every steamer, and it is reported that the daily issues from the Royal Arsenal at Woolwich exceed any experience of the kind even during the days of the Crimean War.

FROM A WRITER TO THE WORLD

I suppose few people know, or have taken the trouble to inquire, what was the value of the commissions of the officers who have lately lost their lives in the Zulu war. It will, no doubt, astonish a good many to learn that no less than £13,500 was lost by eight officers of the 24th Regiment alone in the battle of Isandhlwana.

FROM A CAPE PAPER

If the eighty men at Rorke's Drift had gone out in skirmishing order against 2,500—ten here, twenty there—would they not have been simply strangled by weight of numbers and wiped out, and must not a similar end have resulted if 800 went out in skirmishing order against 20,000, as happened at Isandhlwana?

Isandhlwana Revisited – from an Unnamed Source

Nearly two months after the fight and massacre there, the field of Isandhlwana has been visited. To Major Black, of the 24th, again belongs the honor of heading a gallant performance. It will be remembered that he it was who charged in the darkness up the "neck" that separated his column from the death-strewn valley; he it was too who headed the party which recovered the lost colors of the regiment, and secured decent burial for the remains of Lieutenants Melville and Coghill. On this occasion he led a party of 27 mounted volunteers, mostly irregulars, across the Buffalo at Rorke's Drift to the devastated encampment. It seems now generally understood that no one had previously visited the locality. We need not repeat here the account given of the scene which met the eyes of the adventurous party. The remains of the dead were undistinguishable, and could still scarcely be approached. The wagons seemed nearly all to be in working order, and under the General's tent private papers and mementoes of interest were found. The field guns had disappeared, and there were no traces of ammunition. The results of this expedition only serve to intensify the regret and surprise that have all along been felt at the absence of any attempt to revisit the place where so many brave subjects of the Queen lost their lives, and remained unburied.

Isandhlwana Revisited – a Letter from an Unnamed Correspondent

We pushed on very steadily and carefully, and at half-past 9 our advance guard was on the ridge over-looking the valley beyond Isandhlwana. There it lay, a magnificent stretch of country, with undulating plains for miles, only broken by Dongas and small rises, and bordered by high hills on each side.

Who would have thought, looking down on the quiet scene, that it had witnessed one of the most terrific fights and disasters of modern times? The grass had grown up over the whole site of what had once been our camp, and was thickly intermixed with mealie stalks and oat hay, green and growing yet. Among these lay the bodies of our poor soldiers, scattered about in all postures, and in all stages of decay; while the positions of our tents were indicated by the broken remains of boxes, trunks, tins of preserved meats, remnants of the tents themselves, and masses of disordered papers, books, and letters, &c, &c. The only thing, however, that at once drew the attention of a casual observer, was the broken remains of wagons, and the skeletons of horses and oxen.

Everything else was hidden at first sight, and required searching for to be noticed. One thing we had observed coming along the road was the fresh spoor of a wagon or two, and we conjectured that it had been recently used in conveying crops from Usirayo's Valley away into the strong-holds further inland. For some time after our arrival, and while preparations were being actively carried out to harness the horses to the best wagons, all the men, except those on vedette or other duty, were allowed to wander over the scene of the disaster.

The Carbineers, under Captain Shepstone, made immediately for their camp, and tried to find any relics of their dead brethren. Nothing of any consequence was, however, found near their lines, but upon searching over the ground where the bodies of some of them had been seen on the night after Isandhlwana, Capt. Shepstone came upon the bodies of Colonel Durnford, Lieutenant Scott, and nearly all the Carbineers except London and Bullock, and those few who were killed along the Fugitives' Path.

Poor Durnford was easily recognisable, and he had on his mess waistcoat, from the pocket of which Shepstone took a small pocket-knife with his name on it. Two rings were also taken, and are, with the knife, to be sent home in memoriam to the Colonel's father.

Durrant Scott lay partially hidden under a broken piece of wagon, and had evidently not been mutilated or touched after his death. He had his patrol jacket on buttoned across, and although the rest of the body was only a skeleton, yet strange to say the face was like in life, all the hair being still on, and the skin strangely parched and dried up, although perfect.

Both these bodies lay right in the midst of the rest of the young colonists who fell gallantly in defence of their country, and judging from the position in which they all were, they must have made one last gallant stand, and have been killed altogether. None of these so found had attempted to run, but had stuck together in life, as we found them in death. I can only add that Durnford's body was wrapped in canvas and buried in a kind of water-wash, while all the others were covered over with stones, &c, and their names written in pencil, on wood or a stone close by them.

The bodies of the Royal Artillery and Natal Mounted Police were also buried, the only ones left untouched being those of the 24th Regiment, which was done at the express desire of Colonel Glyn and the officers, in the hope of their being able some day to do it themselves.

This appeared, however, very strange to us, and many remarks were made about the seeming dishonor to part of our brave dead. However, let us hope that some day, not far distant, we may be able to return to that once truly blood-red field and bury all the bodies, bones, and relics, that may be left.

Great numbers of wagons have undoubtedly been taken away, as also everything of value in the camp, and many bodies have been, through one cause or another, either wholly or partially removed or disturbed, so as to effectually prevent recognition. I myself did not move far out of camp, and, therefore, may be a bad judge, but from what I saw there cannot have been more than 200 bodies in the camp itself, and out of these not twenty-five Kaffirs. Others who had not perhaps so many bitter feelings, or sorrowful remembrances of those lying round us went further and saw more, although I cannot hear of anyone having recognised any more bodies of officers, except those of Hon. S. Vereker and young Gibson, both Lieuts. in the Native Contingent.

Many interesting relics were found, and brought away by others, and I know of a few cases where letters addressed to relatives at home from those among the killed, were found complete, and will be sent home to be held in loving regard by the living, but will cause many sores scarce healed to be reopened.

The General was anxious, for more reasons than one, to get away quickly, and therefore, as soon as the wagons were ready, we made a start back at twelve, and reached Rorke's Drift at half-past three, without any hitch whatever. Immediately on getting back I went enquiring about among the different parties who had been over that day, and gleaned some other interesting facts from them.

One officer in the Dragoon Guards, while out with his squadron burning kraals, found in one signs of very recent occupation, and the staff of the Queen's color of the 1-24th. He also later on came across a kraal full of skeletons of Zulus, and this fact, taken in conjunction with the finding of large graves on the left of our camp containing bodies of the enemy, goes far to prove and substantiate my statement made in a former letter that the Zulus did move their dead bodies, and as the kraal was some two miles off where skeletons were found, they probably also moved them in our wagons.

The forty wagons we brought away included two water carts in good preservation, one gun limber, a Rocket Battery cart, and three Scotch carts. All that we left behind, in number not more than twenty, were in a partially or entirely disabled condition. Counting all there, therefore, there are still sixty or seventy wagons missing, which have been taken away at different times.

Last week, when Colonel Black and other officers visited Isandhlwana, in coming home by the Fugitives' Drift, they came across the body of Major Stuart Smith, who was killed just before reaching the river. They were not able to bury him on that occasion, being fired upon; but the morning after our visit, a squadron of Lancers, with some Artillery under Col. Harness, went down our side of the river, crossed over at the Fugitives' Drift, and buried the body, returning in the afternoon. Bengough's Battalion has also returned to Landsman's Drift with the Carbineers and the other mounted men, so that Rorke's Drift is again in its natural quietude.

ISANDHLWANA REVISITED:
MAJOR SMITH'S BODY FOUND –
FROM THE TIMES

For the next three miles over most broken ground where we could only proceed in single file, and at a walk, and often were obliged to dismount and lead, we traced the path, and only saw one body, a native, and winding over a ridge and down the slopes to the

Buffalo, guided here and there by a bit of paper, a shield, a pack saddle, &c, we came to the top of the precipitous ravine immediately above the river. It was at this point that the fugitives were obliged to descend pell-mell, being hemmed in by the enemy who, by a short cut, had here caught them up again.

Our party at their leisure led down to the river side more to the right, and then divided: some going down the river to look for the body of Major Stuart Smith, R.A., who was known to have been killed there; and the others crossing the Buffalo. There is still a quantity of water in the river, despite the report in the Witness of the 15th 'that it can be crossed anywhere dryshod,' and the crossing was quite dangerous enough. What it must have been on the 22nd when it was at least 2½ft. higher, and a roaring torrent, makes it a marvel how a single man escaped on that day. As it was we let the Kaffirs take the horses across, several slipping over the boulders and going completely under, and we followed, the current being strong, and the water waist deep.

Meanwhile the others went down the river half-smile and leaving their horses, scrambled up 300 yards to the foot of the bank where they believed the fugitives had come down. Lieutenant Mainwaring soon found the body of Major Smith almost concealed in the rank grass. It was clearly identified by the uniform, and had not been touched since the gallant officer was slain.

Captain Symons proceeded alone to the top of the cliff, it was very steep climbing, and he came every few yards on skeletons of men and horses, and at one point where there was a sheer drop of fourteen or fifteen feet, two men and three horses were lying at the bottom, and the marks on the face of the rock showed where they had crashed down headlong. (Survivors describe how the enemy pressed them sorely at this place.)

Descending again he joined the others, and they were in the act of giving Major Smith a rough burial when ping, ping, ping, came the swish of bullets over their heads. 'Zulus, by Jingo'—and in a few minutes they were back at the Drift where Capt. Banister had waited to show them the way over, and were soon safely across.

Thanks to the forethought of Colonel Black, a company of Major Bengough's N.N.C. had been ordered down to protect our crossing, and their fire checked and drove off the thirty or forty

Zulus who had followed us, and hoped to take us at a disadvantage at the crossing. The enemy having retired out of sight, the party proceeded up the Natal bank, and passing by the graves of Lieuts. Melville and Coghill, marked by the pretty granite cross, the gift of Sir Bartle Frere, rode the five miles back to Rorke's Drift.

On their arrival the signallers stationed on the hill above the laager reported that soon after we left Isandhlwan two small bodies of Zulus, one lot mounted, had appeared about the hill, and then came down towards the Bashee Valley, no doubt expecting that we were going to return by the way we had gone. The wily Zulu, however, was for once out-witted.

The object of the reconnaissance had been fully accomplished. There is no large body of the enemy near this place. Moreover, the officers of the 2-24th Regiment were anxious to search the Fugitives' Path, as they had been told that a very tall officer, riding a chestnut horse, and carrying a color, had been seen on the 22nd between the battlefield and the river. The description answered exactly to Lieut. Dyer, the Adjutant of the Regiment. No sign, however, of the officer or the color could be seen.

ISANDHLWANA REVISITED –
FROM THE TIMES OF NATAL

The scene that met us was at once magnificent and ghastly. The grand Isandhlwana rock on our left, the wonderful colors and shadows evolving by the 'King of Light' rising fresh from his ocean bath; the rich undulating plain stretching away in front, surrounded by mountains of every varied height and color; the intense stillness and silence; the ruins of the stricken camp; the whitening bones of 800 Englishmen—all this in a coup d'oeil—caused us to hold our breath in awe as we sat for a few moments on our panting horses.

Having posted vedettes, we swept the surrounding country with our glasses, without seeing a Zulu. Colonel Black gave us twenty minutes to roam about; long enough, as there was nothing of value to be found, and the grass, which in places had grown to a great height, hid the remains of the brave fellows till we almost trod on them. We counted over 100 wagons and vehicles of all sorts still there, and most of them sound. The diary of Lieutenant Pope, 2-24th Regiment, was picked up, and the following extract, written in ink, and most probably in his tent, could scarcely have been dry before the desperate fight began:

'*22nd January, 1879—4 a.m.—A, C, D, E, F, H, Companies of ours—12-3 N.N.C.—mounted troops and four guns off. Great Firing. Believed by l-24th. Alarm. 3 Columns Zulus and mounted men on hill E. Turn Out. 7,000 (!!!) more E.N.E., 4,000 of whom went round Lion's Kop. Durnford Basutos, arrive and pursue.—Rocket battery. Zulus retire everywhere. Men fall out for dinners.*'

A supplement to the London Gazette, published on the evening of March 17th, contains some important despatches, indicating as they do most plainly who it was that blundered and caused the disaster at Isandhlwana. The Court of Inquiry was held, it will be perceived, immediately (five days) after the disaster, which occured on the 22nd.

Isandhlwana Court of Enquiry
From the London Gazette
March 17th, 1879

Proceedings of a Court of Enquiry, assembled at Helpmakaar, Natal, on the 27th of January, 1879, by order of His Excellency the Lieutenant-General Commanding the troops in South Africa, dated 24th of January, 1879. President—Colonel F. C. Hassard, C.B., Royal Engineers. Members—Lieut.-Colonel Law, Royal Artillery; Lieut-Colonel Harness, Royal Artillery.

The Court having assembled pursuant to order, proceeded to take the following evidence:—

First witness—Major Clery states: I am Senior Staff Officer to the 3rd Column, commanded by Colonel Glyn, C.B., operating against the Zulus. The General commanding accompanied this column from the time it crossed the border into Zululand. On the 20th of January, 1879, at the camp, Isandhlwana, Zululand, the Lieutenant-General Commanding gave orders to Commandant Lonsdale and Major Dartnell to go out the following morning in a certain direction from the camp with their men—i.e., the Native Contingent and the Police and Volunteers, part of 3rd column. On the evening of the following day (the 21st) a message arrived from Major Dartnell that the enemy was in considerable force in his neighborhood, and that he and Commandant Lonsdale would bivouac out that night. At 1.30 a.m. on the 22nd a messenger brought me a note from Major Dartnell to say that the enemy was in greater numbers than when he last reported, and that he did not think it prudent to attack them unless reinforced by two or three companies of the 24th Regiment. I took this note to Colonel Glyn, C.B., at once; he ordered me to take it on to the General. The General ordered the 2nd Battalion 24th Regiment, the Mounted Infantry, and four guns to be under arms at once to march. This force marched out of camp as soon as there was light enough to see the road. The Natal Pioneers accompanied this column to clear the road. The General first ordered me to write to Colonel Durnford at Rorke's Drift, to bring his force to strengthen the camp, but almost immediately afterwards he told Colonel Crealock that he (Colonel Crealock) was to write to Colonel Durnford these instructions, and not I. Before leaving the camp I sent written instructions to Colonel Pulleine, 24th Regiment, to the following effect:— " You will be in command of the camp during the absence of Colonel Glyn; draw in (I speak from memory) your camp, or your line of defence (I am not certain which) while the force is out; also draw in your line of infantry outposts accordingly, but keep your cavalry vedettes still far advanced." I told him to have a wagon ready loaded with ammunition ready to follow the force going out at a moment's notice if required. I went to Colonel Pulleine's tent just before leaving camp to ascertain that he had got these instructions, and I again repeated them verbally to him. To the best of my memory I mentioned in the written instructions to Colonel Pulleine that Colonel Durnford had been written to to bring up his force to strengthen the camp. I saw the column out of camp and accompanied it.

Second evidence.—Colonel Glyn, C.B., states—From the time the column under my command crossed the border I was in the habit of receiving instructions from the Lieut.-General Commanding as to the movements of the column, and I accompanied him on most of the patrols and reconnaissances carried out by him. I corroborate Major Clery's statement.

Third evidence.—Captain Alan Gardner, 14th Hussars, states—I accompanied the main body of the 3rd Column, as acting staff officer to officer commanding 3rd Column, when it left the camp at Isandhlwana on the 22nd January, 1879. I was sent back with an order from the General between 10 and 11 a.m. that day into camp, which order was addressed to Colonel Pulleine. and was that the camp of the force out was to be struck and sent on immediately, also rations and forage for about seven days. On arriving in camp I met Captain George Shepstone, who was also seeking Colonel Pulleine, having a message from Colonel Durnford that his men were falling back, and asking for reinforcements. We both went to Colonel Pulleine, to whom I delivered the order. Colonel Pulleine at first hesitated about carrying out the order, and eventually decided that the enemy being already on the hill on our left in large numbers it was impossible to do so. The men of the 24th Regiment were all fallen in and the artillery also, and Colonel Pulleine sent two companies to support Colonel Durnford, to the hill on the left, and formed up the remaining companies in line, the guns in action on the extreme left of the camp, facing the hill on our left. I remained with Colonel Pulleine by his order. Shortly after, I took the mounted men, by Colonel Pulleine's direction, about a quarter of a mile to the front of the camp, and left them there under the direction of Captain Bradstreet, with orders to hold the spruit. I went back to Colonel Pulleine, but soon after, observing the mounted men retiring, I went back to them, and, in reply to my question as to why they were retiring, was told they were ordered by Colonel Durnford to retire, as the position taken up was too extended. The same remark was made to me by Colonel Durnford himself immediately afterwards. By this time the Zulus had surrounded the camp, the whole force engaged in hand to hand combat, the guns mobbed by Zulus, and there became a general massacre. From the time of the first infantry force leaving the camp to the end of the fight about one hour elapsed. I estimated the number of the enemy at about 12,000 men. I may mention that a few minutes after my arrival in camp I sent a message directed to the staff officer 3rd Column, saying that our left was attacked by about 10,000 of the enemy; a message was also sent by Colonel Pulleine. The Native Infantry Contingent fled as soon as the fighting began, and caused great confusion in our ranks. I sent messages to Rorke's Drift and Helpmakaar camp that the Zulus had sacked the camp, and telling them to fortify themselves.

Fourth evidence.—Captain Essex, 75th Regiment, states—I hand in a written statement of what occurred. I have nothing to add to that statement.

Fifth evidence.—Lieut. Cochrane, 32nd Regiment, states—I am employed as transport officer with No. 2 Column, then under Colonel Durnford, R.E., on the 22nd January, 1879. The column marched on that morning from Rorke's Drift to Isandhlwana, in consequence of an order received from the Lieutenant-General. I do not know the particulars of the order received. I entered the Isandhlwana camp with Colonel Durnford about 10 a.m., and remained with him as acting staff officer. On arrival he took over command from Colonel Pulleine, 24th Regiment. Colonel Pulleine gave over to Colonel Durnford a verbal state of the troops in camp at the time, and stated the orders he had received, viz., to defend the camp. Those words were repeated two or three times in the conversation. Several messages were delivered, the last one to the effect that the Zulus were retiring in all directions. The bearer of this was not dressed in any uniform. On this message Colonel Durnford sent two troops of mounted natives to the top of the hills to the left, and took with him two troops of Rocket Battery, with escort of one company Native Contingent on to the front of the camp, about four or five miles off. Before leaving he asked Colonel Pulleine to give him two companies 24th Regiment. Colonel Pulleine said that with the orders he had received he could not do it, but agreed with Colonel Durnford to send him help if he got into difficulties. Colonel Durnford, with two troops, went on ahead and met the enemy some four or five miles off in great force, and as they showed also on our left, we retired in good order to the Drift, about a quarter of a mile in front of the camp, where the mounted men reinforced us, about two miles from the camp. On our retreat we came upon the remains of the Rocket Battery, which had been destroyed.

Sixth evidence.—Lieutenant Smith-Dorien, 95th Regt., states—I am transport officer with No. 3 Column. On the morning of the 22nd I was sent with a despatch from the General to Colonel Durnford, at Rorke's Drift. The despatch was an order to join the camp at Isandhlwana as soon as possible, as a large force was near it, I have no particulars to mention besides.

Seventh evidence.—Captain Nourse, Natal Native Contingent, states—I was commanding the escort to the Rocket Battery, when Colonel Durnford advanced in front of the camp, on the 22nd to meet the enemy. Colonel Durnford had gone on with two troops, mounted natives. They went too fast, and left us some two miles in the rear. On hearing heavy firing on our left, and learning that the enemy were in that direction, we changed our direction to the left. Before nearly reaching the crest of the hills on the left of the camp we were attacked on all sides. One rocket was sent off, and the enemy was on us; the first volley dispersed the mules and the natives, and we retired on to the camp as well as we could. Before we reached the camp it was destroyed.

Eighth evidence.—Lieutenant Curling, R.A., states— I was left in the camp with two guns when the remaining four guns of the battery went out with the main body of the column, on the 22nd of January. Major Stuart Smith joined and took command of the guns about 12 noon. I hand in a written statement. I have nothing to add to that statement.

F. C. Hassard, Colonel, R.E., President.

F. T. A. Law, Lieut-Col., R.A.

A. Harness, Major, R.A., and Lieutenant-Colonel.

An Isandhlwana Miscellany
from The Natal Mercury

The losses sustained by Natal natives since the commencement of the war have been officially published. They amount to 482, most of whom were killed at Isandhlwana, and twenty wounded. The Amacuna tribe, under Pakadi, who live in Weenen County, suffered the most severe loss, having 240 killed; whilst the Amangwani tribe, under Sikali, had 103 killed and thirteen wounded. The Eden-dale Mounted Horse lost two men. This troop was raised at the Wesleyan Mission Station near Maritzburg, whose name they bear.

Maquende, Cetywayo's brother, who was at Isandhlwana, says the Zulus were defeated by the British soldiers, and about to fly, when the ammunition failed. The Zulus then plucked up courage for a rush. The 24th then stood in double line back to back, and fought with bayonets until killed by the weight of the enemy's force. The Zulu army numbered 25,000, of whom 14,000 attacked the camp, and 11,000 were reserves. Their intention was to enter Natal and lay waste the colony. The reserve made the attack on Rorke's Drift, and their repulse there saved the colony.

"From epileptic Caesar down to the 'hunchbacked dwarf,' who, according to Macaulay, commanded the French, and the 'asthmatic skeleton' who commanded the English, and down to Napoleon and still more modern generals, we see," says the Daily News, "That the battle is not in this sense always to the strong; but the Government now must perceive that Lord Chelmsford is wanting in robustness of a far more important kind."

The latest joke current at Pretoria is that a Zulu prisoner, having been asked what Cetywayo would do with Lord Chelmsford if he caught him, replied that he would send him back at once, for that he could not wish for a better general to command the forces invading his country.

A pathetic story is told of the late Surgeon-Major Shepherd, who lost his life at Isandhlwana. Before leaving London he engaged as body-servant the son of a club-waiter named Green. "I'll make a man of him," he said to the boy's father at parting. Young Green was wounded, and it was while stopping to assist him that his master met his death.

The 1-24th Band.—Volunteers from bands of various regiments have been called for to form a band of the 1-24th Foot, the whole of the band of that corps, having been killed in action at Isandhlwana.

VISIT TO THE BATTLEFIELD OF ISANDHLWANA
BY ARCHIBALD FORBES
CORRESPONDENT OF THE DAILY NEWS

At the top of the ascent beyond the Bashee, which the Dragoen Guards crowned in dashing style, we saw on our left front, rising above the surrounding country, the steep, isolated, and almost inaccessible hill, or rather crag, of Isandhlwaua, the contour of its rugged crest strangely resembling a side view of a couchant lion. On the lower neck of the high ground on its right were clearly visible up against the sky line the abandoned wagons of the destroyed column. No Zulus were seen. Flanking parties covered the hills on either side the track, along which the head of the column pressed at a trot, with small detachments of Natal Carbineers in front of the Dragoon Guards. Now we were down in the last dip, had crossed the rocky bed of the little stream, and were cantering up the slope that stretched up to the crest on which were the wagons. Already tokens of the combat and bootless fight were apparent. The line of retreat towards Fugitives' Drift, along which, through a chink in the Zulu environment, our unfortunate comrades who thus far survived tried to escape, lay athwart a rocky slope to our right front, with a precipitous ravine at its base. In this ravine dead men lay thick -- mere bones, with toughened, discolored skin like leather covering them and clinging tight to them, the flesh all wasted away. Some were almost dismembered heaps of clammy yellow bones. I forbear to describe the faces with their blackened features and beards blanched by rain and sun. Every man had been disembowelled. Some were scalped and others subjected to yet ghastlier mutilation. The clothes had lasted better than the poor bodies they covered, and helped to keep the skeletons together. All the way up the slope I traced by the ghastly token of dead men the fitful line of tight. Most of the men hereabouts were infantry of the 24th. It was like a long string with knots in it, the string formed of single corpses, the knots of clusters of dead where, as it seemed, little groups might have gathered to make a hopeless gallant stand and die. I came on a gully with a gun limber jammed on its edge, and the horses, their hides scored with assegai stabs, hanging in their harness down the steep face of the ravine. A little further on was a broken and battered ambulance wagon, with its team of mules mouldering in their harness, and around lay the corpses of soldiers, poor helpless wretches, dragged out of an intercepted vehicle and done to death without a chance of life.

Still following the trail of bodies through long rank grass and among stores, I approached the crest. Here the slaughtered ones lay thick, so that the string became a broad belt. Many hereabouts wore the uniform of the Natal Police. On the bare ground on the crest itself, among the wagons, the dead were less thick, but on the slope beyond on which from the crest we looked down, the scene was the saddest and more full of weird desolation than any I had gazed upon. There was none of the stark, blood-curdling horror of a recent battlefield; no pool of yet wet blood; no raw gaping wounds; no torn red flesh that seems yet quivering. Nothing at all that makes the scene of yesterday's battle so rampantly ghastly shocked the senses. A strange dead calm reigned in this solitude of nature; grain had grown luxuriantly round the wagons, sprouting from the seed that dropped from the loads, falling in soil fertilised by the life-blood of gallant men. So long in most places had grown the grass that it mercifully shrouded the dead, whom four long months to-morrow we have left unburied.

As one strayed aimlessly about one stumbled in the grass over skeletons that rattled to the touch. Here lay a corpse with a bayonet jammed into the mouth up to the socket, transfixing the head and mouth a foot into the ground. There lay a form that seemed cosily curled in calm sleep, turned almost on its face, but seven assegai stabs have pierced the back. Most, however, lay flat on the back, with the arms stretched widely out, and hands clenched. I noticed one dead man under a wagon, with his head on a saddle for a pillow, and a tarpaulin drawn over him, as if he had gone to sleep and died so. In a patch of long grass near the right flank of the camp, lay Durnford's body, the long moustache still clinging to the withered skin of the face. Capt. Shepstone recognised him at once, and identified him yet further by rings on the finger and a knife with the name on it in the pocket, which relics were brought away. Durnford had died hard—a central figure of a knot of brave men who had fought it out around their chief to the bitter end. A stalwart Zulu covered by his shield lay at the colonel's feet. Around him, almost in a ring, lay about a dozen dead men, half being Natal carbineers, riddled by assegai stabs. These gallant fellows were easily identified by their comrades who accompanied the column. Poor Lieut. Scott was hardly at all decayed. Clearly they rallied round Durnford in a last despairing attempt to cover the flank of the camp, and had stood fast from choice, when they might have essayed to fly for their horses. Close beside the dead at the picquet line a gully traverses the ground in front of the camp. About 400 paces beyond this was the ground of the battle before the troops broke from their formation, and on both sides this gully the dead lie very thickly. In one place nearly fifty of the 24th lie almost touching, as if they had fallen in rallying square. The line of straggling rush back to camp is clearly marked by the skeletons all along the front. Durnford's body was wrapped in a tarpaulin and buried under a heap of stones. The Natal Carbineers buried their dead comrades roughly. The gunners did the same by theirs. Efforts were made at least to conceal all the bodies of the men who had not belonged to the 24th Regiment. These were left untouched by special orders from General Newdigate. General Marshall had nourished a natural and seemly wish to give interment to all our dead who so long have lain bleaching at Isandhlwana, but it appears that the 24th wish to perform this office themselves, thinking it right that both battalions should be represented, and that the ceremony should be postponed till the end of the campaign. In vain Marshall offered to convey a burial party of the regiments with tools from Rorke's Drift in wagons. One has some, sympathy with the claim of the regiment to bury its own dead, but why postpone the interment till only a few loose bones can be gathered? As the matter stands, the Zulus, who have carefully buried their own dead, who do not appear to have been very numerous, will come back to-morrow to find that we visited the place, not to bury our dead but to remove a batch of wagons. Wandering about the desolate camp amid the sour odor of stale death was sickening. I chanced on many sad relics—letters from home, photographs, journals, blood-stained books, packs of cards. Lord Chelmsford's copying-book, containing an impression of his correspondence with the Horse Guards, was found in one of his portmanteaus, and identified in a kraal two miles off. Colonel Harness was busily engaged collecting his own belongings. Colonel Glyn found a letter from himself to Lieutenant Melville, dated the day before the fight. The ground was strewn with brushes, toilet bags, pickle bottles, and unbroken tins of preserved meat and milk. Forges and bellows remained standing ready for the recommencement of work. The wagons in every case had been emptied, and the contents rifled. Bran lay spilt in heaps. Scarcely any arms were found, and no ammunition. There were a few stray bayonets and assegais, rusted with blood. No firearms.

I shall offer a few comments on the Isandhlwana position. Had the world been searched for a position offering the greatest facilities for being surprised, none could have been well found to surpass it. The position seems to offer a premium on disaster, and asks to be attacked. In the rear laagered wagons would have discounted its defects; but the camp was more defenceless than an English village. Systematic scouting could alone have justified such a position, and this too clearly cannot have been carried out.

List of Officers and Men
Killed at Isandhlwana

"N" Battery, 5th Brigade, R.A.: Captain and Brevet-Major Stuart Smith; Brevet-Major Russell, R.A., Rekt. Bat.; Sergeant Edwards, Corporals Bailey, Cooper, Langridge; Bombadiers Parker, Nash; Act.-Bombs. Lequay, McDonnel, Aylett, Boswell; Farrier Whenham, Collarmaker Sheppard, Shoeingsmith Elliott, Gunners Reede, Meade, Woolacott, Wilson, Page, Beach, James, Miller, Lamb, Byrne, O'Neal, King, Williams, McGregor, Smythe, Burk, Regan, Hicks, Collins, Berry, Roscoe, Davies, Marshall, Redman, Wilson, Dickings, Stevenson, Connelly, Harrison, Cockrane; Drivers Barron, Hutchings, Bailey, Clark, Brooks, McKeown, Allen, Jones, Marchant, Cowley, Dailey, Murphy, Hiatt, Joyce, Adams, Spread, Bruce, Bishop.

Royal Engineers: Lieutenant-Colonel Durnford, Lieutenant McDowell, Corporal Gamble, Sappers Cuthbert, Maclaren, Wheatley; Capt. G. Shepstone, Political Assistant to Colonel Durnford.

1st Battalion 24th Regiment: Major and Lieutenant-Colonel Pulleine, Captains Degacher, Mostyn, Wardell, Younghusband; Lieut, and Adjutant Melville, Lieutenants Porteous, Cavaye, Anstey, Coghill, Daly, Hodson, Atkinson; 2nd Lieut. Dyson, Paymaster White, Quarter-Master Pullen, Sergeant.-Major Gapp, Quarter-Master-Sergeant Leitch, Inst. Musketry Chambers, Drum-Major Taylor, Order-Reg.-Sergeant Fitzgerald, Paymaster-Sergeant Mead, Armoury-Sergeant Hayward, Cook-Sergeant Field, Tailor-Sergeant Smedley, Color-Sergeants Brown, Whitlield, Edwards, Ballard. Wolfe; Sergeants Edwards, Heppenstal, Clarkson, Bradley, Fowden, Hornibrook, Piall, Fay, Bennett, Cooper, Upton, Gamble, Parsons, Cohalan, Giles, Ainsworth, Greatorex, Smith; Lance-Sergeants Milner, Reardon; Corporals Ball. Bell, Bellhouse, Board, Davis, Everett, Franks, Knight, Lawler, Markham, Miller, Rowden, Tarbuck, Williams, and Richardson: Lance-Corporals Chadwick, Conboye, Every, Haekin, Hewitt, Horgan, Johnson, Murphy, Thrassell, Wheatherhead, and Young; Drummers Adams, Andrews, Dibden, Haynes, Osmond, Orlapp, Perkins, Reardon, Stansfield, and Thompson; Privates Alingham, Amos, Atkins, Bailey, Baker, Barry (727), Barry (466), Bartles, Bastard, Beadon, Beckett, Benham, A. Bennett, R. Bennett, Benson, Betterton, Birch, Bishop, Blackhurst, Blower, Bodmin. Boulton, Boylan, Bray, Breese, Brew, Brodrick, J. Brown, Wm. Brown, Bugby, Bud, T. Burke, Wm. Burke, Burns.. Busby, Butler. Bye, Cahill, Calahan, Campell, Camp, Canhillon, Carpenter, Carrol, Casey, Ceiley, Chalmers, Chapman, Chatterton, Christian, Clarke, Clements, Clutterbuck, Cole, Coleman, D. Collins, T. Collins, Colston, C. Conmelly, J. Conmelly, Cormers, Cook, Cooper, Coughlin, J. Cox, T. Cox, M. Clarke.

Cullen, A. Davis, E. Davis. W, Davis, Diggle, Diggles, Dobbin, Dobbs, Donohoe, Dorman, Doran, Dowde, Dredge, Duck, Duckworth, Duffey, Dugmore, Dunn, Dyer, J. Edwards, W. G. Edwards, Wm., Egan, T. Egan, Elderton, Eldrington, Ellis, Ellisan,.J. W. Evans, D. Evans, Ellsmone, Faircloth, Farmer, Fay, Ferris, Fitzgerald, Fortune, Flint, Freeman, Gilder, Gillan, Gingle, Glass, Graham, Goddard. Goddchild, Gass, Green, Greig, Gregson,Grifflths, Hall, Hadden, Hall, Hannaford, Hannard, Hamey,T. Harris,Wm. Harris, Hayden. Hedges, Hemmings, Hibbard, Hickin, Hicks, Hitchin, Hines, Higgins, Holland, Holden, Home, Hornbuckle, Horrigan (Rorke's Drift), D. Harrington, T. J. Harrington, Haugh, E, Hughes, Jno. Hughes, John Hughes, Owen Hughes, S. Hughes, Iggulden, Ilsley, Ivatts, Jas. Jenkins, Wm. Jenkins, Wl. Jenkins, G. Johnston, H. Johnston, Job Johnson, Jno. Johnson (381), Jno. Johnson (144,) Jno. Johnson (1465), Jas. Johnson, Johnstan, E. Jones, Jno. Jones (360), Jno. Jones (428), T. Jones, Wm. Jones (341), Wm. Jones (1681). Keene, Keegan, Kempsall, Kempster, A. Kelly, J. F. Kelly, Jas. Kelly, F. Kelly, Knight, Lamb, Lambert, Leach, Leaver, Lee, H. Lewis, R. Lewis, Lenain, Ling, Lippet, Lisbeck, Lloyde, C. Lowe, R Lowe, Lockett, Lovell, Lyons, Lycett, Lawrence, Mack, Maney. Mann, Martin, McDonald, McFarlame, McHale, McKenzie, Mail. Mahoney (Rocket Battery), Malarey, Marley, Meredith, Millen, Miller, Moore, Jno. Morgan, Wm. Morgan, Morris, Morse, Jno. Murphy, P. Murphy, Murray, Nash, A. Newbery,

T. Newbery, E. Nickolas (Rorke's Drift), Wm. Nickolas, Nye, Oakley, Odey, Ogden, Padmore, Painter, Jno. Parry, R. Parry, Patterson, Petus, Jno. Phillips, J. N. Phillips, Pickard, Plant, Plunkett, Pallen, Pope, Potton, Powell, Procter, G. Prasser, Jno. Prasser, Wm Pugh (182) Wl. Pugh (856), Quirk, Remmington, Retford, Richards,Richardson Rigney Rettman, Roberts, Rowan, Rodgers, Rowbery, Rule, Rutter Ryan, Salter Sainey, Sears, Sellwood, Sharp, Shaw, Shea, Sheather, Shrimpton, Silcock, Skelton, C. Smith (506), C. Smith (1867) E Smith, Jas. Smith, G. Smith, Speed, H. Stevens,W. Stevens, Strange, Jno Sullivan P. Sullivan, Sutton, Swaffer Taylor Tate, Terry, Theobold J. B. Thomas, Jno. Thomas, Thomett; Tillisard Tuneny, Todd, Townsend, Trottmann,Turner (Mounted Troop) Trowell,Tullett,Vines,Waller,Walker, Thos. Walsh (285) Thos Walsh (493), Walhan, Wamer, Watkins, Watley Watts Webb Welsh,Whealon Whelan, Wilks,Wilkinson, Ellis Williams Jno., Williams, E.Williams, P.Williams, M. Williams, Thos Williams (534), Thos. Williams (624), Jas. Williams, Wilson, A Wollendak J. Wollendale, Wood, Wooley, Worthington, Wright Whybrow

2nd Battalion, 24th Regiment:

Lieutenants Pope, Austen and Dyer; Sub-Lieutenant Griffiths; Quarter-Mstr. Bloomfield; Band-Master Bullard; Quarter-Master-Sergeant Davis; Sergeants Lines Chew Ross Reeves, Carse, Shaw, and Wilkins; Lance-Sergeants McCaffry and Haigh; Corporals Henshaw, Sims, Lowe,Thompson Mortlock, and Greenhill; Lanee-

Corporal Elvey; Drummers Anderson and Holmes; Privates J. Byrne, Quinn McGuire T White, Mockler, Sherwood, Malley, J. Smith, Horrocks, J Flynn, Hawking ,T., Jones, Broderick, Kelley, Kennedy, Phillips, Howells, Evans, P. Smith, Long, T., Jones, Emerson, Lynch, E., Edwards R., Smith, Prichard, Buerly, T. Jones, W. Jones, Sathand, Mack, Stevens, Pedler, Watkins, Woods, J., White, Bryant, Carroll, Cornish, J. J., Davis J., Davis, Hacker, C. Hall, McCormack, Hudson, Hopkins, Slade, Thompson, Ball, J., Hall, J., Davis, Fortune, Lewis, G., Williams, Montgomery, Perkins McCaffry, Waterhouse, Bishop, Byard, Turner, McCracken, Fitzpatrick, Watson, Hill, King, Nobes, Machin, Neagle, Quelford, Farr, Allen, Bevan, Bennett, J. Byrne, Buckley, Bray Bridgewater, Cleary, Charles, G., Davis, Cherry, D., Davis, Dowle, Donegan, J., Edwards, Earish, Finn, Fitton, D., Flynn, Fry, Fox, Gee, Ghost, W., Hall, W., Griffiths (V.C.), Hughes, Healy, Hunt, Johnstone, Jenkins, J., Jones, E., Jones, J., Jones, Llewellyn, Martingale Marsh, Moore, Morris, Morrissey, Morgan, Murphy, McDoon, Poole, Popple, H., Price, J., Price, O'Keefe, Rees, Rice, W., Roche, M., Roche, Sheane, C. M., Smith, H., Smith, D. Smith, F., Smith, Ferrett, Thomas, Treverton, Walker, E., Williams, E., Williams, E., Williams, E., Williams, Williamson, Wright, Young Scott, Waters, Muiroy, B., Hall, Shuttleworth, Barton, Wightman and Saunders; Boys— Gordan, Gurney and McEwan.

Army Service Corps: Corporal Pritchard, Privates Cole and Jaques.

Army Hospital Corps: Lieutenant of Orderlies Hall Corporal Lee, Privates Kremer, Lewis, Dean, Hughes, Munn, Gillman Hogan Keen, Baker.

Army Medical Department: Surgeon-Major Shepherd Boy-Green, servant to Surgeon-Major Shepherd.

Mounted Infantry: 80th, Quarter-Mstr.-Sergeant Johnson, 9th Lancers, Farrier Sampson; 6th Dragoon Guards, Private McStravick; 2-3, Privates Shaw, Wheatley; 1 -24th, Turner; 80th, Chesterton, Holman, McDonald, Shoeing-smith Seymour, Private Whitehouse.

Civil Servant: Popworth, Wm., servant to Captain Gardner, special service; Turner, Robt., servant to Captain Hallam Parr, 13th Regiment.

Natal Mounted Police: Corporal Lally, Lance-Corporal Campbell, Troopers Banger, Berry, Blakeman, Clarke, Capps, Daniels, Dorey, Eason, Fletcher, Hunter, Lloyd, McRae, Meares, Neil, Parsons, Pleydell, Pollard, Secretan, Siddall, Stimson, Thicke, White, Winkles, and Pearce.

Natal Carbineers: Lieutenant Scott, Quarter-Master London, Quarter-Master-Sergeant Bullock, Troopers Blackie, Borain, Christian, Deane, Davis, Dickenson, Hawkins, Hayhow, Haldane. R. Jackson, F. Jackson, Lumley, Macleroy, Mendenhall, Moodie, Ross, Swift, Tarboton, and Whitelaw.

Newcastle Mounted Rifles: Captain Bradstreet, Quarter-Master Hitchcock, Sergeant Swan, Troopers Barnes, Greenbank, McAlister, and Dinkelman.

Buffalo Border Guard: Troopers Eary, Guttridge, and Wehr.

1st Battalion 3rd Regiment, N.N.C: Captains Krohn and Lonsdale, Lieutenants Avery, Holcraft, and Jameson; Acting-Surgeon Bull, Quarter-Master McCormick, Interpreter Grant, Sergeants Connock, Cole, Church, Welsh, Patterson, Golling, Bryant, Atkins, Russell, Donnell, Golding, McCarty, and Humphries; Corporals Sibley, Anderson, Palmer, Balmore, Duprie, O'Connell, O'Neil, Davidson, Quinn, Willey, Pearson, and Price; Hospital Sergeant Cane, Conductors Doyle and Le Roue, Cook Neil.

2nd Battalion, 3rd Regiment, N.N.C: Captains Erskine, Barry, and Murray; Lieutenants Pritchard, Young, Gibson, Standish, and Rivers; Quarter-Master Chambers; Quarter-Master-Sergeant Farr; Sergeants Schaap, Phillips, Brebner, Murray, Hamilton, Allen, Mowbray, A. Broderick, M. Broderick, Moore, Kemp, and Elversou; Corporals Walker, Green, Delaharpe, Sturk, Harrington, Willis, Styles, Caufield, Welsh, Allen, Schneither, De Villiers, Stapleton, Laughin, Pitzer.

Rorke's Drift

Rorke's Drift

Descending the steep and circuitous road from Helpmakaar the valley of the Buffalo River, at and above its junction with the Blood River, is comparatively open; whilst below, on the right, just at Rorke's Drift, a spur of the Biggarsberg shuts it in completely. Upon an elevated terrace of rock (which forms a sort of pedestal for the terminating hill of the range) stood a neat homestead, about three-quarters of a mile from the Drift.

The buildings were erected by a former border agent named Rorke, and, together with the farm, were recently purchased by the Rev. Otto Witt, on behalf of the Swedish Church, for the purpose of establishing a Zulu Mission; and the fine hill at the back was named Oscarsberg, in honor of the King of Sweden.

The house stood within a few feet of the edge of the rocky terrace, overlooking a well-enclosed garden of two or three acres in extent, planted with standard grape vines, and many fine orange, apricot, apple, peach, quince, fig, pomegranate, and other fruit trees. There was a road running parallel with the front of the house, between the garden and the terrace, with a strong stone wall along the terrace side; whilst the sloping ground between the walk and the summit of the terrace was occupied by a grove of fine Cape poplars, some large gum trees, and a luxuriant growth of bushes and shrubs of various kinds.

The dwelling-house standing as above described was over eighty feet in length, the side wall on the left running back nearly sixty feet.

Forty paces to the left, but with its frontage line of eighty feet running parallel with the extreme back wall of the dwelling-house, was another block of buildings, consisting of large store-rooms, wagon-house, stable, &c. These buildings extended back fifty-two feet. Almost parallel with the extreme left wall of this block of buildings, with only a space of ten or twelve feet intervening, a stone wall extended to the edge of the ledge of rocks, forming the right wall of a kraal some fifty feet square, which was divided in half by another similar and parallel wall.

Passing out of the semi-enclosure to the left, between the storehouse and the kraal, one saw the neat double row of tents occupied by B Company, 2-24th Regt., under the command of Lieut. Bromhead; whilst all along at the back, and running parallel with the buildings, juts out another and very precipitous rocky ledge, some thirty or forty feet high, full of caves, thoroughly overlooking, and within 350 yards of the premises.

The dwelling-house had been fitted up by the medical authorities as a base hospital for the column, and nearly all the rooms, as well as the large verandah in front, which had been carefully screened with blankets, were occupied by patients—thirty-six in number, including some who had been wounded at the taking of Usirayo's kraals, on Jan. 12.

The large store-house was occupied by the commissariat department, and was full of provisions of all kinds.

On Wednesday afternoon, January 22nd, after the slaughter at the camp at Isandhlwana, three companies (or regiments) of Zulus were formed upon the neck of land above the late camp, and marched towards Rorke's Drift; each company appeared to be from 1,000 to 1,500 strong. No. 1 company (we will call it) marched on in advance in open order, and "drove" every mealie garden, firing heavily all the while, killing many Europeans and natives who were trying to escape from Isandhlwana. They crossed the Buffalo River about four miles below Rorke's Drift, just below where the river makes a bend, almost at right angles, between precipitous rocky sides, firing repeatedly into every cave, bush, and crevice that might have afforded shelter for refugees. Being satisfied with the result, so far, they came on to a small green hill, sat down, and—took snuff all round.

Companies 2 and 3 then followed the example of No. 1, keeping some distance apart. They also advanced in open order—after going through various exercises, dividing off (apparently) into hundreds, then into tens, wheeling and quickly reforming; they crossed the river just above the bend, repeatedly firing amongst the bushes and rocks on both sides. They remained a long time in the river, forming a line across it, either for bathing or to assist one another in fording the stream.

By the time they had gained the rising ground upon this side, and had sat down to take snuff, up started ten men of No. 1, and ran on in advance up the valley, which lies between the high land at Helpmakaar and the hills at the back of Rorke's Drift.

In the meantime another party of Zulus, who must have crossed the river some miles lower down, had set a European house and a Kaffir kraal on fire, about four or five miles away at the back of Rorke's Drift.

No. 1 company followed their advanced guard at an easy pace. No. 2 company started off, bearing away to their left, apparently to join and support No. 1.

No. 3 company started off' two men straight for Rorke's Drift, who ran as hard as they could, followed by ten others who took it more easily; and then came on the rest, headed and led by two very corpulent chief's on horseback.

Whilst these Zulu warriors, reeking with British blood, are pressing on "like a steady rain," to plunder the Government stores, and (incidentally, of course) "wipe out" the handful of men that may attempt to defend them; let us see what preparations for defence have been made by the little band, if only they have been warned in time.

About 3 p.m., or shortly after, several mounted men arrived from the camp at Isandhlwana, and reported the terrible disaster which had occurred.

Lieut. Bromhead, commanding the company (B) of 2-24th Regt., at once struck his camp, sent down for Lieut. Chard, R.E. (who was engaged with some half-a-dozen men at the ponts on the river), to come up and direct the preparations for defence, as in the absence of Major Spalding the command of the post devolved upon him.

The windows and doors of the hospital were blocked up with mattresses, &c, loop-holes made through the walls, both of the hospital and store-house. A wall of mealie and other grain bag's was made, enclosing the front of the hospital, and running along the edge of the rocky terrace to the stone wall of the kraal, which has been described as coming from the far end of the store-house at right angles to the front of that building, down to the edge of these rocks.

Other mounted men arrived from the late camp, and told of the horrors they had escaped, and the dangers that were about to overwhelm us. Doubtless the poor fellows had seen terrors enough for one day, and were possessed by an earnest desire to warn the people at Helpmakaar in time, and so, like many before, and several after, on they gallopped to carry out their laudable intention.

A praiseworthy effort was made to remove the worst cases in hospital to a place of safety; two wagons were brought up, after some delay, and the patients were being brought out, when it was found that the Zulus were so close upon us that any attempt to take them away in ox wagons would only result in their falling into the enemies' hands. So the two wagons were at once utilised and made to form part of the defensive wall connecting the right hand front corner of the store-house with the left hand back corner of the hospital—about 40 paces long; sacks of mealies forming the remainder, and being also used as barricades' underneath and upon the wagons. A barricade, filling up the small space between the left front corner of the store-house and the stone wall of the kraal before referred to, and the blocking up of the gates of the kraal itself, made the outer defensive work complete. The men worked with a will, and were much encouraged by the unremitting exertions of both the military officers, the medical officer, and Assistant-Commissary Dalton, all of whom not merely directed but engaged most energetically in the construction of the barricades.

The water cart in the meantime had been hastly filled and brought within the enclosure.

The pontman Daniells and Sergt. Milne, 3rd Buffs, offered to moor the ponts in the middle of the stream and defend them from their decks with a few men. But our defensive force was too small for any to be spared, and these men subsequently did good service within the fort.

About 100 men of Durnford's Horse, who came in from the camp, had been drawn up for an hour or so, upon some rising ground, half a mile off. As soon as firing was heard, they rode off in a body to Helpmakaar, and then a noble body of some 350 loyal natives, who had been left specially to protect this post, and had consumed one or two oxen daily, at the expense of a paternal Government, and had got fat in the process, were seen hurrying away like a flock of sheep to the summit of a distant hill.

The anxiety which had been displayed for the safety of Helpmakaar, Fort Pine, Dundee, and other distant places, had considerably lessened the number of those whose help had naturally been calculated upon for the defence of the place. Seeing this, Lieut. Chard had a retrenchment of a double row of biscuit boxes placed from the right hand front corner of the store-house, straight down, and at right angles to the barricade, running along the ledge of rocks in front, thus dividing our whole enclosure (roughly speaking) in half.

Between this retrenchment and the kraal wall on the left, were two large pyramids of sacks of mealies and oats standing side by side.

About 4.30 p.m., the Zulus came in sight, coming round the right hand end of the large hill in our rear; only about 20 at first appeared, advancing in open order. Their numbers were speedily augmented and their line extended quite across the neck of land from hill to hill. A great number of "dongas," on their line of approach, a stream with steep banks, the garden with all its trees and surroundings, gave them great facilities for getting near us unseen. The garden must have soon been occupied, for one unfortunate Contingent corporal, whose heart must have failed him when he saw the enemy and heard the firing, got over the parapet and tried to make his escape on foot, but a bullet from the garden struck him, and he fell dead within 150 yards of our front wall. An officer of the same corps who had charge of the 350 natives before referred to, was more fortunate, for being mounted, he made good his escape, and "lives to fight another day."

But the enemy are upon us now, and are pouring over the right shoulder of the hill in a dense mass, and on they come, making straight for the connecting wall between the store-house and the hospital; but when they get within fifty yards, the firing is altogether too hot for them. Some half of them swerve round to their left, past the back and right end of the hospital, and then make a desperate attempt to scale the barricade in front of that building: but here too, they are repulsed, and they disperse, and find cover amongst the bushes and behind the stone wall below the terrace. The others have found shelter amongst numerous banks, ditches, and bushes, and behind a square Kaffir-house and large brick ovens, all at the rear of our enclosure. One of the mounted Chief's was shot by Private Dunbar, 2-24th, who also killed eight of the enemy, in as many consecutive shots, as they came round a ledge of the hill; and as fresh bodies of Zulus arrive they take possession of the elevated ledge of rocks overlooking our buildings and barricades at the back, and all the caves and crevices are quickly filled, and from these the enemy pour down a continuous fire upon us.

A whisper passes round amongst the men— "poor old King Cole is killed." He was at the front wall, a bullet passed through his head, and then struck the next man upon the bridge of the nose, but the latter was not seriously hurt. Mr. Dalton, who is a tall man, was continually going along the barricades, fearlessly exposing himself, and cheering the men, and using his own rifle most effectively. A Zulu ran up near the barricade; Mr. Dalton called out "pot that fellow," and himself aimed over the parapet at another, when his rifle dropped, he turned round quite pale, and said that he had been shot. The doctor was by his side at once, and found that a bullet had passed quite through, above the right shoulder. Unable any longer to use his rifle (although he did not cease to direct the fire of the men who were near him), he handed it to Mr. Byrne, who used it well.

Presently, Corporal C. Scammell, N.N.C., who was near Mr. Byrne, was shot through the shoulder and back; he crawled a short distance and handed the remainder of his cartridges to Lieut. Chard, and then expressed his desire for a drink of water; Byrne at once fetched it for him, and whilst giving it him to drink, poor Byrne was shot through the head, and fell dead instantly.

The garden and the road—having the stone wall and thick belt of bush as a screen from the fire of our front defences—were now occupied by a large force of the enemy; they rushed up to the front barricade and soon occupied one side whilst we held the other; they seized hold of the bayonets of our men, and in two instances succeeded in wrenching them off the rifles, but the bold perpetrators were instantly shot. One fellow fired at Corporal Scheiss of the N.N.C. (a Swiss by birth, who was a hospital patient), the charge blowing his hat off; he instantly jumped upon the parapet and bayoneted the man, regained his place and shot another, and then repeating his former exploit, climbed up the sacks and bayoneted a third; a bullet struck him in the instep early in the fight, but he would not allow that his wound was a sufficient reason for leaving his post, yet he has suffered most acutely from it since. Our men at the front wall had the enemy hand to hand, and besides, were being fired upon very heavily from the rocks and caves above us in our rear. Five of our men were here shot dead in a very short space of time; so by six p.m., the order was given for them to retire to our retrenchment of biscuit boxes, from which such a heavy fire was sent along the front of the hospital, that although scores of Zulus jumped over the mealie bags to get into the building, nearly every man perished in that fatal leap; but they rushed to their death like demons, yelling out their war-cry of "Usutu," "Usutu." Shortly after, they succeeded in setting the roof of the hospital on fire, at its further end. As long as we held the front wall, the Zulus failed in their repeated attempts to get into the far end room of the hospital; Lieut, Bromhead, several times, having driven them back with a bayonet charge. When we had retired to the retrenchment, and the hospital had been set on fire, a terrible struggle awaited the brave fellows who were defending it from within.

Private Joseph Williams fired from a small window at the far end of the hospital. Next morning fourteen warriors were found dead beneath it, besides others along his line of fire. When their ammunition was expended, he and his companions kept the door with their bayonets, but an entrance was subsequently forced, and he, poor fellow, was seized by the hands, dragged out, and killed before their eyes. His surviving companions were Private John Williams, No. 1395, and two patients. Whilst the Zulus were dragging forth our men's late brave comrade, the latter succeeded in making a hole in the partition with an axe, and got into another room, where they were joined by Private Henry Hook, and he and Williams, turn about, one keeping off the enemy, the other working, succeeded in cutting holes into the next adjoining rooms.

One poor fellow, Jenkins, venturing through one of these, was also seized and dragged away, the others escaped through the window looking into the enclosure towards the store-house, and running the gauntlet of the enemy's fire, most of them got safely within the entrenchment. Trooper Hunter of N.M.P., a very tall young man, who was a patient in the hospital, was not so fortunate, but fell before he could reach the goal. In another ward Privates 593, Wm. Jones, and 716, Robt. Jones, defended their post until six out of the seven patients in it had been safely removed. The seventh was Sergt. Maxfield, who was ill with fever, and delirious. Private R. Jones went back to try and carry him out, but the room was full of Zulus and the poor fellow was dead. The native of Umkungu's tribe who had been shot through the thigh at Usirayo's kraal, was lying unable to move; he said that he "was not afraid of the Zulus, but wanted a gun." When the end room in which he lay was forced, Private Hook heard the Zulus talking with him; next day his charred remains were found amongst the ruins.

Corporal Mayer, N.N.C., who had been wounded under the knee with an assegai, at Usirayo's kraal, Bombadier Lewis, R.A., whose leg and thigh were much swollen from a wagon accident, and Trooper R. S. Green, N.M.P., also a patient, all got out of the little end window within the enclosure. The window being high up, and the Zulus already within the room behind them, each man had a fall in escaping, and had then to crawl (for none of them could walk) through the enemy's fire, inside the retrenchment. Whilst doing this, Green was struck in the thigh with a spent bullet. Some few escaped from the front of the hospital, and ran round to the right to the retrenchment, but two or three were assegaied as they attempted it. Gunner Howard. R.A., ran out of the hospital, and managed to hide himself in the long grass on the upper side of the stone wall below our front parapet. He covered himself as well as he could with twigs and grass, and there, in company with a dead pig, and four of our horses (which had been shot where they were tied up), he lay unobserved all night, and came in unharmed at day-light. Another, Private Waters, 1-24th, secreted himself in a cupboard in the hospital, and killed many Zulus who entered the room, he himself getting wounded in the arm. At last he put over him a black cloak, and ran out of the burning building amongst the bushes, in one of which he lay concealed and unharmed until morning, with hundreds of Zulus moving about during the night upon all sides of him.

Whilst the hospital was being thus gallantly defended, Lieutenant Chard and Assistant-Commissary Dunne, with two or three men, succeeded in converting the two large pyramids of sacks of mealies into an oblong and lofty redoubt, and, under heavy fire, blocking up the intervening space between the two with sacks from the top of each, leaving a hollow in the centre for the security of the wounded, and giving another admirable and elevated line of fire all round. About this time the men were obliged to fall back from the outer to the middle, and then to the inner wall of the kraal, forming our left defence.

The Zulus do not appear to have thrown their assegais at all, using them solely for stabbing purposes.

Corporal Allen and Private Hitch both behaved splendidly. They were badly wounded early in the evening, and incapacitated from firing themselves, but never ceased going round and serving out ammunition from the reserve to the fighting men.

The light from the burning hospital was of the greatest service to our men, lighting up the scene for hundreds of yards around; but before ten p.m. it had burned itself out. The rushes and heavy firing of the enemy did not slacken until past midnight, and from that time until daylight, a desultory fire was kept up by them, from the caves above us in our rear, and from the bush and garden in front.

At last daylight dawned, and the enemy retired round the shoulder of the hill by which they had approached. Whilst some remained at their posts, others of our men were sent out to patrol, and returned with about 100 rifles and guns, and some 400 assegais, left by the enemy upon the field; and round our walls, and especially in front of the hospital, the dead Zulus lay piled up in heaps. About 350 were subsequently buried by us. They must have carried off nearly all their wounded with them.

Our loss was 15 killed, two mortally wounded, and 10 others less seriously wounded. But we were not to be left alone, for between 7 a.m. and 8 a.m. the enemy re-appeared in great force, in the same direction as before, when, fortunately, the General, with the remainder of the column, was seen coming in the opposite direction, and, crossing the Buffalo, came straight to our relief, and the Zulus made off as they approached.

Whilst all behaved so gallantly, it was hardly possible to notice other exceptional instances, although all their comrades bore testimony to such in the conduct of Color-Sergeant Bourne, 2-24th, Sergeant Williams, 2-24th (wounded dangerously—since dead), Sergeant Windridge, 2-24th, and Privates McMahon, A.H.C., and Roy, 1-24th.

It was certainly of the utmost strategical importance that this place should not be taken. Perhaps the safety of the remainder of the column, and of this part of the colony, depended on it.

The determined and successful resistance which by God's help the brave fellows were able to make seems to have surprised the enemy, who have not shown themselves near the place since.

Whatever signs of approval may be conferred upon the defenders of Rorke's Drift from high quarters, they will never cease to remember the kind and heartfelt expressions of gratitude which have fallen both from the columns of the colonial press and so many of the Natal colonists themselves.

The Official Report of the Defence of Rorke's Drift

The Lieutenant-General Commanding the Forces in South Africa has much satisfaction in publishing for general information the official report of the gallant defence of Rorke's Drift post, on the 22nd and 23rd January.

The Lieutenant-General feels sure that the gallant conduct of the garrison will receive most ample recognition. He trusts that the example set by those few brave men, and the success which attended their noble efforts, will be taken to heart by all under his command.

The odds against them were nearly thirty to one; but by taking advantage of the materials which lay to their hand, and by hastily constructing with them such cover as was possible, the gallant little garrison were enabled to repulse, for twelve hours, the determined attack made upon their position; and inflicted a loss upon the enemy, in killed alone, of more than three times their own number.

Rorke's Drift, 25th January, 1879.

Lieutenant Chard's Report

Sir—I have the honor to report that on the 22nd inst. I was left in command at Rorke's Drift by Major Spalding, who went to Helpmakaar to hurry on the company of the 24th Regiment ordered to protect the ponts.

About 3.15 p.m. on that day I was at the ponts, when two men came riding from Zululand at a gallop, and shouted to be taken across the river. I was informed by one of them, Lieut. Adendorff, of Lonsdale's regiment (who remained to assist in the defence), of the disaster at Isandhlwana camp, and that the Zulus were advancing at Rorke's Drift. The other carbineer rode off to take the news to Helpmakaar.

Almost immediately I received a message from Lieutenant Bromhead, commanding the company of 24th regiment at the camp near the Commissariat stores, asking me to come up at once.

I gave the order to inspan, strike tents, put all stores, &c, into the wagon, and at once rode up to the Commissariat store, and found that a note had been received from the third column to state that the enemy were advancing in force against our post, which we were to strengthen and hold at all cost.

Lieutenant Bromhead was most actively engaged in loop-holing and barricading the store, building, and hospital, and connecting the defence of the two buildings by walls of mealie-bags and two wagons that were on the ground.

I held a hurried consultation with him and with Mr. Dalton, of the commissariat, who was actively superintending the work of defence (and whom I cannot sufficiently thank for his most valuable services), entirely approving of the arrangements made. I went round the position, and then rode down to the pont and brought up the guard of one sergeant and six men, wagon, &c.

I desire here to mention the offer of the pont man, Daniells, and Sergeant Milne, 3rd Buffs, to moor the ponts in the middle of the stream, and defend them from their decks with a few men. We arrived at the post at 3.30 p.m. Shortly after an officer of Durnford's Horse arrived and asked for orders; I requested him to send a detachment to observe the drifts and ponts, to throw out outposts in the direction of the enemy, and check his advance as much as possible, falling; back upon the post when forced to retire, and assisting in its defence.

I requested Lieutenant Bromhead to post his men, and having seen his and every man at his post, the work once more went on.

About 4.20 the sound of firing was heard behind the hill to our south. The officer of Durnford's returned, reporting the enemy close upon us, and that his men would not obey his orders, but were going off to Helpmakaar, and I saw them, apparently about 100 in number, going off in that direction.

About the same time Captain Stephenson's detachment of Natal Native Contingent left us, as did that officer himself.

I saw that our line of defence was too extended for the small number of men now left us, and at once commenced a retrenchment of biscuit boxes.

We had not completed a wall two boxes high, when, about 4.30 p.m., five or six hundred of the enemy came in sight, around the hill to our south, and advanced at a run against our south wall. They were met with a well sustained fire, but, notwithstanding their heavy loss, continued the advance to within fifty yards of the wall, when they met with such a heavy fire from the wall, and cross fire from the store, that they were checked, but taking advantage of the cover afforded by the cookhouse, ovens, &c., kept up a heavy fire. The greater number, however, without stopping, moved to the left, around the hospital, and made a rush at our north-west wall of mealie-bags, but after a short but desperate struggle were driven back, with heavy loss, into the bush around the work.

The main body of the enemy were close behind, and had lined the ledge of rock and caves overlooking us, about 400 yards to our south, from where they kept up a constant fire, and advancing somewhat more to their left than the first attack, occupied the garden, hollow road, and bush in great force.

Taking advantage of the bush which we had not cut down, the enemy were able to advance under cover close to our wall, and in this part soon held one side of the wall while we held the other. A series of desperate assaults were made, extending from the hospital along the wall as far as the bush reached, but each was most splendidly met and repulsed by our men with the bayonet, Corporal Schiess, N.N.C., greatly distinguishing himself by his conspicuous gallantry.

The fire from the rocks behind us, though badly directed, took us completely in reverse, and was so heavy that we suffered very severely, and about six p.m. were forced to retire behind the entrenchment of biscuit boxes.

All this time the enemy had been attempting to force the hospital, and shortly after set fire to its roof.

The garrison of the hospital defended it room by room, bringing out all the sick that could be moved before they retired, Privates Williams, Hook, R. Jones, and W. Jones, 24th regiment, being the last men to leave, holding the doorway with the bayonet, their own ammunition being expended.

From the want of interior communication and the burning of the house, it was impossible to save all. With most heartfelt sorrow, I regret we could not save these poor fellows from their terrible fate.

Seeing the hospital burning and the desperate attempts of the enemy to fire the roof of the stores, we converted two mealie-bag heaps into a sort of redoubt, which gave a second line of fire all round, Assistant-Commissary Dunne working hard at this, though much exposed, and rendering-valuable assistance. As darkness came on we were completely surrounded, and after several attempts had been gallantly repulsed were eventually forced to retire to the middle, and then the inner wall of the kraal was on our east. The position we then had we retained throughout. A desultory fire was kept up all night, and several assaults were attempted and repulsed; the vigour of the attack continuing until after midnight; our men firing with the greatest coolness, did not waste a single shot, the light afforded by the burning hospital being of great help to us.

About 4 a.m. on the 23rd, the firing ceased, and at daybreak the enemy were out of sight over the hill to the south-west. We patrolled the grounds, collecting the arms of the dead Zulus, and strengthened our defences as much as possible. We were removing the thatch from the roof of the stores, when about seven a.m. a large body of the enemy appeared on the hills to the south-west.

I sent a friendly Kaffir who had come in shortly before, with a note to the officer commanding at Helpmakaar, asking for help. About 8 a.m., the third column appeared in sight, the enemy, who had been gradually advancing, falling-back as they approached. I consider the enemy who attacked us to have numbered about 3,000. We killed about 350.

Of the steadiness and gallant behaviour of the whole garrison I cannot speak too highly. I wish especially to bring to your notice the conduct of Lieut. Bromhead, 2-24th regiment, and the splendid behaviour of his company B; Surgeon Reynolds A.M.D., in his constant attention to the wounded under fire, where they fell; Acting-Commissariat Officer Dalton, to whose energy much of our defences were due, and who was severely wounded while gallantly assisting in the defence; Assistant-Commissary Dunne, acting Storekeeper Byrne (killed), Color-Sergeant Bourne 2-24th, Sergeant Williams 2-24th (wounded dangerously), Sergt. Windridge 2-24th, Corporal Schiess 2-3rd N.N.C. (wounded); Privates Williams and Jones 2-24th, McMahon, A.H.C., R. Jones 2-24th, H. Hook, Roy, 1-24th.

The following return shows the number present at Rorke's Drift, 22nd January, 1879.

Twelve wounded (list already forwarded by medical officer) of whom two have since died, viz., Sergeant Williams, 2-24th regiment, and Private Beckett, 1-24th regiment, making a total killed of 17.

I have the honour to be,

Your obedient servant,

(Signed) Jno. R. M. Chard, Lieut. R.E.

To Col. Glyn, C.B., Com. 3rd Col.

Forwarded, J. R. GLYN,

Col. Com. 3rd Column. Rorke's Drift, 3rd Feb., 1879.

Such is the accurate account of this memorable defence; and old hands not given to sensational remarks have pointed out the serious likelihood of the Zulus continuing their victorious march onwards, penetrating even to Cape Town, and so driving every white man into the sea, had not Chard and Bromhead and the trusty men under them stemmed the fierce martial torrent. It will be also plainly seen that if the Zulus had been victorious at Rorke's Drift, Lord Chelmsford and his column, which in straggling form wearied out and down-cast, were marching towards the latter place, were entirely at their mercy—and we know what that is.

Private Hook Receives Victoria Cross
by the Natal correspondent of a Cape Paper,
Rorke's Drift, August 4th

General Sir Garnet Wolseley and head-quarters staff arrived on Saturday afternoon. The General yesterday during the morning held a parade of the 24th to witness him decorate Private Hook, of that regiment, with the Victoria Cross for bravery at Rorke's Drift last January. The General made a little speech, saying it was always a pleasure to a General to have to present such a decoration, being the highest that the Queen could give a soldier, but that the pleasure was greatly increased on this occasion because he was able to present it on the scene of the act of bravery which it rewarded. He said that in the future history of the world and on the regimental records the memory of the splendid defence of Rorke's Drift would outlast fame. Private Hook was then called up, and had the coveted cross pinned to his breast by the General, who afterwards with his staff visited the scene of the defence.

Roll of Officers, Non Commissioned Officers, and Men present at the Defence of Rorke's Drift, 22nd January, 1819

Royal Engineers: Lieutenant J. R. M. Chard (in command), Private Robson.

Royal Artillery: Bombardiers Cantwell and Lewis, Gunners Evans and Howard.

General's Staff: Sergeant Maybin.

3rd Buffs: Sergeant Milne

2-24th Regiment: Lieutenant Bromhead (commanding), Color-Sergeant Bourne, Sergeants Gallaghar, Smith, Windridge, Maxfield (killed); Lance-Sergeants Williams (wounded died 25th January) and Taylor; Corporals Allen (wounded), French Lyons, and Saxty; Drummers Hayes, Keefe, Mecham, and Galgey; Lance-Corporals Bessell, Halley; Privates Ashton, Bennett, Chas. Bromwich, Joseph Bromwich, Buckley, Bush, Camp, Chester, Clayton, Cole (killed), Collins, Timothy Connors, Anthony Connors, Deacon, Deane, Dicks, Driscoll, Dunbar, Edwards, Fagan(killed), Gee, Hagan, Harris, Hitch (wounded), Hooke, Jobbins, Wm. Jones, Robt. Jones (wounded), Jones (970), Jones (1179), Jordes, Judge, Kears, Riley, Lines, Lockhardt, Lloyd, Lodge, Marshall, Martin, Mason, Michan, Moffatt, Frederick Morris, Augustus Morris, Morrison, Murphy, Neville, Osborne, Pitt, Robinson, Savage, Sherman, Stephens, Tasker (wounded), Thos. Taylor, Frederick Taylor, Thomas, Thompson, Tobin, Todd, Tongue, Wall, Whetton, John Williams, Joseph Williams (killed), Wilcox, Woods, Lyons, Pears, Manley, Scanlan (killed), Chick (killed), Adams (killed), Hayden (killed). Williams, Cooper, Cole, Connolly, Partridge, and Evans.

l-24th Regiment: Sergeant Wilson; Privates Nicholls (killed), Jenkins (1083), Horrigan (killed), Desmond, Paton, Turner, Waters (wounded), Jenkins (841—killed), Bekett (wounded—since dead), and Roy.

90th Light Infantry: Corporal Graham.

Assistants-Commissary: Dunne, Byrne (killed).

Acting-Commissary: Dalton (wounded).

Army Service Corps: Lance-Corporal Attwood.

Dr. Reynolds, A.M.D.: Pearse (doctor's servant).

Army Hospital Corps: Corporal Miller; Privates McMahon and Luddington.

Rev. Geo. Smith, Chaplain, Vicar of Estcourt.

Natal Mounted Police: Troopers Green, Hunter (killed), and Lugg.

Natal Native Contingent: Lieutenant Adendorff; Corporals Doughty, Mayer, Scammell (wounded), Anderson (killed), Scheiss (wounded), and Wilson.

Ferryman: Daniels.

Private (native Umkungu's tribe), Natal Native Contingent (killed).

Eshowe

Eshowe

On the same day (January 22nd, 1879) that the battle of Isandhlwana was fought, Colonel Pearson, who had entered Zululand near to the sea with one column, encountered the enemy near Eshowe, or Itshowe, at a spot called Ingangane. The following is an accurate account of the engagement:

THE BATTLE OF ESHOWE
AN UNATTRIBUTED ACCOUNT

Never in the annals of Zulu history has a more signal defeat been administered to the Zulu army. On Wednesday morning, the 22nd, Colonel Pearson reached the rough and woody Ingangane, and the head of the column had just got into a little rising ground, and were in the act of piling arms, to prepare for breakfast, when the mounted scouts on in front were heard to fire rapidly. Colonels Pearson and Parnell at once took in the situation—about as unfavorable a one as could be. To the left lay a short hill, while in the front large hills covered with dense bush, and along the lowland to the right where the men and wagons were slowly coming up, the bushes also thickly dotted the landscape.

The enemy were seen on the hills in considerable force, and it was at once perceived that a heavy battle must ensue. There were but two companies of the Buffs in front, the remainder of the regiment being further back with the wagons, as were also the Engineers and the men of the 99th Regt.; but with admirable coolness and true military tact, the leading two companies were at once doubled up a short hill on the left; one company being sent round the right brow to encounter the large body of the enemy which was coming down the opposite hill, and whose forms could only be discerned when they with lightning rapidity started from one clump of bushes to the other.

A moment's look at the position seemed to convince the Colonel that the Zulu tactics were to surround the column, for in addition to pouring in a rapid fire on the right, the vast horde of savages were to be observed pushing into the lowland at the base of the hill, on which position had been taken up, and from thence pouring in a heavy and continuous fire, showing that they had plenty of rifles. To counteract this movement, the other company of the Buffs had to face down hill in reply to the challenge of the enemy. Lieut. Lloyd, R.A., had his men well in hand, for at a moment's notice his two guns were also facing the valley, down which it could be seen Zulu soldiers were densely crowding, no doubt with the intention of pressing still further on and attacking the wagons.

The mounted men, including all the volunteer forces, were at once placed on the side of a hill to the left to guard off what was evidently intended as a flank movement. This was about the position of affairs when the fighting commenced at 7 a.m. The company to the right fired volley after volley into the bush on the opposite hill, but, with the most dogged resistance, were answered back, while missiles of every description came fast and heavy, rattling and whirring through the air. Colonels Pearson and Parnell actively superintended all arrangements, exposing themselves frequently to the fire of the enemy in giving directions in the combat. Both their horses were shot dead under them during the fight.

Being afterwards annoyed by a heavy fire, which, however, was noticed frequently to fall short, and the rifles being unable to silence the enemy, the guns were brought to bear on the bush, and poured shot and shell among the black occupants hot and heavy, and caused great destruction. This they were evidently unprepared for; the Martini rifles they could stand, even if they did make them grin, but shot and shell bursting and crashing amongst them, and making them (or such of them as escaped from its effects) leap, dance, and tumble from their hiding quarters, they seemed not quite able to understand. Still with a brave determination for victory at all hazards, when hunted from one quarter they only opened with renewed vigor from another.

On they still pushed through the bush, shouting and roaring out their stentorian war-cries, frequently drafts no doubt supplying the gaps in the ranks of their comrades in the lowlands; but this place again getting rather too warm for them, their picked companies seemed suddenly to centre with a rush on the Colonel's right flank, and the fire went on hotter than ever. In the meantime the rockets from a neighboring hillock were making it very hot for the bronzed Zulus, while the game was considerably heightened in danger to the blacks and in general interest by the Blue Jackets getting their Gatlings into position from the opposite side. Then the fun became fast and furious, and the whizzing missiles, wrecking and tearing all before them, literally mowed down the branches and the brushwood around, and the Zulus fairly fell like locusts; but after scampering out of the bush in question they still retreated in an orderly manner, and kept up a rapid fire, though volley after volley from the Buffs must have caused many a Zulu to bite the dust.

Whilst matters were thus progressing, a daring attempt was made by a body of the enemy to the rear of the hill on which the guns were playing to turn the left flank, but here they were met by the Volunteers, who gave them such a reception as will long be remembered by Cetywayo's tribe. But though bullets went in hundreds after them into the bush, still would they reply, hoping that the British would give way, and confident in their large numbers. The horde which had come down the bush on the right now tried to force their way by dint of rushing on to the place where the wagons had been drawn, but little did they calculate the reception which awaited them.

The men of the Buffs, Naval Brigade, Royal Engineers, and men of the 99th Regiment poured such death-dealing volleys on them that they fairly reeled, staggered, and ultimately broke, totally defeated, and in their retreat exposing themselves to grape shot and bullets, while one of the Gatling guns, which had again attained a good position, played havoc wherever a group of darkskins was to be seen; and so nothing more was heard of the gentlemen who so injudiciously endeavored to turn a British flank. After 10 o'clock the enemy were chased through the wood by some companies of the Buffs, the 99th, cavalry, and Native Contingent, and thus completely routed out, great numbers being seen scrambling over the hills carrying their wounded and numbers of their dead with them.

The fight lasted two hours and a quarter, the English fighting all through under great disadvantages, but with much coolness, and upon ground selected by the Zulus themselves, a spot round which martial tradition hangs as being the scene of one of the proofs of their invulnerability, when they conquered with much slaughter their old enemies the Dutch.

They left upwards of four hundred counted dead upon the field. How many died uncounted is unknown, as the Zulus, according to their custom, do all they can to conceal their dead in the thick bush, throwing them in holes and between rocks, or anywhere where they can be effectually hidden; so that, reckoning these and others carried over the hills, some seven or eight hundred fell. A high chief of Cetywayo's taken prisoner, said that their orders were to retire before Colonel Pearson, whom they watched crossing the Tugela River, but on no account to allow the troops to advance beyond the old battle-ground just described. There were four thousand in the attacking force, and Cetywayo told them that if they did not "eat up" the white men never to show their faces before him again.

The Intombi River
Massacre

The Intombi River Massacre

A Detailed account of
the Intombi River Massacre from
a Letter in the Transvaal Argus

It is with the deepest sorrow I write to convey the sad, sad news of the disaster that occurred this Wednesday morning, the 12th of March, 1879, between the hours of four and five o'clock, at the Intombi River, about four and a half or five miles from Luneburg, which resulted in great loss of life—1 captain, 1 civil surgeon, and 40 noncommissioned officers and men being found assegaied and butchered on the scene of the action, 20 being still unaccounted for, only 43 turning up at Luneberg out of 105. The circumstances in detail, as far as can be accurately known, are as follows:—On Saturday, 1st March, D Company, 80th Regiment, in command of Captain Anderson, accompanied by Lieutenant Daubeney, was sent out from Luneburg to act as convoy to wagons from Lydenburg and Middleburg via Derby, laden with ammunition, stores, and provisions. They met the wagons some distance on the other side of the Intombi River, and took them in charge.

On Wednesday, the 5th, Captain Anderson and his company were recalled, abandoning the wagons which were in their charge to care for themselves. On Friday, the 7th March, Captain Moriarty, accompanied by Lieutenants Johnson and Lindop, with Dr. Cobbin, civil surgeon, went out with 103 non-commissioned officers and men, to complete the escort duty the first company sent out were detailed for. Captain Moriarty, on arrival at the Intombi River, halted and pitched his camp on the Luneburg side of the river, as owing to its being very much swollen through the incessant rain, it was found impossible to get across. Eventually a raft was constructed, and the men passed over in groups, Captain Moriarty and Lieutenant Johnson accompanying them, leaving about 35 men behind under command of Lieutenant Lindop, as a working party, to cut down the drift, and to prepare and forward supplies to those who had crossed. Lieutenant Johnson, with a party of men, went on at once to meet the wagons, Captain Moriarty with another party following, leaving a sergeant and a few men on the Derby side of the river to pitch the tents.

The wagons were first reached by a few mounted men, when it was found they had been tampered with by the Kaffirs in the absence of one company being recalled and the other coming out. All the wagons were eventually got to the bank of the river by 2 o'clock on Tuesday, the 11th, the escort returning with them. I omitted to mention that it was stated 46 oxen were taken in addition to the stores being interfered with from the wagons. It was raining very heavily at this time, but ceased about 4 in the afternoon. Captain Moriarty caused the wagons to be laagered in the shape of a triangle, the river being the base, the wagons on the sides resting within twelve or fifteen yards of the river; inside the laager the men, about seventy-nine, were stationed, also the oxen.

Everything seemed perfectly safe and secure, every precaution being taken. It was impossible to get the wagons across on the Luneburg side, as the river was swelling more and more, and the current running six or seven knots an hour. About 4.15 a.m., the never-to-be-forgotten 12th March, a shot was heard, and reported by the sentry to Lieutenant Harwood (who had been sent out to relieve Lieutenants Johnson and Lindop, the former acting-commissariat officer, the latter acting-ordnance officer, the evening before the 12th).

Lieutenant Harwood sent over at once to the other side of the river to report the circumstance to Captain Moriarty. The men at once stood to their arms. At this time there was a very heavy mist and fog. No sooner had the rain ceased, and the fog partly cleared away, so that those in the laagar could distinguish fifty yards in front, than a volley was poured into the laager by an impi of Zulus, who had crept up to within about 100 yards of the laager. They then threw down their guns, and charged, assegai in hand, on the laager, which was most heroically and bravely defended till overwhelmed by over 4,000 Zulus. Then the butchery began, the gallant fellows being assegaied in all directions.

Seing their laager taken, the few who were left took to the river, and endeavored to reach the little party on the Luneburg side. They were followed into the river by the Zulus and assegaied, not more than twelve or fifteen escaping from the laager.

The party on the Luneberg side of the river, in command of Sergeant Booth, was all this time keeping up a heavy fire on the Zulus on the opposite bank, and protecting their comrades who were attempting to escape through the river. This sergeant and little party fought most bravely till, at last, outflanked by hundreds of Zulus, who had crossed the river on both sides of them with intent to cut them off, they retired, disputing the ground into Luneberg, and being followed for over two miles by hundreds of Zulus.

A great many of those saved owed their lives to Sergeant Booth and Lance-Corporal Burgess, who collected the few straggling men, and kept pouring volley after volley upon the advancing Zulus, as they retreated into Luneberg. Lieut. Harwood, who was on the Luneburg side of the river, rode in with all speed to convey the news of the attack to Major Tucker. It was about 6 when Lieutenant Harwood arrived with the sad news. Major Tucker immediately mounted every one for whom a horse could be found, and, accompanied by Lieutenants Harwood and Johnson, and a little body of horse, rode with all speed to the scene, followed by two companies, C in command of Lieutenant Chamberlain, and H in command of Lieutenant Potts, accompanied by Lieutenant Lindop; D Company, in command of Captain Anderson, being left to guard the fort at Luneburg.

As the mounted party neared the scene of the attack, they could plainly see the Zulus moving over the hills like so many ants, the impi being estimated between four and five thousand. On arrival at the laager a most ghastly and horrid sight presented itself. There lay our poor fellows, butchered and assegaied, and otherwise disgracefully illused, amongst whom were Captain Moriarty and Civil-Surgeon Cobbin and 35 men. Major Tucker caused the whole of the bodies to be collected, a large square grave dug on the bank of the river, and all, with the exception of Captain Moriarty and Dr. Cobbin, who were brought to Luneburg, buried. The funeral service was read, and the honors of war fired over them. Captain

Moriarty and Dr. Cobbin were buried with military honors in the little graveyard of Luneberg, as also four other poor fellows who were found on the way to Luneburg. Evidently they were previously wounded and were trying to effect their escape, but, being overtaken, were killed and disembowelled.

Almost all the poor fellows were disembowelled that were assegaied. Too much could not be said for the exertions and labor of Lieutenant Chamberlain, who caused the bodies, which were in many cases dreadfully disfigured, to be carefully identified, and an inventory taken of anything that might have been found on them. Almost in every case the bodies were stripped of their clothing.

On a careful inspection of the camp being made, it was found that the whole of the ammunition had been carried away, also blankets, rifles, &c. What was left was taken from off the wagons, and was strewn all over the place; biscuit, tins of preserved meat, and mealies, lay scattered in all directions. The rockets and rocket apparatus were taken out of the boxes, but received no serious damage. All the oxen were carried off, and thirty Zulus were found killed, numbers being carried off. From the traces of blood all over the place, numbers of Zulus must have been wounded.

Two Zulus were found alive badly wounded. It was ascertained from the wounded Zulus that Umbeline himself was with the impi, and their strength was about 9,000. When asked why they fled so quickly, they said they dreaded the other red-coats coming down on them.

They also contemplated attacking the fort at Luneburg three days before this. Now that this sacrifice of life has occurred, perhaps steps will be taken in future to avoid sending a handful of men as a convoy to wagons, and in the eyes of justice we trust a thorough investigation will be made, as this demands it, more especially as it was well known to the military authorities at Luneburg for some days previous that Umbeline with an impi of Zulus was hovering about close by. All sorts of precautions are taken in the fort (Fort Cleary), a company being told off nightly as an outlying picket, the officers and men being exposed to the weather and being frequently saturated through.

When Captain Moriarty was shot through the breast he cried out, 'Fire away, boys, death or glory, I am done', and was then surrounded and assegaied.

Mr. Josiah Sussens, went down to the Zulu border in charge of some Government wagons and managed very providentially to escape the fate of the poor fellows who were slain at the recent massacre at Intombi River.

THE INTOMBI RIVER MASSACRE
BY JOSIAH SUSSENS

I was in the wagon, sleeping, and early in the morning I got up to see if it was daylight, and saw the Kaffirs swarming around within twenty yards of me. The alarm was given, and Captain Moriarty called out 'Guards out.' I ran back to my wagon to get my rifle (which belonged to No. 1 company Transvaal Rifle Volunteers of which corps I am a member), but in the confusion of the bullets flying about me, I could not get it out. I now found it so dangerous that I determined to try to bolt, if I could, without remaining to take out my clothes. As I emerged from the wagon for the last time, I heard Captain Moriarty cry out, 'Fire away, men, I am done. I then went to the adjoining wagon to call Whittington (also a Pretoria man), and I told him the niggers were around. He immediately came out and jumped down, but was caught almost as soon as he got to the ground, and assegaied on every side. The poor fellow shrieked out, but without avail, as no assistance was at hand. Seeing that I was powerless to do anything, having no arms of any kind, I ran down between the oxen, and made for the river, which was about 60 yards off. I found the Zulus shooting and stabbing the people in all directions. The sight was a most horrifying one, and one never to be forgotten. I had to dodge about to save myself, and am now surprised to find that I managed to get through at all. As soon as I got to the river, I jumped in and made a dive, as swimming was too dangerous, the Zulus standing on the banks, and at the edge of the river, as thick as thieves, throwing assegais and aiming their guns wherever they saw a head. I came up about the middle of the river, but the moment my head was out, I saw several Zulus pointing their guns, and ready to fire. I therefore dived again, and came out on the other side.

The river was very full at the time, and a strong current running. In crossing I had torn off my shirt, the only garment I possessed, and, therefore, when I landed I was entirely in a state of nudity. I now found that fighting was still going on on all sides of me, and that it was almost impossible I could get any further, and in my desperation I contemplated throwing myself in the water, to be drowned peaceably, rather than suffer the death by torture of many of those I saw around me. I, however, got into a courageous spirit again, and dashed off, keeping as much out of the way of the enemy as I could. Several shots were fired at me, and assegais were flying in all directions, but somehow I happened to be fortunate and got clear of the encampment. I made for Meyer's station as fast as I could, and overtook one soldier on the road, who was shot dead just as I got up to him. I overtook two others shortly after, who were also shot. Getting further on, I fell in with Sergeant Booth and about a dozen men, who were keeping up a retreating fire, and fighting very pluckily. I rested for a few minutes with them, during which time I espied the Zulus coming round the hill to intercept us. I informed Sergeant Booth of this, and he kept up a steady fire upon them, and made the enemy retire back into the hills. I cannot speak too highly of the conduct of Sergeant Booth on this occasion; he fought most pluckily, and lost four of his small band here. It was entirely owing to their doing so well that any of us managed to get through at all. The Zulus would have entirely surrounded us, and not a soul could have escaped. Seventeen leaders and drivers were killed altogether, amongst them being Whittington, Campbell, and Goss. As I got in camp, I met Major Tucker going out with his men to the relief.

Eight of us managed to get into Luneburg, and perhaps it would not be out of place if I were to state how I was received. Arriving in a state of nudity, with the exception of a soldier's overcoat, got from a native on the road, I applied to the authorities for blankets to sleep under, but was refused. They said they had none. Eight of us only had two blankets between the lot. To add to our annoyance two wounded Zulus were brought in (one was on my own cartel) and were put into a nice tent and covered with blankets, whilst we had to take our chance as best we could underneath the wagons. Only a very few of us survivors had any clothes on when we arrived, and we managed to get along as best we could—a shirt from one soldier, trowsers from a second, boots from a third, and so on. A sale of clothing, &c, took place afterwards, when we were allowed to buy a few things. And so we got on.

Hlobane & Kambula

Hlobane and Kambula

Last week has been eventful to this column with varied fortune, pregnant with sorrow and joy; sorrow for the brave men that we have lost, and joy over the great and important victory won by our gallant troops against an overwhelming superiority of numbers of the savage foe, who had been dispatched by their ruler on an errand of extermination of the white race. Their orders were to wipe everything white off the face of the earth before they returned to him again.

I have been an actor in these great events, and as actors in a fight are generally bad narrators, I shall only give what came under my personal observation. Other correspondents will, no doubt, supply the public with what I am deficient in, regarding occurrences at other points of the Hlobane Mountain.

On the 27th a force consisting of detachments of the Frontier Light Horse, Raaffs Corps, Weatherley's Rangers, Baker's Horse, and the Burgher Force, under their respective Commandants, started from the camp. This force consisted of about 400 horsemen, and the Native Contingent, under Major Leet, l-13th Regt, and Lieut. Williams, 58th Regt. We left camp at 8 a.m., another column consisting of mounted infantry, Kaffrarian Mounted Rifles, under Commandant Schermbrucker, Wood's Mounted Irregulars Colonel Wood and his staff were to leave later; the whole to attack the west point of the mountain, so as to create a diversion.

Colonel Buller's column halted at 12 noon, near the old camp on the 23rd February, on the south side of Zinguin Neck. Colonel Weatherley, with his corps, arrived half an hour later. At 3 p.m. saddled up, leaving the Rangers, as we supposed, also saddling up to follow. As the column passed the south side of the Hlobane two shots were fired with an elephant gun from the mountain, and three fires were lit on a shelf of rock near the summit. We passed on out of range of fire, diverging towards the Kukuze valley to mislead the enemy, and halted six miles distant just at sundown, lit fires and cooked coffee and green mealies; but just as the moon set we saddled up and rode in a north-easterly direction. This march was performed in silence, a precaution necessary, as several spies had been seen near our camp before dark. Commandant Uys acted as guide. At about 10 p.m. we halted in a valley, tying the horses together with their reims in a line, each man lying down in front of his horse, which stood saddled and bridled.

At 1 a.m. a heavy thunderstorm came on, raining very heavily for four hours. At 4 a.m. we silently saddled up and rode on towards the east side of the mountain, which we reached at daybreak. I forgot to include Major Tremlett and the artillery men with rocket tube in the force of the column. As we approached the pass, Commandant Uys, Colonel Buller, Majors Leet and Tremlett taking the lead, the Zulus did not open fire, but allowed us to approach within five hundred yards of the top before they did so; then they commenced with volleys from some hundreds of guns. It was a cross fire, but it only killed Lieut. Williams and one horse. Several horses were severely wounded, and a few men slightly, and the mountain was gained; but some severe fighting continued for about another hour, the brunt of it falling on the Light Horse, killing two officers and two troopers. After silencing the fire of the Zulus who had done this damage, Colonel Buller and Commandant Raaff rode to the westward end of the mountain, where the track divides it.

The Zulus had fortified the pass with stone walls, from which they were annoying our rear, where Commandant Uys, with the Burgher Force, had attacked. In the meantime parties of Raaff's, Baker's Horse, and the Burgher Force kept up a hot fire on the Zulus under the krantzes on the north-west side of the mountain where the Zulu troops had built huts for encampment. These operations occupied us four or five hours; and as Colonel Buller. Commandant Raaff, and Commandant Uys returned from silencing the force at the pass, where the enemy only fired occasional shots, a body of Zulus made their appearance on the northern extremity of the mountain, and Colonel Buller rode off to attack them; but before he could get half way he perceived that strong bodies of Zulus were climbing every available baboon path, with the intention of cutting us off from the only two passes by which it was possible to descend. At the same time two large columns were seen approaching along the top of the mountain to the eastward, and another dense black mass of men, the main Zulu army, were observed coming on from the southward. Colonel Buller passed us at a gallop, ordering us to ride hard for the pass over the krantz at the neck, the only road open.

This pass may well be termed the Infernal, or Devil's Pass. The descent is at an angle of ninety degrees, full of huge boulders. How a single horse got down alive is a perfect miracle, more especially when crowded within such a narrow space; but hundreds of men did tumble or roll down without knowing how they got there. Many did not attempt to try to get their horses, but abandoned everything on the top, and were saved on the cruppers of those who luckily saved their horses; but the greatest disaster of the day was the loss of Mr. P. L. Uys, who was stabbed by the Zulus while returning up the hill to save one of his sons who was in danger of falling into their hands. Although Colonel Buller, Commandant Raaff, Majors Leet and Tremlett did all that they could to rally sufficient of the fugitives to cover the retreat of those descending, the loss here was seven men.

The other column suffered serious loss of valuable lives, amongst them being Captain the Hon. Ronald Campbell, Lieut. Lloyd, Mr. Charles Potter, and Mr. Duncombe; Calverly was also killed. In justice to the latter, who will be called to account in another world, it is right to say that no proof has been adduced of his actual presence at the attack on the General's camp at Isandhlwana. Captain Campbell and Lieutenent Lloyd were buried in a grave dug on the spot, under fire, by the Colonel's mounted escort. Colonel Wood's horse was shot under him, and he had a couple of narrow escapes. Besides, Colonel Weatherley's Rangers missed their road by not up-saddling when the rest of the column did, and the last that was seen of him was when surrounded by the Zulus; he was then seen slashing at his foes with his sword, and of his troop of 52 men, only one officer and seven men escaped destruction. The brave Captain Barton, of the Frontier Light Horse, who had been delegated to perform some duty on the left, is supposed to have fallen into an ambush and was cut off. The last time that he was seen, he was trying to escape, carrying young Weatherley on the crupper of his horse, and it is feared that he, in his humane endeavour to save a fellow-creature, exhausted the strength of his horse. The loss on the day has been estimated at over one hundred and twenty belonging to the various corps, and the escape of so many is a miracle. The Zulus came on like hell-hounds, killing all that came in the way, white and black, and were on the Zinguin Keck before the first of the fugitives were in camp. A number of Oham's men and a large number of women and children, who were on their way here, were killed.

On the following morning one of our natives, who had hid himself in a hole, around which the Zulu army encamped, heard the conversation of the Zulus and their intended plan of attack on our camp. He learnt that the Zulu chiefs were opposed to the attack, but were overruled by the young soldiers, who said it was the King's orders to wipe off and destroy everything white before they returned to him. At 12 a.m., immense black masses of Zulus were visible from the camp. When they arrived at the Jagt Path, they divided, one column of two miles in length, which diverged to the right, and another to the left, while the main body marched on in the centre.

The right division was first engaged with our horse under Colonel Buller and Commandant Raaff, I am in advance with my story, so I must go back. The alarm sounded at 1.06 p.m. All the tents were struck and the contents removed inside, and all necessary preparations made to receive the shock of the Zulu force when it attacked. Everything that could be done was done in the coolest and most systematic manner possible, Colonel Wood and staff superintending. Boxes of cartridges were placed at short distances, unscrewed, ready for use, and buckets of water placed under every wagon for drinking. At 1.26 p.m. the first shot was fired (but the Zulus kept up a fusilade as they marched down the road from 3,000 to 4,000 yards away) by the Horse, which made the Zulus halt and extend into skirmishing order when the Artillery opened on them from the mountain guns at the fort and the four field pieces at the laager, throwing shell at 2,500 yards with admirable precision.

Our horsemen drew them on, but kept up a retreating fire until the Zulus were within rifle range of the fort and laager. The first shell was fired at 1.45 p.m., and notwithstanding the heavy loss of the enemy they pressed forward to surround the laager and take up positions under cover, a dodge they have learnt to perfection. While the right wing was keeping us employed on the north-east side of the laager, the left wing was hastening to attack the west and south-west side, and when these had commenced, the two wings were re-inforced by the main body, who also advanced to attack the fort and the cattle kraal, and before 2 p.m. we were surrounded on all sides.

The most desperate attack was made on the cattle kraal; the troops defending it had to retire, and the Zulus took possession of several wagons, from which they opened fire on the laager at short range, and made an attempt to advance on the wagons; but two companies of the 90th regiment made a sortie to drive the Zulus back, and charged them with the bayonet. Here the 90th were ex-posed to a heavy cross-fire, suffering severely, losing Major Hackett and Lieut. Bright wounded (the latter since dead), while a sergeant and ten men were killed and wounded. The Zulus made a similar attempt on the south-west corner of the laager, and were driven back at the point of the bayonet by a company of 1-13th. Both these sorties were most gallant affairs, and many acts of heroism were performed by both officers and men, which no doubt will be mentioned in the despatches.

Many of our troops were shot in the back by the enemy in the rear while they were firing at those in front, for the bullets whizzed across the camp like a perfect hailstorm, killing and wounding sev-eral horses near the picket lines. An officer of Raaff's Contingent was killed in the laager, and several of the troops killed and wound-ed in the fort and laager.

The Zulus would not face the bayonet, and soon after some charges from the troops and a few wholesome discharges of can-ister-shot from the cannon at fifty yards range, the Zulus began to run, and the horsemen and artillery, with one gun, and our Na-tive Contingent started off in chase, playing fearful havoc amongst them, from 4.45 p.m. until nightfall, when the exhausted state of the horses compelled us to retire. The Zulus were also completely done up; and had there been two hours more light, and fresh hors-es, few would have been left to tell the tale of their disaster. The last shot was fired at a quarter past five, but after that great numbers were killed with assegais, the men economising their ammunition.

Prisoners captured say that nine regiments were sent to attack this column. There were 23,000 when they left Undine, and many more joined on the road; the lowest estimate would be 25,000 in all. They also say that on the day the King sent them away, he sent five regiments to reinforce his army on the coast, and attack Colonel Pearson's column. The loss the army sustained that attacked this camp on the 29th instant cannot be estimated at less. than 3,000 killed; 1,500 lay about the vicinity of the camp, and great numbers have been seen in ditches and rivers at a distance. Over 600 stand of arms have been brought in, and a great number have been kept as trophies by those who fought on the eventful and glorious day—a day of redemption for South Africa.

On Sunday, Monday, and Tuesday, fatigue parties with wagons have been fully employed collecting and burying the slain.

On Monday four bodies of the enemy were seen at the Hlobane, estimated at from 200 to 500 each, as near as could be estimated from the distance of four miles. Umpepe, Tyingwayo, Mnyamane, and one of Masipula's sons were the commanders. One of the wounded in hospital here told me that Oham's people are at the King's kraal, Undine, with the Indabakaombe regiment.

THE HLOBANE MASSACRE FROM A LETTER BY A MEMBER OF BULLER'S HORSE

We have had two hard days of it, and have lost some fine fellows. The storming of the Zlabane was a sad affair. We took the hill all right, only losing-poor Williams of our regiment; he fell as we went up. It was warm work, and the Kaffirs gave it to us from two sides. As soon as we got to the top we took up our different positions along the ridge of the mountain. The Kaffirs were down below us in holes and behind rocks, &c. They had splendid cover, and made the most of it, by keeping us continually under a very heavy fire. We lost another officer on this ridge, poor Von Stietencron; he was shot dead through the head. We also had about five men wounded there; but all would have gone well had the Hlobane Kaffirs not been reinforced by a very large impi, which we saw coming down from the opposite range. The order was then given to stand to our horses, and we had to ride about a mile along the top of the mountain before we reached the path which led down. When we got there we got all jammed up, and the confusion was something awful. Horses tumbled down and rolled over their riders. Hundreds of Kaffirs bore on to us in no time, and, I am sorry to say, most of our poor fellows were assegaied. It was an awful sight, and one I never wish to see again. Weatherley's men were killed by the impi; they went down another path. Poor Barton was with them, also Williams, 58th regiment, who was attached to the Native Contingent. Calverly and Potter were killed there also. The following-day the impi, about 20,000 strong, attacked our camp. The fight lasted about four hours, and we gave it to them properly. When they retired Colonel Buller led his mounted men out, and away we went after Cetywayo's army, shooting a tremendous lot. I do not know what the Colonel estimates the enemy's loss at, but it was very heavy. Our loss was 19 killed and 55 wounded. Lieut. Nicholson, of the artillery, was among the killed. He is not in returns, so I mention it here. The Kaffirs on the Hlobane alone were about 3,000 strong. The Zulus simply fought splendidly, and tried once or twice to rush us, but the fire was too heavy. No men could have fought more bravely. The artillery did great service.

Hlobane & Kambula by Captain D'Arcy of the Frontier Light Horse, a Letter to His Father Published in the Eastern Star

I sent a telegram to you on the 30th of last month, telling you I had pulled through two hard fights, in which the Frontier Light Horse suffered severely. Poor Barton, the Baron, and another officer called Williams were killed, whom you perhaps know.

Now to give you a short account of the two events.

All the mounted men had to take a very strong position on a mountain called the Hlobane. We got up there, driving the natives before us at every point, although they fought very well. Williams was killed as we charged up the hill, the Baron on the top while he was in command of his troop, a Zulu spotted him from above and shot him right through his head. Barton was sent down a hill with C troop, and just as we got down we saw about three thousand Zulus below us, trying to get between us and our camp; we at once crossed the hill to come down a most awfully steep place; the Dutchmen got to the place, rushed to their horses, and bolted as hard as they could go.

My troop was left behind, and Blaine, myself, and Hutton got them to go quietly down the hill, which was really a fearful place. I had of course to leave the top of the hill; the Zulus all this while were giving us awful pepper from Martini rifles. I saw, I thought, all our men down, and then considered I had to think of myself, and got half-way down when a stone about the size of a small piano came bounding down; I heard a shout above, "look out below," and down the beastly thing came right on my horse's leg, cutting it right off. I at the same time got knocked down the hill by another horse, and was nearly squeezed to death. I had taken the bridle off, and was about to take the saddle, when I heard a scream; I looked up, and saw the Zulus right in among the white men stabbing horses and men. I made a jump and got down somehow or other, and ran as hard as I could with 70 rounds of ball cartridge, a carbine, revolver, field-glass, and heavy boots. I went some 300 yards when a fellow called Francis got a horse for me, but no saddle or bridle, a riem did for both, when one of the Frontier Light Horse got wounded through the leg, and I had to jump off, put him on my horse, and run again.

Colonel Buller saved my life by taking me up behind him on his horse, then Blaine, who had been keeping the natives off in the rear, saw me (as after I got my breath I got off the Colonel's horse) and he nearly cried when he met me, all the fellows thinking I had been killed on the top of the hill. He behaved as he always does, and stuck to me, and pulled me through the second time. The third time a major of the Artillery, Tremlett by name, took me up behind. Our men and officers all behaved well, but the other volunteers were what Major Robinson would call a 'big rabble.' We lost many white men and a number of natives.

The Frontier Light Horse lost 3 officers and 34 non-commissioned officers and men and 66 horses. Each of our men arrived in camp with another man behind him.

The next day our colored brothers came on and attacked the camp in numbers from 20,000 to 23,000, and after six hours' hard fighting they bolted. We killed a little over 2,300, and when once they retired all the horsemen in camp followed them for eight miles, butchering the brutes all over the place. I told the men 'no quarter, boys, and remember yesterday,' and we did knock them about, killing them all over the place. On the line where I followed them there were 157 dead bodies counted next day. We have buried 800 of them that were killed close to the camp, but there are hundreds and hundreds of men some miles off, that are being eaten by dogs and vultures. We got about twenty or thirty of the 24th rifles, some carbines belonging to the men we lost the day before, and a number of little things taken from the General's camp, besides 500 odd rifles of various descriptions.

We are all in high feather at having had such a good fight with the Zulus. I never saw such a lot of blacks together in my life as came on the day of attack. They fought well, and kept rushing in the most plucky way, but I knew what the result must be. All the men were killed and wounded, with two exceptions, from Martini rifles; their fire was very hot, but badly aimed (much too high). I am afraid we gave them such a dressing that they won't attack an encampment again. We went out and attacked them, then we retreated, so as to bring them on, and you ought to have heard them yell, thinking that they had the camp like the General's, but they found out their mistake.

I am sure you will be sorry to hear that my Dutch friend, Piet Uys, commandant of the Dutch, was one of the killed at the place where I nearly came to grief; his two sons pulled through. He was as plucky as possible.

Captain Ronald Campbell's Heroism
in the Transvaal
by Sir Evelyn Wood
from Pearson's Magazine

It having been decided to invade Zululand, three main columns, right, centre, and left, moved across the border; but the incident with which I am now concerned took place in the operations of the left or northern column, which was under my command.

On the 22nd of January, 1879, the centre column was overwhelmed at a place called Isandlwhana, i.e., the Little Hand, nearly every man, in all some 1,500, being destroyed.

The news of the disaster, carried by a mounted native, reached us on the 24th January, just as we were driving before us the Amaqulisi tribe, which we had surprised between the Zungi range and the northern side of the Inhlobane mountain. We pursued the enemy for a mile or two, and I then; moved the column back over the Umvelosi river, and proceeded to one of the lower, features of the Nagaba-ka-Hawane mountains, where water, and firewood which covered the southern slopes of that range of hills, were plentiful. The infantry remained in this position, called Kambula, till the final advance on Ulundi, the mounted men, under Colonel Redvers Buller, being constantly employed in making raids, which were carried far into the enemy's country.

Ronald Campbell, second son of Lord Cawdor, born at Stackpool Court, Pembroke, in December, 1848, was educated at Eton, and joined the Coldstream Guards in 1866. He was adjutant of the 1st battalion from 1872 to 1878, when, having been nominated as a "Special Service Officer" for duty in South Africa, he reported himself to me, as the officer commanding the troops at Utrecht in the Transvaal, shortly before Christmas.

I gave Captain Campbell charge of the Adjutant-General's duties, and as he messed with me, I saw a great deal of him and became greatly attached to him. A tall, powerful, well-made man, with strikingly handsome features, he showed towards me, his commanding officer, the greatest consideration and devotion in small matters of everyday life, while on the 28th of March he manifested them in their highest aspects.

About twelve miles from the ridge on which Kambula camp was pitched, the elevated tableland comes to an end with a steep fall to the southward. Three miles further south, a hill, named the Inhlobane, stands up 1,200 feet above the adjoining country. It is about four miles in length and one and a half miles in breadth. It is absolutely precipitous on the northern side, and also on the upper part of its southern face, and can be climbed only with great difficulty at the eastern and western ends, the former end being the easier of approach.

Colonel Buller and I had often discussed the practicability of

taking this stronghold of the Amaqulisi tribe. Early in the month of March he had been up on a ridge which lies 150ft. under the western crest of the mountain, from which he had carried off a great many of the enemy's cattle. It was impossible to tell the exact number of the fighting men on the mountains, but we estimated them at from 800 to 1,000.

About this time the Commander-in-Chief was preparing to advance to relieve Ekowe, and hearing that his force was to be strongly opposed, he suggested to me that I should make some movement to attract the attention of the Zulus from the southern side of Zululand. We believed it would be possible to take the Inhlobane, and my only anxiety was lest while engaged thereon, the Zulus on it might be strongly reinforced from the southward. This indeed actually occurred.

Early on the 27th of March, Colonel Buller left Kambula with a force of 400 mounted men and 30 natives, and after marching some thirty miles, bivouacked at dusk about five miles south-east of the mountain, changing his position, however, twice during the night in order to guard against being surprised while dismounted.

I had no intention of taking part in the attack, but with an escort of eight men of the 90th Light Infantry and seven natives, one being Umtonga, a half-brother of Cetewayo's, I left Kambula late in the afternoon, and bivouacked under the western end of the mountain. The party, besides the escort, consisted of Captain the Honourable Ronald Campbell, Mr. Lloyd, political agent, who had shown marked courage in leading friendly natives in an expedition against Sekukuni, and Lieutenant Lysons (90th Light Infantry), aide-de-camp.

Starting at 3.30 a.m. on the 28th, we rode under the southern face of the mountain, hoping to arrive in time to see Colonel Buller ascend its eastern point.

We failed to overtake him, for he had left his bivouac, ten miles further to the eastward, at 3.30 a.m., and ascending a steep path, hardly passable for single men when mounted, he led his force up a gulley at the break of day, under cover of the morning mist, surprising the Zulus, a few of whom only could fire before he, at the head of his men, gained the summit.

When we came in sight of the eastern angle of the mountain,

the rear of Buller's column was just gaining the summit, and at this time we met a party of mounted Irregulars who had got off the track, and were marching westward.

Hearing the firing, I directed them to turn round and follow Colonel Buller, and, moving faster myself, passed on to the front with my escort, accompanied by half a dozen of the Irregulars: we soon came under a shower of bullets from the front and both flanks, poured in by men behind huge rocks. Turning towards the foe, we wandered still further from Colonel Buller's track, which we had in the first instance followed, but which we had lost on getting to a place where there was only bare rock, without even enough soil to take the imprint of horses' feet. We continued to advance towards the fire directed on us, and presently arrived at a part of the mountain where further progress on horseback was impossible.

Dismounting the men, we left the horses in the charge of two or three soldiers and the natives, and proceeded to climb the steep face of the mountain. I had retained my horse, endeavouring to make it follow me, while Captain Campbell, walking behind, drove it on. While thus engaged, Mr. Lloyd, who was climbing alongside on my left, touched me with his elbow, saying, "That man won't hit us in the face, anyhow," and raising my eyes I saw, about thirty yards above us, a Zulu who was looking down the sights of his gun, which was apparently directed at the lower part of my body. While Lloyd and I were getting out our revolvers the man fired, and pulling the muzzle of his gun off to the right, shot my friend through the stomach and backbone.

He fell, saying, "I'm hit," and to my inquiry, "Badly?" replied, "Yes, I fear very badly."

Letting go my horse I lifted him from the ground, when Captain Campbell, a much stronger man, relieved me and carried him down the hill to where we had left the horses, while I ascended to the rock whence the Zulu had fired. He had, however, disappeared, and almost immediately afterwards another Zulu fired from underneath some large boulders of granite, killing my horse stone dead, the animal's head striking me as he fell and knocking me down.

Captain Campbell now rejoined me, still some seventy feet

from the summit, and agreeing that it was impossible to get much further up the precipitous rock in our front, we retraced our steps to the little ledge where we had left the horses.

Some thousands of years before the date of which I am writing, irregular masses of rock must have fallen from the precipitous sides of the Inhlobane, and these lie piled in confusion about the base of the cliffs, forming caves, some of which are big enough to hold several men. As all the effective fire seemed to come from one of these caves, I directed the Irregulars who had now arrived to advance and storm it. The order was taken by Captain Campbell, who returned saying that the officer in command thought it was impossible to force the passage through the rocks. This view the officer endeavoured to impress on me, but I realised that while the Zulus held their position it would be difficult, if not impossible, to remove some wounded who were lying near the ledge, and I repeated the order for an attempt to be made. Captain Campbell had seen the entrance of the Zulu stronghold, and fully recognised the risk to the leading man who should try to enter it. He took the second order, and being again met by objections, shouted "Then I will do it myself," and, jumping over a low wall, he ran up the entrance of the cave, being followed by Lieutenant Lysons and three 90th Light Infantry, men of my mounted escort. One of these, Bugler Walkinshaw, I called back, as I wanted him to attend to Mr. Lloyd, who was now dying.

The small party disappeared, passing up a narrow passage 4ft. wide, the sides of which were about 8ft. or 10ft. high, and moving over great boulders of rock. No one was seen in the passage, but the north side of the mountain above them was lined with Zulus with firearms. Their bullets, however, all passed over the little band, which was protected by the walls of the passage, and Captain Campbell, climbing over the rocks in the most determined manner, led it on for thirty yards to where the passage came to an end.

He and those following him all knew that though no Zulus were in sight, yet their guns were covering the party, and, as all officers of experience are aware, the unseen is the most appalling form of danger. Captain Campbell, determined to secure the safe removal of the wounded, never hesitated a moment, and, while peering down into a cave at his feet, he was shot in the head. Lieutenant Lysons and Private Fowler passed his body, and firing into the cave killed one of its occupants, the others creeping away by a subterranean passage, to reappear higher up the mountain. The resistance, however, at this point terminated, and the Irregular Horse, regaining Colonel Buller's track, reached the top of the mountain without further casualty.

Ronald Campbell gave his life indeed, but attained the object, for he cleared the cave of some good Zulu marksmen who, secure under cover in their apparently impregnable position, made advance or retreat or the removal of the wounded almost impossible.

How Colonel Redvers Buller cleared the summit of the mountain, seizing all the Amaqulisi cattle, and eventually, on the main Zulu army coming into sight, had to retire down the nearly precipitous face of the mountain, belongs to another story. He covered the retreat, and after bringing three men out of a crowd of Zulus, returned again into the fight to keep back the oncoming wave of black men, and thus allow the footmen to escape. Buller, in holding the ridge, the only avenue of escape, indeed emulated "Horatius who kept the bridge in the brave days of old."

While the cave was being cleared by Captain Campbell's party, seeing that Mr. Lloyd was dying, I remembered that I had a prayer-book in the wallet of the saddle on my horse lying dead some sixty or seventy feet above me, and, calling Bugler Walkinshaw, desired him to climb up the mountain, and at any risk to bring back the prayer-book, which had been lent to me by Captain Campbell, it being the property of his wife. I told Walkinshaw that if he was not fired on heavily he might also bring the saddle, which was underneath the horse as it lay dead with all four feet in the air. The bugler, although he was under heavy fire, succeeded in bringing away the saddle without being touched.

I now attempted to put the dead bodies of our friends on one of the ponies, but the Zulu bullets striking around on the rocks, made the animal so unsteady that it was impossible for me to arrange the bodies on the pack-saddle.

The men were taking cover, for though the Zulu fire was indifferent, it had already hit fourteen out of the twenty-six horses left on the ledge. Bugler Walkinshaw, coming forward, asked me to hold the pony, when he soon adjusted the mournful loads, and then we moved down the hill to where we could obtain soil enough to bury the bodies, and I read the burial service from the prayer-book over my two friends. If Ronald Campbell had lived he would have received the Victoria Cross, as Lieutenant Lysons and Private Fowler did; Bugler Walkinshaw received the distinguished service medal.

Fourteen months later, Captain Campbell's widow visited the spot with me in order to place a head-stone over her late husband's grave. This memorial was carried up the mountain by some of the tribe engaged in the fight.

THE BRAVERY OF COLONEL BULLER
BY SIR EVELYN WOOD
FROM PEARSON'S MAGAZINE

During a successful attack at the eastern end of the Hlobane mountain in Northern Zululand, Captain the Hon. Ronald Campbell gave up his life to save others, two of those following him earning the Victoria Cross. I propose here to describe how two more of the coveted decorations were gained in the retreat from the western summit of the mountain. No other battle-field has ever been marked by the grant of the reward "For Valour" to four persons out of a force numbering only 400 men.

The chief actor, Redvers, son of Wentworth Buller, of Dowries, Crediton,— who represented his fellow-countrymen for many years in the House of Commons,—was born in December, 1839. After leaving Eton, he entered the army just too late for the Indian Mutiny campaigns, but he served in the China War of 1860, and ten years later, during the Red River expedition, made a reputation which has steadily grown in the last quarter of the century. Having taken an important part in the Ashanti Expedition of 1873-4, he commanded a corps of Irregulars during the Kafir War of 1878, being actively engaged in the suppression of the Gaika outbreak. He harassed the insurgent natives continuously until, on the death of Sandilli, the Gaika Chief, the rebellion collapsed.

In Zululand he had been employed on many raids and expeditions at a distance from Colonel Evelyn Wood's camp, and, acting as that officer's right hand, came out "one of the bright spots" in the war. In an unsuccessful skirmish on the 20th January, 1879, a trooper having fallen from his horse, it escaped and galloped off towards the enemy, but Buller followed, and while under close, though badly aimed fire, turned and caught the horse, and helped the disabled man to remount and escape.

On the 27th of March, 1879, Lieutenant-Colonel Redvers Buller left Kambula camp with a force of 400 mounted men and 150 friendly Zulus of Uhamu's tribe; that chief having abandoned the cause of his brother Cetewayo and taken refuge with the " flying column." After a march of thirty miles, Colonel Buller led his force, in the grey dawn of the 28th of March, up the north-eastern face of the Hlobane mountain, which is an elevated table land of about 3000 acres. It stands 1200ft. above the surrounding country, being absolutely precipitous on the northern, and the upper part of the southern sides, and can be ascended only on its north-eastern and western extremities.

Colonel Buller cleared the top of the mountain with a loss of two officers and one man killed, and several minor casualties, and the warriors of the Amaqulisi tribe, who had held the mountain, were driven into their fastnesses amongst the bush-covered rocks, abandoning 2000 head of cattle. These were collected and driven down the western end of the mountain, on to a ridge 150ft. lower than the summit. There were goat paths at the north-western point of the mountain, nearly at the apex of the salient angle of the two long faces, and these Colonel Buller determined to use for his return to camp, thus avoiding the long round by the eastern extremity up which he had ascended.

While giving orders on the summit, he perceived a Zulu army approaching from the southward, estimated then at 20,000, but which in reality numbered 23,000. This army was still six miles off, and it was calculated that the British force on the Hlobane would have an hour's start ere it could be seriously harassed by the oncoming Zulu columns. However, the Amaqulisi tribe, encouraged by the approach of the main Zulu army, now came forth from their hiding places to attack Buller's men as they descended the rugged paths. These paths passed over a series of ledges of rock from 2ft. to 10ft. wide, separated by vertical distances of from 3 to 6 feet.

Colonel Buller sent down first of all the native portion of his force, keeping his own personal command, the Frontier Light

Horse, on the summit to form a rear-guard. The steepness of the tracks caused considerable delay, and the Amaqulisis, advancing on either face of the mountain, occupied the rocks above and below the line of the paths, and fired at short range into the stream of straggling dismounted horsemen.

The difficulties of the descent may be partly realised from the fact that in May, 1880, when on the mountain with the then friendly Amaqulisis, I turned ten ponies loose, and drove them down, allowing them time to pick their way. Nevertheless, one only got down without a fall, and though none were hurt, some rolled for thirty or forty yards on losing their foothold, as, after jumping from the higher crags, they landed on the narrow ledges of rock.

The scene on the 28th of March, 1879, was very different. Down the rugged mountain side streamed and tumbled a resistless surging torrent of black creatures, which, constantly smitten with leaden hail, and checked by the difficulties of the descent, broke indeed, but, like a huge on-coming wave, only to spread out in encircling foam-like smaller bodies, which, gathering in volume, again swept on with renewed force down and round the track.

I will first narrate what happened to the Commandant of Wood's Irregulars.

Major Leet, of the 13th (Somerset) Light Infantry, had dislocated his knee in the early part of the month, and was unable to walk; but mounted on a pony he was conspicuous throughout the day by his cool courage, and he remained on the summit of the mountain until Colonel Buller said to him: "Go down and wait for us at the bottom." There were two main goat paths down the mountain, one on the right and the other on the left, and when Colonel Buller had ordered Leet down, he himself went back to cover the retreat.

Major Leet, Lieutenant Smith, and a private of the Frontier Light Horse, descended by the right-hand path which Colonel Buller had intended should be used by all his men, but he found later, when he himself turned to retreat, that apparently the string of foot-men were all moving on the left-hand path, and Major Leet and his two companions not being visible from the summit thus became isolated from the remainder of the party.

The Zulus, who were following up the troops, being checked by the fire of Buller's covering party standing on the plateau, swarmed down the sides of the cliffs, and some of them came across Major Leet and his two comrades, who were slowly and with great difficulty descending the steep mountain side. The trooper was stabbed when about half-way down, and Lieutenant Smith's horse was shot. In a shower of assegais Smith turned round, and shot the foremost Zulu with his revolver, but others pressing on were nearly up to him when Major Leet, stopping his pony, called Smith and made him catch hold of the saddle. The Lieutenant begged the Major to go on and not imperil his own life, but Leet insisted, and taking Smith up behind him, both eventually escaped.

When the last of the troops had left the plateau, Buller was heard to say to Commandant Piet Uys, who was in command of thirty Dutchmen: "You go down, Piet; I'll stop up here! And when you get to the bottom halt some men to cover us as we come down." Turning then to Lieutenant Everitt, of the Frontier Light Horse, he ordered him to halt ten men, who, as a covering party, were to descend last of all. Mr. Everitt could only collect seven men, but these kept the Zulus back for some time, descending later with the enemy close upon them; four of the little party were almost immediately killed, and Lieutenant Everitt's horse was assegaied.

Buller, a tall and powerful man, now seizing Mr. Everitt, who was exhausted, by the collar of the coat, pulled him out of the way of the pursuing Zulus, who were themselves greatly impeded by the rugged nature of the cliffs, and standing over his breathless Lieutenant, received from him a carbine and ammunition, saying: "Get on down as quick as you can!" and with the three men remaining alive out of the rear-guard of seven, Buller covered the retreat of the last of those descending the cliff.

As Everitt reached the lower ridge, 150ft. from the summit, he passed Commandant Uys and saw him shoot one Zulu, and then, stabbed by another with an assegai, fall dead in sight of his two sons. Uys had previously reached the lower ridge in safety, but seeing that his youngest son, sixteen years old, could not get his horse down, the Commandant had re-climbed, for a short distance, the path on which he was killed.

Buller's command was now demoralised; and one very brave officer of an Irregular corps, who had often shown great personal courage, burst into tears when his men refused to obey his order

to form up to cover the retreat of the Frontier Light Horsemen, who were still descending the mountain. He himself remained, and assisted Colonel Buller in rallying the men, and had not this been effected, none of the wounded, nor those who had lost their horses, could have escaped.

Buller himself was ubiquitous, and to my knowledge rescued four men that day, three of whom lived for years afterwards; the fourth man, whom he pulled out of the middle of a struggling crowd of Zulus and carried, holding on to his stirrup, down the hill, was eventually wounded much lower down, and lost his life.

Trooper Randal, Frontier Light Horse, told me five days later, that in the retreat, his horse was completely exhausted, when he was overtaken by Colonel Buller, who was falling back with the rearmost men, and that the Colonel put him up on his own horse and carried him for some distance; then dropping him, returned again to the fight, this time picking up Captain C. D'Arcy also of the Frontier Light Horse. This officer had lost both his horses, and when panting along on foot with the Zulus less than a hundred yards behind him, was rescued by Colonel Buller, who took him up on his horse.

The first man to ascend the eastern end of the mountain in the grey dawn, Buller acted throughout the retreat as the rearmost man of the rearguard, although he knew from experience that any man who was wounded was sure to be ripped up by the ruthless enemy.

The casualties that day were heavy. Colonel Buller lost twelve officers, and eighty of other ranks killed, and thirty of all ranks wounded, out of a total of 400. This was in addition to a large number of Wood's (native) Irregulars, who, with Messrs. Williams and Potter, were killed under the western end of the mountain.

That evening we were sitting in our sodden tents, for the rain was falling heavily. We had seen the Zulu army bivouacing seven miles off our camp, and while we did not feel doubtful of the result of any open attack, yet our native allies had disappeared, and the 1800 British soldiers had a stern task awaiting them on the morrow.

Buller and his men had been almost continuously in the saddle for 100 consecutive hours, during which time they had skirmished once, fought twice, and marched over 170 miles. Nevertheless when, at nine o'clock, a solitary fugitive from a detachment, of which some few men had escaped over the eastern end of the Hlobane, crawling into camp reported that half-a-dozen more stragglers were trying to reach Kambula, the indomitable Buller had no difficulty in immediately mounting a dozen volunteers, whom he led forth on their jaded horses into the pitchy darkness of the night, returning later with the last of the survivors of the bloody fight of the 28th of March. Both Colonel Buller and Major Leet were granted the Victoria Cross in June, 1879.

HLOBANE & KAMBULA
BY LIEUT. ALFRED BLAINE
FROM A LETTER TO HIS COUSIN

Kambula Camp, March 31, 1879

Before this reaches you, you will have heard of our fight.

On the morning of the 27th we started with Col. Buller for the Hlobane: our strength was about 500 mounted men and natives. The first night we slept about four miles from the mountain; our horses stood ringed and saddled-up the whole night. In the morning, before day-light, we started for the mountain, which we reached just as the day began to break. As soon as we got to the foot of the mountain, one shot was fired by the enemy. We then got the order to go up in skirmishing order as fast as we could, which we did to the best of our ability.

The Zulus poured bullets into us from two spots as we went up, and we did the same to them. We lost one of our officers — poor Williams—and two or three horses. As soon as we got up, we mounted our horses and rode along the top for a little way, then dismounted and took up our positions all along the ridge of the mountain. There we fought for two or three hours: Kaffirs kept up a tremendous fire the whole time, which we, of course, returned. They were behind us in holes and behind enormous rocks.

We lost another officer there—poor Von Steitencron—two or three men, and about five wounded. At last an order came for us to retire to the other side of the mountain, which we did, and immediately we moved off the Kaffirs came out in hundreds and let us have it.

We had not gone very far when another order came to tell us to go back to our positions. as the first order was a mistake, and only one corps was intended to retire, so we rode back as hard as we could, and found the positions we had just left occupied by the Kaffirs.

We succeeded in taking our place, and we fought with the Kaffirs for about half-an-hour, when, to our horror. we saw an enormous Kaffir impi coming down from the opposite range to reinforce the Hlobane Zulus. We saw at once that it would be all up with us if we did not cut quickly, so the order was given to stand to our horses and retire, which we did in good order until we got to the steep, stony krantz, which we had to go down. It was just possible for men to go down with horses in single file; but the Kaffirs were behind us in hundreds, and every one was so anxious to get down that we got all jammed up.

Then an awful confusion took place—horses fell on top of the rocks, broke their necks and legs—you saw horses on top of men. I was under my horse for about two or three minutes, and thought it was all up with me, but succeeded in getting out. We shouted to the men not to hurry, but to take it coolly. The Kaffirs got in amongst us and assegaied our fellows. We could not hit them even with our carbines, for we were too jammed up. The officers could not even use their swords.

A lot of us got down, and then we rallied our fellows and made a stand for a time, shooting the Kaffirs down as fast as we could. We retired fighting the whole way, the Kaffirs following us for about ten miles. D'Arcy and myself were, with Colonel Buller, the whole time behind. We picked up carbines from our men that had fallen and shot at the Kaffirs from our horses. As we retired, the Zulus were the whole time within a hundred yards behind us, sometimes even closer. They did not fire much, but were evidently trying to assegai.

We lost no end of horses, and men jumped up behind others. Both Buller and myself were riding one for some time. D'Arcy's horse fell down the krantz and broke his leg, so he was dismounted, but we soon put him up behind us. The Hlobane retreat was a most awful affair. Never do I wish to see another day like it. We retired well, but I shall never forget the Kaffirs getting in amongst us and assegaing our fellows. Some of the cries for mercy from the poor fellows brought tears into our eyes.

We lost over a hundred officers and men. Weatherley's corps suffered most; they lost over forty-six. We lost thirty killed and five wounded. Our fellows behaved really splendidly, and stuck to their officers. We brought in our wounded. No men ever fought more pluckily than the Zulus—they are brave men indeed. On the following morning we sent put small patrols all over the country, to see if we could find any men who had escaped. Commandant Raaff's corps went out to the south-east with about twenty of his men, our Sergeant-Major went out to the north-east with ten of our men, and I went out to the south with ten men. When I had got about eight miles out I met Raaff riding towards me. He shouted out, "For God's sake, Blaine, ride back as hard as you can; you are right on to the Zulu army."

I looked, and saw thousands of Kaffirs coming over the hill in front of us, running. I put the men about and rode into the camp with Raaff, the Kaffirs following, but we soon left them behind. We warned the camp, and succeeded in getting all our cattle and horses into laager. We saw some mounted men riding for camp as hard as they could. They crossed about a thousand yards in front of the right wing of the Zulu army, which was about 6,000 strong, the Zulus tiring at them as they rode past.

The mounted men turned out to be our Sergeant-Major and his patrol. They got in safely. As soon as the right wing had got about two thousand yards from the camp, Colonel Buller led all the cavalry out to go and meet, them. We had a grand skirmish, and then retired back to camp, the Zulus following. Men lost their horses, and the horses ran back to camp, but we succeeded in putting the men up behind us.

Those in camp said this skirmish was a very pretty sight. We lost one man killed and two wounded out there. The Zulus then drew in their horns, and the main body came on with a rush. A heavy fight lasted for about four or five hours. The Zulus tried once or twice to rush us, but were repulsed; the fire was too heavy. As soon as the Kaffirs retreated we cheered tremendously.

Buller led us out to shoot them down as they retreated. The soldiers cheered us as we went out, and we all declared that now we would pay them out for the day before. 'Remember yesterday,' we all shouted out, and I can assure you we did, and had our revenge.

We shot two or three hundred. The guns did great service. The loss in camp was about twenty-two killed and sixty-four wounded? the enemy's about two thousand killed, and about five thousand must have been wounded. We all admire the pluck of the Zulus. I wish you could have seen it. Under tremendous fire they never wavered, but came straight at us. They got into the cattle kraal, which was only twenty yards outside tie laager. A company of soldiers had to retire from there.

The Zulu army is still near us, but I do not think they will attack the camp again. At Hlobane D'Arcy and myself lost our pack horses and all our thing's, which we hope Government will compensate us for. Buller has told us to make a claim. The correspondent to the London Standard has just arrived. As we are so far off, I suppose we shall be the last to be reinforced. I must tell you that when the Zulu army came at the camp nearly all the wagon-drivers and natives bolted away, and sat on the hill behind the camp, but most of them came back as soon as the Zulus retreated, and joined in the chase after the Kaffirs, using their assegais properly.

I have written this letter in a great hurry, but I thought you would like to hear something about our defeat at Hlobane and victory at Kambula.

A Disastrous Day for the British Army
from the Correspondent of the Cape Argus

Another disastrous day for British arms and British prestige dawned with the morning of the 28th March. Several thousand head of cattle had been observed on the Hlobane mountain, some fifteen or eighteen miles from our camp, and information reached those in command that the enemy was likewise there in considerable force. On the morning of the 27th about 400 horsemen, consisting of the Frontier Light Horse, Weatherley's Horse, Baker's Horse, and Raaff's men, with some mounted Basutos, left camp at about 9 a.m., and, marching all day, bivouacked at night about three miles to the rear of Hlobane. At 4 a.m. on the 28th this force was ready to start, with the exception of Weatherley's Horse, which had become detached, and rejoined the column late in the morning.

The arranged plan of attack was for the column to take the mountain in the rear at an accessible point, while the mounted infantry under Colonel Russell, some mounted Basutos, and Schermbrucker's corps were to attack from the front; their attack, however, to be only a feint, and a diversion in favor of the main attacking column. Day had just broken, and a mist was still hiding the summit or the Hlobane, when the head of the column advanced. Every corps was quickly engaged.

The ascent is at the best of times difficult on foot, and proved doubly so when the men were compelled to dismount and lead their horses up the steep incline, everywhere studded with loose stones and heavy boulders. From behind every stone on the summit of the hill a heavy fire was being poured upon the advancing column. Up, however, they went, and on reaching the summit the two officers leading the Frontier Light Horse were shot dead, viz., Lieutenants Williams and Baron von Steitencron. Two troopers were also killed and one wounded. However, our men pushed on, and, driving back the enemy, the summit was reached by all, with only the loss of one more man, a trooper belonging to Baker's Horse, which corps brought up the rear of the column. When all had surmounted the rise and were safely on the summit, Colonel Weatherley and his troop could be discerned at the foot of the hill.

The main column on the Hlobane extended along the summit and drove back the few Kaffirs before them in a very short time, and reaching a deep, precipitous and almost impassable gorge, that divides the hill near the centre, this force then halted and communicated with the mounted infantry, and Schermbrucker's corps, which had taken the mountain from the front, was halted on the brink of this ravine. All the cattle on the left slope of the hill were soon collected, and were being driven off.

The main column were preparing to descend the mountain by the same route they had ascended. Meanwhile Colonel Wood in person, attended by Captain the Hon. Ronald Campbell, Mr. Lloyd, chief interpreter, and a small escort, joined Colonel Weatherley's Border Horse, and attempted to surmount the mountain, when a hot fire was opened upon them from the rocks quite near, and Colonel Wood gave the order to Colonel Weatherley to send men in and clear the rocks.

The call for volunteers was promptly met, and Lieutenants Poole and H. Parminter, of Weatherley's corps, along with Captain Campbell, rushed forward, leading the men on. Almost touching his head with a rifle, a Zulu blew poor Captain Campbell's brains out. Mr. Lloyd fell here, too, and at last the troop reached the summit, and were ordered down the mountain again to hold that means of exit.

Colonel Wood had already descended with his escort and returned to camp, thinking, no doubt, all was well, and that an immense take of cattle would be the day's result. To return to the main column under Colonel Buller, which had already commenced its homeward journey. It had not proceeded very far towards the edge of the Hlobane, when news came of an immense impi of Zulus at the foot of the hill, and, true enough, the main body of the enemy could clearly be defined on the slope of the hill, and various other large bodies of Kaffirs studded the plain below, completely barring our return to camp at that side.

An immediate halt was called, and after a moment's deliberation the column was ordered back again to attempt a descent by the steep gorge already alluded to, which divided the mountain. Captain Barton and a troop of Frontier Light Horse went down to join Colonel Weatherley, and attempted to reach the camp by the open ground. As soon as the enemy saw our men retreating precipitately, from behind every boulder and rock a Zulu seemed to appear, and ran firing after the column, which, reaching the ravine, commenced its perilous descent.

To attempt to describe this descent will be impossible. In places the horses had to jump perpendicularly down three and four feet, many of them rolling down the hill and breaking legs and necks, and impeding the progress of others. The retreat now became a regular stampede. The Zulus were coming on behind, when a few men were rallied by Colonel Buller, Piet Uys, and several officers of the mounted corps, and were keeping them off as best they could. Suddenly the Zulus, seeing the confusion that the whole body of men were thrown into, profited by the occasion, and rushed in amongst our men, stabbing with their assegais, and killing a large number of the poor fellows, who, after they had discharged their carbines, were quite at the mercy of their assailants.

When the main column first commenced its disorderly descent, the mounted infantry, under Colonel Russell, and Schermbrucker's men, were on the opposite rise, and if they had remained there until the main column had crossed they could have covered its descent, and not a man would have been killed. However, whether acting under orders or not, the whole of them turned about and galloped off as hard as they could. Commandant Schermbrucker is said to have protested against this, but was overruled by his superior officer.

When Captain Barton joined Colonel Weatherley at the foot of the hill the latter moved forward rapidly, in the hopes of being able, by a hard ride along the enemy's flank, to get clear away. The moment, however, he got into the open he saw how futile this plan would prove. The enemy had already outflanked him on the one side; the Hlobane presented an insurmountable obstacle on the other, and from the hills in the rear a mass of Zulus were descending, and had already collected. They were thus caught in a trap. Collecting themselves in one mass, they charged the enemy, and managed to break through their dense masses, and gained a neck of the Hlobane, where they hoped to find a gentle incline to the plains on the other side of the mountain, but, alas, they were doomed to disappointment.

A steep, rocky ravine there met their view, and while attempting the descent the Zulus came on, and out of fifty-four men that formed the troop only one officer and six men escaped. Captain Denison, of Rustenburg, was that fortunate officer, and he says none could have behaved with greater courage than the whole of the men during that fearful time. Their gallant colonel fell fighting to the last, cutting down Zulus with his right hand, while grasping his son, a lad of fourteen, with the other. Every man who fell was assegaied by the ruthless enemy. The enemy pursued and kept up with the mounted men for more than eight miles, many poor stragglers with knocked-up horses falling into their hands who would otherwise have been saved had even a small detachment of Russell's Horse been allowed to cover the rear of the demoralized and retreatinig force.

Scarcely was the last word written when the alarm was given that a large impi was discerned in the distance, and at once all tents outside the camp were struck and brought into laager, all entrances closed, and the men placed in position. It appears that a friendly native who had escaped from Hlobane by hiding himself amongst rocks reported that he had overheard a conversation in which it was stated that Cetywayo intended attacking the camp at noon on the 29th.

This report, though not quite believed. seemed so probable an event that a sharp look-out was kept, and we were able to see dense masses of the enemy advancing in perfect order, in four columns. Their end seemed never to come, and no doubt many in camp were doubtful whether they would be able to resist the rush such masses could make. Colonel Wood seemed of a different opinion, and was happy, without doubt, that the enemy would attack him.

Throughout the engagement nothing could have exceeded the good management of the troops. Every occasion was seized upon in the nick of time to harass the attacking party. Sorties were made, and the cannons were directed against the various points with judgment that reflected every credit upon our colonel, who, however, requires no more eulogies. A more deservedly popular man, and one, too, in whose pluck, discretion, and judgment greater confidence is placed, could not be found in the whole British army. But to return to the attack.

The enemy was advancing in force on the left flank of the camp, and the Frontier Light Horse and mounted Basutos were ordered out to meet them, and entice them near to the camp, so as to meet their attack before the dense masses in the front and on the right flank were able to come up. This they did with great spirit, firing and retiring with admirable regularity and precision, and drawing on the enemy rapidly. Suddenly they received the order to retire, and fall back upon the camp.

The retreat was covered at once by a discharge of shell from the fort and the battery drawn up in front of the camp. At the same time a terrific fire of small arms was opened upon the Zulus from the front by the 99th Regiment, which lined the wagons of the laager on that side.

The enemy wavered for a moment, and then fell hastily back, and eventually effected a junction with the main attacking columns in the front and right of the camp. Here they came on in thousands, making rushes for the cattle laager, which is on the slope of the hills and protected by both camp and fort. Then the 99th and 13th made two sorties, inflicting great slaughter on the enemy and retiring into camp again, though not without considerable loss to themselves, Major Hackett, of the 13th, being shot through the head. The doctors hope to save him, but unfortunately at the expense of both his eyes.

After repeated rushes upon the camp from the right flank, in which the enemy succeeded in getting into the cattle laager, and up to within 10 yards of the camp, they seemed to tire and their firing was not nearly as well sustained as during the earlier part of the day. Suddenly it ceased, and they were seen to retire at every point simultaneously.

The colonel gave the word for every mounted man to follow in pursuit. The guns run out, then commenced a slaughter. The horsemen, desirous of wiping out the previous day's failure, shot down hundreds, and pursued the flying until night fell, when they found themselves five miles out of camp. The infantry and natives scoured the immediate neighbourhood of the camp, and killed many who were hidden away.

The attack lasted from 1 p.m. until half-past 5, when the enemy's retreat commenced, which was greeted by every one with a ringing cheer; and as the horsemen rode out of the camp at their quickest pace they were saluted from camp and fort by thunders of applause, which plainly told them how willingly the regulars would have liked to share in the revenge they were going to take.

The loss was 26 killed and about 50 wounded. The enemy's loss is estimated at between 1,500 and 3,000; the probability is that the former number is the truth.

VICTORY AT KAMBULA
A PARTICIPANT'S ACCOUNT

Yesterday (March 29), about 10 o'clock, we saw the Zulus advancing over the plains in two bodies to attack us. They were attempting to surround the camp. We were ordered to saddle-up, and the footmen fell into their places in the laager. When the right wing of the Zulus had come within three miles of the camp all the cavalry were ordered out to the attack. I think this was done to draw the enemy on to attack the laager early, as they did not care to leave the Zulus to take their own time, and wait for night. We attacked and retired into the laager, the Zulus chasing us. I think we only lost one man. The Zulus then attacked the laager, and we had hard fighting for over four hours, when, finding they could not take the place, they commenced retreating; the cavalry were then ordered out, and we chased the enemy for seven miles, till it was too dark to see. We killed a fearful lot in the retreat, shooting them down at ten and fifteen yards, and having a good many hand-to-hand struggles. The Zulus were quite knocked up and some laid down and got into holes and hiding places. I should not care to count how many I killed, and every man did the same. The Zulus numbered, we think, from 20,000 to 25,000—a tremendous mass; and thank goodness we cut them up and defeated them. There is no doubt the Zulus fight splendidly. They rush up straight, and don't seem to fear death at all. The cannon worked first-rate; so differently to the firing at Isandhlwana. We lost at the camp thirty killed and forty wounded, nearly all mortally. We lost only one of our lot (Natal N. Horse) yet they were in the thick of the fight. They behaved splendidly. We could not get them to retire for some time. There is no question as to their bravery; everyone in camp praises them, so there will be no nasty insinuations cast at them this time. The mounted infantry think no end of them. We got back into camp between seven and eight o'clock. The infantry behaved well, and drove the Zulus out of the cattle laager splendidly.

THE BATTLE OF KAMBULA
FROM A NATAL PAPER

During the attack of the Zulus on this column on the 29th ult., I had the opportunity of observing all that passed in the camp, and admired the cool and systematic manner in which all the orders were carried out by officers and men, and the short time it took to establish. a thorough preparedness for fighting; and after every one was at his station, their countenances showed a stern determined purpose of meeting the foe with British pluck and courage; and the volleys that they delivered were something terrible, especially on the side where the 1-13th were stationed, that being the centre and main attack of the Zulu army. Colonel Wood and his staff-officers were conspicuous for their bravery in directing the defence of first the fort and then the laager, under

153

a very heavy cross fire from the enemy; Captain Woodgate especially exposing himself to the enemy's fire, and directing the two companies of the 90th at the sortie where to go, marching as leisurely and unconcernedly as if he was pacing a piece of ground for cricket wickets.

Major Hackett received a dangerous wound, the ball passing through the head, whilst gallantly leading on two companies 90th L.I.; he is in a most precarious state. Lieut. Smith, 90th L.I., assistant director of transport, was wounded, ball through left arm, while gallantly bearing a stretcher to carry a wounded man, under a heavy fire. Color-Sergeant McAllen was wounded in the arm, and after the wound was dressed ran out to his company, performing his duty till shot dead.

Acting-Sergeant Quigley, R.A., exhibited great energy and zeal in working his gun in the fort, and did excellent service after his officer had been mortally wounded. Sergeant Brown, 80th Regt., attached to Royal Artillery, exhibited similar energy and zeal in working the other gun in the fort, being severely wounded in doing his duty. Private Grosvenor, 1-13th, when his company had to retire from the cattle laager, remained behind to assist Sergeant Fisher, who was wounded, losing his own life by his bravery.

Captain Vaughan, R.A., after Lieutenant Nicholson received his death wound, was indefatigable in working the gun personally, under a heavy cross-fire. Major Tremlett, Lieutenants Bigge and Slade, showed great coolness and courage while commanding the field guns, which received the special attention of the enemy, who poured in a heavy fire on the guns, wounding two of the gunners, and damaging several portions of the wheels.

Captain Leetheridge, a patient in hospital, left his bed, and sitting in a chair, cheered on his men with encouraging words, and exposed himself to the fire of the enemy. Every man did what England expected he would; even the three little buglers, among whom Tommy Finn was conspicuous again, did their duty like men, carrying buckets of ammunition out to the companies of the 90th engaged with the Zulus. One of the buckets was shot through with a Zulu bullet.

A Soldier's Account of the
Attack on Kambula Camp

On the 29th March we had a severe engagement with the enemy that attacked our camp, in round numbers 20,000. They were sighted about 10 a.m., coming towards our camp in the shape of horns, and about 1 p.m. the alarm sounded, and every man was at his post, fully resolved to avenge our comrades' lives that had been lost on the 22nd January; only too well known throughout the wide world.

When the enemy was within half-a-mile from our camp, the cavalry was sent out to break the right horn, and succeeded in felling a good few of them. Notwithstanding, they still came on, but our six guns, seven-pounders, fired shell and case shot into their midst, which scattered them like chaff before the wind. I never saw the like; nothing frightened them, as when any of their numbers were shot down others took their places, and this lasted to nearly 6 p m., when they fled in confusion, the infantry firing, and artillery throwing rockets and shells.

The cavalry also followed them up for about eight miles, killing every one they could lay hands upon. It was a most awful sight. For miles round our camp the dead lay very thick; it took us three days to bury them. Close upon seven hundred were buried, but there are a good number that have been wounded and died on the road. Our loss was but small; we had thirty killed and fifty wounded. There have been a few deaths every day since, men dying of their wounds; God knows when this war will be over for us.

We have fearful bad weather, and have to be very watchful; the whole column is under arms one hour before daylight, ready for any attack that may take place. The Zulus are very cunning. We found rifles and belts on the Kaffirs belonging to the 24th regiment. This is what they shouted when they were near our camp: "We are the Boys from Isandhlwana"—so the Dutchmen told us, as they understand them; but their mission was fruitless.

Kambula camp, says the correspondent before alluded to, has been shifted for sanitary and strategical reasons higher up the ridge. There seems to be some question about who assisted Captain Gardner to get away from the foot of the Devil's Pass at Hlobane on the 28th March. I can affirm that the honor on that occasion is due to Lieutenant-Adjutant Biecher, of Wood's Irregulars, for

I was standing within three yards of the gallant captain, when he implored Biecher to assist him; and I saw him carried on Biecher's crupper across the Nek, between the Pass and the lower plateau, and through a heavy cross-fire from the Zulus.

A monument has been erected over the graves of the brave men who fell at Kambula. It is built of freestone, quarried on the battle-field. The inscription records the services of each corps engaged on that glorious day. The ladies of Pretoria have acted nobly, and will be gratefully remembered for their kindness in providing the wounded and sick soldiers with pillows, books, tobacco, and other comforts.

THE BRAVE BOER: PIET UYS
FROM THE HUMANSDORP ECHO

Piet Uys came from a family whose names are celebrated in connection with the earliest Kaffir wars. He was born at Brakfontein, near the mouth of the Kromme River. The family left this neighborhood for Natal in 1837, and in 1838 Piet Uys's father and brother were killed whilst fighting against Dingaan—not Tshaka, as has been erroneously stated. From letters received by his relatives here, we learn that Piet Uys was determined to avenge the death of his father and brother, and so was the first to come forward and offer his services against his and our enemies. His very last letter is full of the reasons by which he was actuated. He says:— 'I fight in a good faith, and a righteous cause. I must avenge the death of my father and brother, although in doing so I am almost sure to lose my life; yet I cannot restrain myself when I remember how they were slain.' Brave, noble Piet Uys! Your last letter had no need to be answered. As the recipient of that letter was standing outside the post office here the news of his tragic death arrived, and the answer, ready to be posted, was never sent. There were few men in the field against the Zulus whose death will be more deeply deplored than that of the gallant Dutch leader, Piet Uys.

THE DEATH OF PIET UYS
FROM A NATAL PAPER

The death of Mr. Piet Uys is a national calamity. So loyal a citizen, so patriotic a burgher, so brave a man, deserves all the praise that such qualities call forth. With his little band of forty burghers,

he had rendered invaluable service throughout the campaign to Colonel Wood, to whom his advice and experience were of the highest importance. We know nothing of how he met his death, but this we know—for it goes without saying—that he died a soldier's death in the field. Honor to his memory. As we write, the following passage in a letter in the Cape Times catches our eye:—
'The name of Uys is associated in my mind with what is generous, brave, religious, hospitable, and, in the truest way, refined. I have felt pity for such of my countrymen, as being comparatively strangers, could slight these men because they lacked the conventional polish that probably would not have been found in Abraham or Isaac, many of whose grand qualities these Boers possessed. The name Uys is one among several in my mind—a typical name. It appears in the accounts of frontier skirmishes. It is historical.'

Piet Uys from a Report by F. O. Brissenden Friend of the Free State Correspondent with General Wood's Column

By-the-bye, Commandant Uys has made such a good name for himself by his brilliant performances in this campaign, that his idea of the future conduct of the war is worthy of listening to, though any comfort-lover would shrink from taking part in his scheme:—He says we can subdue the Zulus in two months from the present time in the following manner: 2,000 volunteers must be well mounted, and supplied with a few pounds of coffee and sugar each, and a little extra ammunition. We go into the enemy's country without wagons or food, kill what oxen we want for meat, and eat what mealies we can, and destroy the rest; attack small bands of Kaffirs, burn villages, and capture oxen wherever we can, and always avoid the large impis.

In two months Commandant Uys calculates that such a clearance would be made of the Zulu's foodstuff, that the now defiant Kaffirs, worn with hunger and privation, would come and lay their guns at the white man's feet and ask for food. How likest thou the picture, reader?

From what I have seen of the performances of regular— and I suppose the South African volunteer will be termed an irregular combatant—I should be most happy to venture my lot amongst the irregular 2,000, and back with my humble life old Commandant Uys's scheme for a speedy solution of the Zulu problem, believing at the same time that I should have just as good a chance of furnishing particulars of events which might transpire as now (in camp) with a cordon of wagons around me, and one of the big impis, for aught I know, making tracks for these very identical wagons and their defenders.

The Battle of Umgungunhlovo

The Battle of Umgungunhlovo

THE BATTLE OF UMGUNGUNHLOVO
EYE-WITNESS REPORTS FROM A NATAL PAPER

We are enabled, through the courtesy of eye-witnesses to place before our readers this morning, many interesting details of the battle of the 2nd of April, 1879, and of subsequent occurrences. These statements generally bear out the skeleton facts already made public, but. they also shed light upon matters that seemed obscure.

The approach of the enemy on the morning of the 2nd was first seen by Captain Buller, one of Lord Chelmsford's aides-de-camp. About half-past 5 in the morning, just at daybreak, a long coffin-shaped mass of the enemy was seen to come over the hill beyond the Inyezane, on this side of which our column was in laager.

The camp was a small and compact one, the wagons being in the centre, the 57th, the 60th, and the 91st Regiments being on three sides, the detachments of the 88th and the Buffs on the other side: a Gatling at each of two corners, and a nine-pounder at the other two corners. The camp was entrenched.

Orders were at once issued, and the troops were silently drawn into line. On crossing the river the Zulus threw out in admirable order two flanking bodies. which swiftly encompassed the camp, while a large and solid mass remained in the front and centre of the attack.

When the enemy was about seven hundred yards distant. our men and the Gatlings opened fire at 6.04 a.m. The Zulus continued at first to advance, and found good cover in small clumps of thick bush, but were checked by the reception they met, and firing ceased in front at 6.30. The shining of bayonets in the rear appears to have led them to believe that the Native Contingent was there, and that the weakest point of the camp would probably be found in that direction, and a most determined attack was accordingly-made there on the 91st Highlanders. This attack lasted about twenty minutes, when they wavered and then fled. Meanwhile, at half-past 6, when the enemy retired from the front, the order was given for Barrow's mounted men to pursue, when they at once rode out and kept up a running fight with the retreating Zulus, who often turned and fought boldly with their pursuers. The retreat, however, so far from being "sullen," was, we are assured, a most precipitate flight. At 6.45 the Native Contingent was poured out upon the flying foe, and it did much execution. At 7.10 firing ceased, and twenty minutes later all was over, barring the continued pursuit by Barrow's men.

The battle had been short but sharp, and the defeat was a crushing and complete one. The little river across which the enemy retired was choked with guns, not less than four hundred, filling at least a wagon and a half, being recovered. They were mostly old weapons, only forty or fifty being Martini-Henrys.

The Gatling is said to have behaved well, no hitch interfering with its successful handling. Our informant did not at any time consider that the tiring was very heavy when compared with other fights.

The youthfulness of our soldiers, and their consequent lack of training and steadiness, had its effect in one or two instances; but the general bearing of the troops was excellent. High praise is accorded to the 57th, who, we are informed by Captain Stanley, did splendid service; discipline and morale being alike most efficient. Our losses were two officers and five men killed; two officers and twenty-eight men wounded. The native losses, which were not large, have yet to be made known.

Colonel Northey's death is immensely lamented by all. He was a most zealous and gallant officer of about forty-eight years of age, and he owed his death to the impulse which led him, while he was lying wounded under a wagon, to jump up and cheer on his men —an effort which brought on a violent hoemorrhage.

The average shots fired per regular was 6.2; the average for the whole force was 10. Much execution was done by the rockets. Fourteen Zulus were killed by one charge alone.

The Naval Brigade behaved admirably, and were as steady as possible. Commodore Richards was, of course, in chief command of this branch; but Captain Brakenbury, of the *Shah*, led the attack. Lieutenant Carr, of the *Boadicea*, had charge of the Gatling.

We are told that all possible credit is due to Major Barrow, whose mounted men were handled in a masterly manner, and whose ceaseless efforts in scouting and patrolling, from first to last, were of the utmost value. Those of our volunteers who were present were conspicuous for their coolness and steadiness, and the behavior of the Native Contingent is spoken of in terms of the highest praise.

ZULUS FIGHT BRAVELY AT UMGUNGUNHLOVO
BY THE SPECIAL CORRESPONDENT OF
THE LONDON DAILY TELEGRAPH

As the enemy drew out of the grass and thorn-bushes into a dense semicircle of advancing warriors, the whole front of our camp broke out into a sheet of fierce flame which ran from corner to corner without intermission, in rattling volleys of a frightful close-range musketry.

Nothing, it might be thought, could live before this terrible and perpetual roll of the breech-loader, and yet our gallant though savage foes crowded their way onward through the hail of death. While spreading now to the right, now to the left, as if to find some break in the wall of fire, their central swarms kept desperately pressing forwards past the falling bodies of their comrades. Those behind sprang to the front over the corpses of their fellows, only to sink to the ground themselves and be succeeded by fresh desperadoes.

It was impossible for men to perish with more magnificent contempt of death, but they could not quite reach even our outer trenches. After again and again charging up to within twenty or thirty yards of the muzzles of our Martini-Henrys—despite the withering tempest of bullets rained upon them, to say nothing of the Gatling fire and the rockets—these heroic savages gave the game up at last upon this face of the camp, leaving the front of our defences piled with dead and wounded.

Another large body had meanwhile concentrated on the other flank of our laager, and just as the first attack was failing a second and most spirited attempt to rush our positions was tried in this new quarter. If the courage of the enemy was admirable, so was the coolness with which the men of the 91st and 57th met the swarms of yelling thousands which closed in towards the trenches. This last effort was led by a chief of high rank named Dabulamanzi, who was mounted on a good horse, and rode in the thick of his regiments close up to the laager.

The onset was for some minutes very formidable, and once inside our lines such men might have done anything; but the never-ceasing rattle of the breech-loaders could not be confronted, and on the point of forcing on that hand-to-hand fight which they wanted, the daring barbarians melted away again, and finally abandoned the attack.

A ringing British cheer was raised upon this second retreat of the enemy, and the word was given for the mounted troops to dash out. This was done by the cavalry and Barrow's mounted infantry, accompanied by some of the swift-footed Native Contingent, who flew forth from the shelter of the wagons and pursued the now disheartened survivors. Once turned and beaten, the Zulu makes no further stand, and in the headlong hunt which ensued almost as many of the foe as had fallen before the musketry and the fire of the Gatlings were overtaken and dispatched in the bush.

A SEMI-OFFICIAL ACCOUNT OF THE AFFAIR AT UMGUNGUNHLOVO

The engagement now became general, and a heavy fusilade from both sides was kept up for an hour and a half, with slight losses on our side, and doubtful ones on the other. The Gatlings, both 9-pounder guns, and rocket tubes were all in action, and added to the men in the trenches some good work was done by men, non-combatants, who had rifles and took up positions on the wagons, picking off Kaffirs whenever they showed themselves.

The General and staff throughout the whole action were constantly round and round the trenches encouraging the men and telling them to fire steadily and low. Lord Chelmsford was not mounted, but his staff were. Colonel Crealock was slightly wounded in the arm, and lost a horse, and Capt. Molyneux had two horses shot under him. Lieut. Milner had a bullet through his clothes. At about half-past seven the mounted men and those of the Native Contingent were got ready to charge and drive the enemy from their positions in the grass, and upon a cheer being given, out they went driving the Zulus before them. In a few cases the enemy when retiring fired upon their pursuers, but as a general rule they fled as fast as they could in all directions, and after being chased four miles, large and disjointed masses of them were seen in the distance, going over the surrounding hills, to our front, left, and right. A good many assembled together on some of the hills, and quietly waited to see what followed, but after receiving a few shells amongst them, they cleared out for good.

Then commenced the work of scouring the surrounding ground for dead bodies, wounded men, and firearms. Until we had been at this for some time we had no idea what number we had killed; but as 473 were found in heaps within four hundred yards of the laager, we were in hopes that their losses had been pretty severe. This idea was confirmed when three hundred more bodies were also found within it centre of 1,000 yards.

Preparations were then made during the rest of the day for an early start next morning, with a flying column, which was intended to go through to Itshowe in one day, and return the next. The laager was altered to suit the reduced garrison, and the evening passed through quietly. Early next morning the flying column started, and consisted of the 57th, 60th, and 91st regiments, with about 100 of the naval brigade, John Dunn's scouts, and some mounted men.

We reached the Inyezane at about 11, and as the sun was setting, came in view of the large hill behind which lay Itshowe. Colonel Pearson, who had been communicated with regularly by the heliograph, came on to meet the General by the new road with 500 of his men, and then turned round and went back again with the General. The head of our column got to Itshowe about seven, and came in in straggling order until about midnight.

The temporary camp of our relieving column was placed over the little stream beyond the fort, but within 250 yards of it. The garrison had got everything ready to depart in the morning, and moved off after noon.

The General with the mounted men went out a few miles and burnt a large kraal belonging to Dabulamanzi, who was present on the hill above and witnessed his men's destruction. Col. Pearson's force laagered that evening about five miles from Itshowe, the next on the Matikulu, Sunday at the Inyoni where a convoy of goods wagons met him, and early on Monday morning they all reached Fort Tenedos without the loss of a single man. The General bivouacked on Friday evening near Itshowe Fort, and left early next day passing Colonel Pearson's column on the road, but just after turning off to the left, so as to reach our laager at Umgungunhlovo by a short cut over the Inyezane, lower down. His column was not able to reach the laager the same day, and had again to bivouac out, this time in a very bad place.

At about 3.30 on Sunday morning, a picket of the 60th Rifles thought they saw some figures moving about in the dim light, and fired at them. Some of Dunn's scouts who were in front rushed back immediately, and unfortunately the men of the 60th behind the trenches, thinking that their picket was attacked by the enemy, fired into the midst of them, killing one and wounding five of their own men; also two of Dunn's scouts and six others were wounded.

This affair cast a gloom over all, which was not dispelled when the color-sergeant who had charge of the party was court-martiailed, and sentenced to five years' penal servitude. After this unfortunate contretemps, the General moved his force back to a new position nearer the Mati-kulu than our old laager, which was by this time becoming unfit to live in or near.

The stench arising from the numerous surrounding dead bodies, several hundred more of which had been found since the General's departure, added to the foulness of the water from the same causes, made it imperative that our quarters should be changed.

UMGUNGUNHLOVO
FROM A LETTER TO THE NATAL WITNESS

Feeling the fire so heavy, and the work of the Gatling gun, which was brought to bear on them, so effective, they had to retire; but some old Zulu chief haranguing them 'as to what the Zulu maidens would say when they heard the Zulus had fled before British dogs,' the force came on again, and was literally mowed down. Their superiority of numbers was of no avail—the fire from our line was too effective, the big guns doing their work well, till the ranks of the large force dwindled down, and they became disorganised. A panic seized them, and they fled, throwing down their ammunition and rifles. Just then the mounted party was let loose on them, and committed the greatest havoc, slashing them with their swords as they fled. Particular mention must be made of Sergeant Anderson, 6th Carbineers, whose conduct on this occasion reflects the greatest credit on him. The havoc he committed was tremendous, and his heroism not alone redounds to his own honor, but also to the corps to which he belongs. I understand his conduct, coming as it did under the General's eye, elicited his warmest praise, and good things in store are spoken of as likely to be the lot, at no distant day, of the brave young fellow. Aware of the presence in the bush of a large force which was acting as a reserve, the place was well shelled until the enemy fled in dismay. I must mention that among the number of the dead men were found several Zulus, clothed in the accoutrements of the 24th Regiment, belts and pouches being pretty plentiful, while one gentleman went so far as to embellish his person with an officer's sword.

Umgungunhlovo
from a Letter by an Officer of the
Natal Native Contingent
Published in the Watchman

I expect ere this reaches you you will have heard of our battle on the 2nd April. I will give you a true account of the whole thing.

On the evening of the 1st I was out on outlying picket with fifty natives and a company of the 60th Rifles. It rained nearly all night, and next morning, at about daylight, one of my boys came to me and asked if I saw Zulus down in the valley. I saw nothing. But a few minutes afterwards I saw swarms of them all rushing for the laager about half-a-mile off, I at once fell my men in and ran for the camp. I heard the Gatling gun go, and then firing began all round the camp from the trenches, and the natives were all round it in swarms, shooting as fast as they could. Fancy, there were some of them twenty yards from the trench. Talk about pluck! the Zulu has all that. They were shot down one after the other, and they still came on in hundreds.

The fight lasted for about an hour and a half, and then the Native Contingent jumped over the trench and chased them all off. The soldiers buried 473, and the marines 127. That was within a radius of 1,000 yards. There are any amount of dead Zulus lying further away that were wounded and died on the hill. The whole country stinks most fearfully. I can only swear to one man that I shot. He was creeping in the long grass about one hundred yards from me. I took a good steady aim, and saw him jump in the air, and when the fight was over I went and looked at him. I hit him, just where I aimed, in the ribs. The ball passed right through him, so I have done some good for Natal in ridding it of one Zulu, I may have shot more, only I can't tell, so many firing at once.

Death of the
Prince Imperial of France

Death of the Prince Imperial of France

The following particulars relating to the death of the Prince Imperial have been brought by Mr. Phil. Robinson, special correspondent of the Daily Telegraph, who speaks from information received direct from the four troopers in Bettington's Horse, who escaped with Lieutenant Carey from the fatal spot:

THE DEATH OF THE PRINCE IMPERIAL
BY PHIL ROBINSON, DAILY TELEGRAPH
SPECIAL CORRESPONDENT

The escort with which the Prince left camp consisted of Lieut. Carey, of H.M. 98th Regiment, six selected men of Bettington's Horse, and one Kaffir. Six mounted Basutos had been told off to accompany the party, but the Prince, with that disregard of danger which has always distinguished him, left camp without them. It will be remembered that a few days ago the Prince, accompanied by Major Bettington, Lieutenant Carey, and a party of Basutos visited a Zulu kraal, where they were fired upon by a large party, the Prince being on that occasion conspicuous for gallantry amounting almost to rashness.

The advance of two forces within the last few days has been in this direction, and the Prince, it can easily be imagined, knowing the ground, conscious of the vicinity of Lord Chelmsford's camp on the one hand, and General Wood's on the other, approached the familiar spot with confidence and a sense of security which betrayed him to his death. The party started at about half-past 9, and on their way were joined at the site of Lord Chelmsford's camp of the second, that is on the neck of the Incenzi Mountain, by some officers who, after riding with them some distance, turned off towards the left, in the direction of General Wood's camp, the Prince and his companion keeping to the right.

After crossing the spruit, which in rainy weather helps to fill the Ityotyozi River, they arrived at the flat-topped hill, nameless on our maps, which is a conspicuous feature of the landscape of this portion of the Zulu frontier, and here the Prince, directing his men to slacken girths for a while, took a sketch of the country. We may here digress to say that the Prince's talent with pen and pencil, combined with his remarkable proficiency in military surveying—(that great gift of recognising at once the strategic capabilities of any spot which so distinguished the First Napoleon)—made his contributions to our knowledge of the country to be traversed of great value.

His sketch finished, the Prince and Lieutenant Carey returned, and the order was given to resume the march, the Prince en route pointing out the kraal at which he had been fired upon on his previous visit, and turning off to another close by, which was found empty. A third kraal was then sighted about a mile further on, and towards this the party descended, the Prince having observed that a small river, the Mbazani, as the Kaffirs called it, would enable the escort to water their horses, and make themselves some coffee.

The kraal is situated some two hundred yards from the river, and consisted of five huts, one with the usual small kraal (stone cattle enclosure). Between the kraal and the river stretched a luxurious growth of Tam-bookie grass five feet or six feet in height, with, after the fashion of all described Zulu kraals, mealies and Kaffir corn interspersed. This dense cover did not, however, completely surround the kraal, for in front there was an open space, apparently used by the Zulus, from the ashes and broken earthenware strewn about, as a common cooking ground. Here the party halted, and the Prince gave the order to off-saddle for an hour.

The huts betrayed no signs of recent occupation, but two or three dogs were still lingering about the spot. The presumption, of course, was that the animals, attached to their masters' homes, had remained there after the Zulus had deserted the kraal; but seen in the light of the dreadful event that immediately followed, it is more than probable that the dogs belonged to the Zulus who were then actually stalking the Prince and his companions, who were completely off their guard, and chatting together. All the party having turned their horses into the grass and grain crops, and sent the Kaffir down to the river for water, sat down in the open space and made themselves some coffee.

The Kaffir, meanwhile, went off again to see that the horses kept together, and so the hour wore on. It is horrible to think of what was passing behind them all this time. Concealed by a deep donga, which lay right across the path taken afterwards by the fugitives, some 40 or 50 Zulus were creeping on their victims. Stealing out of the donga, they made their way. completely concealed by the rank vegetation, along the water's edge, and there, it is probable, lay waiting until the bustle of preparation for the start should give them a favorable opportunity for rushing upon the Prince's party

While thus in ambush they must have been surprised by the Kaffir, for one of the Zulus left his concealment, and crossing the river, was seen by the Kaffir making off up the opposite hill. The Kaffir at once returned to the Prince, but at first was not understood. Corporal Grubb however, knowing the language well, asked him what was the matter, and then interpreted his answer to the Prince. The Prince, meanwhile, had looked at his watch. It was 10 minutes to 4. "You can give your horses 10 minutes more," he then said; but the Kaffir's intelligence at once roused suspicion, and the order was given to saddle up at once. Every man went in search of his horse, and in a few minutes all was ready for the start.

The Prince for a minute was busy looking to his bit. All stood to their horses waiting for the order to mount—waiting for death! "Prepare to mount." The word was hardly spoken when, with a startling crash, there burst through the cover a volley from some 40 rifles. The distance was not 20 yards, and the long grass swayed to the sudden rush of the Zulus, as, with a tremendous shout, they charged towards the Prince and his companions. "Usutu" was their cry. "To the English cowards!" The horses all swerved at the suddenness of the tumult, and some broke away.

Rogers, of Bettington's corps, was shot before he could recover his horse, and the Prince was unable to mount his charger, a grey of 16 hands high, always difficult to mount, and on this occasion, frightened by the firing, worse than ever. One by one the party galloped past, the Prince in vain endeavoring to mount. He was passed by Private Letocq. *Dépêchez vous, s'il vous plait, Monsieur*, he cried, as he dashed by, himself only lying across his saddle, but the Prince made no answer, already striving his best, and in a minute he was alone.

The Zulus burst from their covert, yelling and firing after the fugitives. The Prince's horse followed, and the Prince was seen by Letocq holding his stirrup leather with the left hand, the saddle with his right, trying to keep up with his horse and to mount. He must have made one desperate effort to leap into the saddle by the help of the holster, and the holster must have given way, and he then fell. The horse trod upon him, and galloped off.

The Prince regained his feet, and ran after the fast retreating party. Letocq turned in his saddle to look behind him, and saw the Prince was running on foot, with some twelve or thirteen Zulus only a few feet behind. They all had assegais in their hands—and then—no one saw the awful end. The rest of them galloped on towards General Wood's camp, and after going some three miles met General Wood himself and Colonel Buller.

They made their report, and those officers, looking through their glasses, saw the Zulus leading away the horses they had taken—the trophies of their successful attack. Troopers Rogers and Abel and the Kaffir were killed, Abel being shot in the back by a Martini-Henri bullet as he was galloping from the kraal; Rogers before he could get on to his horse.

Survivors of the Prince Imperial's Escort
Tell Their Story –
from The Home News

Lieut. Carey, who accompanied the reconnoitring party which the Prince commanded, sends the following account of the circumstances leading to the Prince's death:

"Having learnt that His Imperial Highness would proceed on June 1st to reconnoitre the country in advance of the column and choose a site for the camp of the following day, I suggested that, as I had already ridden over the same ground, I should accompany him. My request was granted; but at the same time Colonel Harrison, acting quartermaster-general, stated that I was not in any way to interfere with the Prince, as he wished him to have the entire credit of choosing the camp. Shortly before starting I found that no escort was prepared, and applied to the brigade-major of cavalry. I received the necessary orders, and at 9.15 six men of Captain Bettington's Horse paraded before head quarters.

"With these and a friendly Zulu, provided by the Hon. Mr. Drummond, we started. Six Basutos of Captain Shepstone's corps were also under orders to proceed with us, and before crossing the Blood River I sent on to him to ask for them.

"The messenger returned to say that they would meet us on the ridge between the Incenzi and Itelezi hills. I again sent the man with orders to bring the escort back with him. On our right and left flanks I saw large bodies of Basutos scouting. Arrived upon the ridge we dismounted, wishing to fix the position of some hills with our compasses.

"Colonel Harrison then rode up and told us that General Marshall's cavalry was coming up. When he had left I suggested to the Prince to wait for the remainder of the escort. 'Oh no; we are quite strong enough.'

"At a mile and a half we ascended a commanding and rocky range of hills beyond Ityotyozi River. I proposed that we should here off-saddle, but the Prince said that he preferred to off-saddle near the river. We remained for half an hour sketching and surveying the country with our telescopes. Seeing no one, we descended to a kraal in a valley below and off-saddled. No precautions were taken, as no Zulus were expected to be in the neighborhood.

"The Prince was tired, and lay down beside a hut. The men made coffee, and I reconnoitred with my telescope. At 3.35 I suggested saddling up. His Imperial Highness said, 'Wait another ten minutes;' but in five minutes gave me the necessary order. I repeated it, and then went to fetch my horse from the mealie fields. I had saddled and mounted on the home side of the kraal when I heard His Imperial Highness give the order, 'Prepare to mount.' I looked round and saw his foot in the stirrup. At the same time I said, 'Mount,' and as the men vaulted into the saddle I saw the black faces of Zulus about twenty yards off, rushing towards us through the mealie fields.

"They shouted and fired upon us as we rode off. I thought that all were mounted, and, knowing that the men's carbines were unloaded, I judged it better to clear the long grass before making a stand. Knowing from experience the bad shooting of the Zulus, I did not expect that anyone was injured. I therefore shouted, as we neared the donga, 'We must form up on the other side. See to the retreat of everyone.' On looking back I saw one party following us, while another on our left was attempting to cut off our retreat across the ridge. Meanwhile we were under a heavy fire, and after we had crossed the donga a man said to me, 'I fear the Prince is killed, sir.' I paused, looked back, and, seeing the Prince's horse galloping on the other side of the donga, asked if it was any use returning.

"The Zulus had already passed over the ground where he must have fallen, and he pointed out the men creeping round our left. I paused for our men to come up, and then galloped on to find a drift over the Tombocto River."

The following are such points of the evidence of the surviving members of the escort as differ from the report of Lieut. Carey or throw fresh light on the subject. The names of the men were Sergeant Willis, Corporal Grubb, and Troopers Letocq, Cochrane, Abel, and Rogers. Abel and Rogers were killed. Willis mentions that when the native who accompanied them returned to the kraal with the horses, which he had been sent to bring out of the mealie field whither they had strayed, he told them he had seen a Zulu. He continues:

"We saddled as quickly as possible. All mounted and left the kraal except Rogers, who was trying to catch a spare horse he was leading. I heard a volley fired, and saw Rogers fall against a hut. I saw two men fall from their horses. The Zulus followed us for about 200 yards from the spot. I should say they numbered about fifty."

Grubb states that the kraal was 100 yards from the Mbazani River, and that when they entered it they saw some dogs and signs of Zulus having lately been there. The native told them that he saw a Zulu go over the hill on the other side of the river. He further says:

"I heard a volley, and the Zulus rushing forward shouting 'Nanga amagwala amangisi' ('Here are the English cowards'). As I rode off I saw Rogers, who was dismounted behind a hut, level his carbine. On nearing; the donga I saw Abel, who was just before me, struck below the bandolier by a bullet. From its whiz I could tell it was a Martini. Letocq now passed me, crying, 'Put spurs to your horse, boy. The Prince is down.' I looked and saw the Prince clinging to the stirrup and underneath his horse. The horse galloped a few lengths, and then the Prince fell and was trampled upon. I turned and tried to fire, but my horse tumbled into the donga, and in striving to keep my seat I dropped my carbine. I saw Lieut. Carey put spurs to his horse. We all did the same and followed him."

Cochrane in his statement says:

"I was next to the Prince. He did not mount. At the shots of the Zulus our horses were frightened, and we could not hold them. After I crossed the donga I looked back, and saw the Prince running. About a dozen Zulus, all armed with guns and assegais, were following and within three yards of him. His horse was galloping away. No order was given to rally, fire, or help the Prince. We galloped for two miles without stopping. Nothing was said about the Prince."

Letocq says:

"The Prince asked the question, 'Are you all ready?' We answered, 'Yes, sir.' He then said, 'Mount.' When the volley was fired I dropped my carbine, and dismounted to pick it up. I could not again get into the saddle, for my horse was frightened and galloped away with me, my left foot being in the stirrup and my stomach across the saddle. My horse followed the others. I was unable to stop him as I passed the Prince, who had hold of the stirrup leather and was attempting to mount. I said, '*Dépêchez vous, s'il vous plaît, Monsieur, de monter.*' He did not answer. He had not hold of the reins. I saw him fall down; his horse trampled on him. Carey was leading, and we galloped two or three miles. Noticing that Grubb and Willis could not catch us up, I advised Carey to wait for them. He said, 'We will cross the spruit, and then go on to the high road and wait.' No order was given to rally, halt, fire, or try to save the Prince. All Lieutenant Carey said was, 'Let us go quick; let us make haste.'"

The Times correspondent adds:

"Capt. Bettington, by whom, in the presence of Captain Shepstone, the evidence was taken, says that the escort was selected from the best men of his corps, and that their evidence, especially that of Grubb and Letocq, who are particularly cool and steady, may be relied upon. Grubb and Letocq may be particularly cool and steady, but they have an odd manner of evincing these qualities, and if the evidence of the escort is not more trustworthy than their boldness the less said about it the better. Lieutenant Carey has also a reputation for coolness and nerve, but on this occasion he seems entirely to have lost his presence of mind. The fact is patent that no one thought to attempt to assist the unfortunate Prince, whereas if only one man had waited to see him mounted and held his horse's head for him he might have been saved. It is a general opinion that the numbers of the attacking party have been exaggerated. The question on whom the blame is to rest is a grave one. Lord Chelmsford, who is too apt to trust to others, gave a general verbal order to Colonel Harrison, in whose department and under whose authority the Prince Imperial immediately was, not to allow him on any expedition without a fitting escort, and in any case not to permit him to incur danger. He knew nothing of the Prince's movements, and was not aware he had quitted the column. Colonel Harrison evidently disobeyed orders; the escort deserted its duty. In the whole event there is not one redeeming feature."

THE DEATH OF THE PRINCE IMPERIAL
FROM THE HOME CORRESPONDENT OF THE SOUTH
AUSTRALIAN REGISTER, 4TH JULY, 1879

Another evil memory has been added to the Zululand campaign in the death of the Prince Imperial. This sad news was brought to Madeira by the *Balmoral Castle* a fortnight ago. The first intimation of it came in a short telegram to Mr. Pender, one of the directors of the Eastern Telegraph Company. As by the preceding mail we had been victimized by a report of the death of Major Chard, there was the less inclination to credit another distressing report of the same kind. By-and-by, however, the Commander-in-Chief got a message from Lord Chelmsford to the same effect. It dispelled all shadow of doubt by announcing, with military brevity, "Prince Imperial killed."

After the House of Commons had been for a short while in painful suspense, and knots of members were forming in the lobby to find out who had the latest news. Colonel Stanley rose in his place, and said he exceedingly regretted to have to read a telegram just received from Madeira, which reported that the Prince Imperial had been killed by the Zulus in a foray. Though the telegram had not been verified till nearly midnight, all the morning papers had articles expressing the grief of the nation and its sympathy with the bereaved mother.

On the 26th, Colonel Stanley, replying to questions put by several members relative to the death of Prince Louis. Napoleon, read an extract from an official letter received from Lord Chelmsford stating that he had attached the Prince to his staff. He also read a number of extracts from letters addressed by Lord Chelmsford to his own relatives in England, referring to the presence of the Prince at headquarters, in which the Commander-in-Chief expressed the utmost solicitude for the health and comfort of his illustrious guest. In the last letter received, dated 21st May, Lord Chelmsford said— "The Prince Imperial went on a reconnaissance a few days ago, and very nearly came to grief. I shall not allow him out of my sight again if I can help it." A Bonapartist meeting was lately held in Paris, and some of the crowd outside gave three cheers for the Zulus. A dozen arrests were made.

The Removal of the Prince Imperial's Body from the South African Correspondent of the Melbourne Argus

Four o'clock, Sunday.—The mortal remains of Prince Louis Napoleon have found a temporary resting-place with the local clergy of the community to which his family belong. Seven days ago to the very hour the young Prince was stricken down under circumstances devoid of any incident which might glorify his fall. The body was recovered early upon the succeeding day, disfigured by assegai wounds, and stripped of everything but a religious token, which the savage, but withal chivalrous, foe had deemed the fallen warrior's charms.

Inquiry into Prince Imperial's Death Announced from the Home Correspondent of the South Australian Register

It is announced from the Cape that Lord Chelmsford immediately ordered an inquiry into the circumstances attending the melancholy event; but that there may be no doubt as to the facts, Colonel Stanley has telegraphed out orders for a full investigation, and a reply at the earliest moment. The Government and the Commander-in-Chief have already cleared themselves of responsibility by stating that the Prince held no commission whatever in the army. He had asked for one, but the Government had thought it advisable he should go out simply as a volunteer. He took with him letters of introduction from the Duke of Cambridge to Sir Bartle Frere and Lord Chelmsford, in both of which the Duke expressed an opinion that he was too eager and heedless of danger.

Something has been done towards clearing Lord Chelmsford, his wife having furnished to Colonel Stanley extracts from his letters respecting the Prince, in which he spoke of the precautions it had been necessary to take to keep him out of danger. Neither he nor General Wood knew that he had been sent on the service which led to his death. Mr. Forbes, in a letter to the Daily News, says he was attached to Colonel Harrison, the Quartermaster-General of the army, and his principal duty was reconnoissances and sketch-taking, of which he was very fond. He was noted for his anxiety always to get into close quarters with the Zulus, and on the day before his fatal expedition he had reconnoitred the very kraal at which he met with his death.

The chief point for the Court of Enquiry will be who sent him out or allowed him to go out with such a small escort. It is said that orders had been given to Captain Shepstone to send six of his black horse with them, but that either the horse were not supplied, or the Prince rashly went off without them. One man will have difficulty in escaping from a serious share of responsibility—Lieut. Carey—who appears to have received from Colonel Harrison special charge of the Prince to keep him out of adventures to which he was notoriously prone.

Carey states that as the party were preparing to mount he saw black faces peeping over the grass, which was five or six feet high round the kraal. He was calling the Prince's attention to it, when a volley was fired from forty or fifty guns. His belief is that the Prince fell within the kraal and never got on his horse at all. The only evidence he saw of what had happened was the riderless horse galloping off.

Sergeant Cochrane, who gave evidence at the court-martial, says that he saw the Prince attempt to mount, and break his stirrup-leather. When the horse bolted the Prince then ran to the gully, and never came out of it. Cochrane's version agrees with the position in which the body was found. Some of the Bonapartist papers have been putting delicate questions as to the conduct of the English troopers in leaving the Prince when they saw his danger. There were at least five of them unharmed by the first volley. It killed two of them, and the Basuto disappeared; but there were still Lieutenant Carey, Sergeant Cochrane, and three men. It was surely their duty to stand by a comrade who had been unhorsed at such a perilous moment. Even had they seen the Prince killed it was their duty, one would think, to recover his body. Had the Zulus known its value they might have used it to inflict upon it a greater humiliation than Isandhlwana itself. With it in his possession Cetywayo might almost have dictated his own terms to Lord Chelmsford. Colonel Buller, however, as soon as he heard of the disaster, had sufficient presence of mind to gallop forward at once in search of the body.

Since the death of the Prince Consort I doubt whether any event has excited a greater sensation, or aroused an intenser personal feeling, than the unexpected death of the Prince Imperial in the Zulu war. In the English royal circle the feeling which the news excited was one of absolute consternation. The Prince of Wales had been the youthful exile's bosom friend. Their friendship began in Paris many years ago. When there they were inseparable companions, and up to the moment that the Prince Imperial left for Natal he was always a welcome visitor to Marlborough House. The Duke of Cambridge, who possesses great command of soldierly language, has, it is said, anathematised the conduct of the Prince's escort in terms which I could hardly ask you to reproduce in your columns. It really does appear that the Prince was, as M. Rouher remarked at Chislehurst, 'abandoned,' and that if a stand had been made by his companions his life might possibly have been saved. But although it is impossible to compliment the survivors upon their gallantry or devotion, it is idle to shut one's eyes to the fact that the original and cardinal mistake was in the Prince going to Natal at all. The Prince had no call to fight the naked and barbarous Zulus. When his mother, for whom the entire country feels such genuine and heartfelt sympathy, first settled in England, she frankly remarked: 'I have loved war too much.' Mexico and Sedan both proved this, and now the justice of the reflection is confirmed by what must he to her a yet deeper and more heart-breaking tragedy.

The Zulu Custom of Disembowlment
by a Special Correspondent to
the Times of Natal

Short of a post-mortem examination, it would, of course, be impossible to speak with any exactitude, but there was one longish wound on the right breast which was evidently mortal, for the assegai has passed through the body, and the point had penetrated the skin of the back. There were two hurts in the left side also which might well be mortal, and less serious wounds all over the upper part of the chest, and one in the right thigh. The right eye was out, but whether by the thrust of an assegai or by the impact of a bullet of some kind was impossible to say. If a bullet or stone from a sling, it could not have been projected with any force. There was a large gash in the abdomen exposing the intestines, which were, as in the case of the trooper, uninjured. Close by the left shoulder of the corpse, half trodden in the bloody mire, was a sock and a pair of spurs, which had evidently belonged to the Prince, and round his neck was found, when Dr. Scott moved the body, a small gold chain, holding a few gold and stone trinkets. I am inclined to think that Zulu superstition had something to do with this being left. The witch doctors carry their magic materia medica round the neck, very much after the same fashion, and I am pretty sure that they looked upon the bunch of trinkets as the Prince's witch apparatus, and thought it best to have nothing to do with it. The gash, too, in the abdomen is not, I feel assured, inflicted with any idea of mutilating the corpse of a slain enemy, but simply because it is a belief among them that if this coup is not given, and the body swells, as it would by the generation of the gases of decomposition, the warrior who had neglected this precaution is destined to die himself by his body swelling. Apart from the gash which was in every case inflicted after death, for no blood had flowed, there was no mutilation whatever. Many of the wounds were so slight that I think they too must have been inflicted after death, all the members of the party probably 'washing their spears,' in pursuance of some ceremonious regulation on the subject of a dead enemy." The above reason for the Zulus disembowelling their victims is correct.

The saddle used by the Prince on his last fatal ride told its own tale. It had attached to it two saddle-bags and two holsters. One of the latter was smooth and uninjured, but the other on the left side had evidently been clutched and squeezed in the death grip of a man holding on to it for life. The connecting band was torn almost, but not quite, in two. It is evident, therefore, that when the Prince failed to vault into his saddle, owing to his horse's bolting, he seized hold of the near holster and held on to it, keeping by his horse's side until the leather gave way, and he no doubt was thrown back and left helpless. The evidence borne by the saddle—which we saw before it was taken on board—scarcely tallies with the statement of Mons. Hellehulle, who said that the saddle turned round the horse. The visible marks on the holster of an ever-tightening grasp were very pathetic in their significance.

Before he started upon his last expedition the Prince wrote a few lines to the Empress, his mother, remarking when doing so that 'You never know what may happen.' He probably shared the fatalistic belief in 'destiny' which possessed both his great uncle and his father. If this were so, it would account for the indifference he displayed to the ordinary risks of savage warfare.

One of the most painful local circumstances connected with the Prince's death was the terrible and overwhelming effect it had upon his faithful intendant—or confidential servant and companion—Mons. Uhlmann. This devoted attendant had been attached to the person of the Emperor before the Prince's birth, and when the latter was six months old he was placed in oversight of the heir-apparent. When asked how long he had been with the Prince he said, mournfully, 'for 23 years.' He was urgent to be allowed to go with his young master to the front, but the latter was very loth to encumber the staff with more personal attendants than he absolutely needed, and believed that his good and faithful custodian would find abundant employment in his behalf as his representative in Durban. We have reason to know that the excellent Uhlmann remained behind in a chronic condition of anxiety and solicitude. He seemed to be oppressed with a presentiment that something might happen to his Imperial charge. When the fatal news reached Durban he could scarcely realise it, and ever afterwards was a crushed and broken-hearted man. He went to Maritzburg by post-cart on Wednesday, the 4th, and put up at the Royal Hotel, where his overpowering grief made him an object of deep sympathy to the other inmates of that establishment.

The arrival of the Prince's remains, and especially their inspection by him, intensified, as was natural, his unspeakable distress. It must have been only by a supreme effort of mind and body that he was able to go through the various ceremonies and journeys that attended the progress of the funeral cortege.

In the Catholic Church of Durban, during the short service that immediately followed the arrival there of the coffin, he succumbed to the long and intense strain and fainted away; nor did he revive until an hour's assiduous attendance on the part of friendly hands brought him back, alas! to the recollection of his woe. On the final day of embarkation he succeeded in passing through the painful ordeal of the great popular demonstration which did honor to the memory of his master; but the sadness of his appearance and expression was beyond description. 'What shall I say to the Empress when she asks me for her son' was the remark constantly on his lips.

The following statement was taken down from the lips, of its author in the office of Mr. Peace, Belgian Consul, and solemnly declared to be true in the presence of that gentleman and the Mayor of Durban:—Mons. C. Hellehulle, of Ghent, who was with the force when the body of the Prince was recovered,said it was found lying on the side in a recumbent position, with one leg bent under him, and close to him were found three empty revolver cartridges, thus showing that he had died only after defending himself against such fearful odds to the very last. Mons. Hellehulle left camp at 10 o'clock on the night of the 2nd June, and arrived in Durban this evening along with the remains of the Prince. I must not omit to mention one fact which may be significant. The native who went with the Prince's party is supposed to have been killed, but neither his body nor his horse, saddle, or bridle have been found. He was a Zulu.

THE COURT-MARTIAL OF LIEUTENANT CAREY
FROM THE LONDON TRUTH

Of course we civilians shall be told that it is absurd for us to form any opinion respecting the august decisions of military men on a military question. But I take the liberty to assert the heresy that, on broad matters of fact, our opinion is as sound as that of all the Generals in the army.

When Lord Chelmsford, after the disaster of Isandhlwana, wrote home a despatch, announcing that his mind was unhinged, and seeking to excuse himself at the cost of his subordinates, reason told us that Sir Garnet Wolseley or some other tried commander should be despatched at once to the Cape to replace him. Our common-sense view, however, was scoffed at by the military authorities, and not until Lord Chelmsford had been given several other opportunities to prove his incompetence was he relieved of his command.

So, too, in regard to the court-martial on Lieutenant Carey. Common sense tells us that the Court had two missions: to whitewash Lieutenant Carey's superiors, and to throw all responsibility on the lieutenant.

Unless there are two Colonel Harrisons at the Cape, it would seem that the very Colonel Harrison who was mixed up in the circumstances that led to the Prince commanding and yet not commanding the reconnoitring party, was actually himself a member of this court-martial; and in any case no evidence was submitted to show whether Lord Chelmsford had disobeyed his instructions as to the position which the Prince was to occupy at head-quarters.

My only surprise is that the entire blame was not officially thrown upon the two troopers who were killed with the Prince.

The military authorities must distinctly understand that they will not be permitted to make Lieutenant Carey the scapegoat of the miserable indecision and the absence of firmness displayed by his superiors in Natal in regard to the late Prince Imperial. Either the Prince was a 'spectator'—and if so, his plucky desire to share danger ought to have been controlled, nor should he have been allowed to make one of a reconnoitring expedition, where an ambush was not only possible, but probable—or he was, like others forming part of the reconnoitring expedition, a soldier accepting like his companions the chances of war.

Lieutenant Carey appears to have pursued his career up to the moment of the unfortunate accident with commendable zeal and discretion. Those who thrust the Prince and him into a false position are responsible for what occurred. Our regret for the untimely fate of the brave French lad must not lead us to view the conduct of Lieutenant Carey in any exceptional manner. A reconnoitring party found itself suddenly surrounded by an overwhelming force of Zulus. A general rush was made to get away, and this was, I believe, strictly in accordance with the usage of war. Unfortunately the Prince and two troopers did not get away. They were killed. We are all sorry for them and their relations, but that one of the victims of war happened to be the late Prince Imperial should make no difference in our feelings towards Lieutenant Carey. Had three troopers been slain and the Prince Imperial been saved, would Lieutenant Carey have been brought before a court-martial, and then sent home to England under arrest? No. And if not, the entire proceeding is an unjustifiable one.

To-day (August 23, 1879,) a home telegram appears in the Adelaide papers to the effect that Lieut. Carey has been cleared of all blame re the death of the Prince Imperial.

THE BRAVERY OF CAPTAIN CAREY
FROM THE BROAD ARROW

A statement of Captain Carey's career and services in the army has now, however, been made public, and one part of it is most significant in relation to the charges which have been made in some of the French journals, and, we are ashamed to say, in English newspapers, too, that this officer is in plain words a coward. It appears that Captain Carey, at a time when London was full of Frenchmen, old and young, who had deserted their country before the German invasion, was daily risking his life as a volunteer with the English ambulance which was taking care of the wounded soldiers of the French army.

That this was a service of no ordinary danger is shown by the fact that Captain Carey was taken a prisoner three times, and as a combatant officer giving aid and comfort to the enemy he must have been in imminent risk of being shot, as the German commanders were not at all the sort of men to draw fine distinctions in cases of this kind. The Society of the Secours aux Blesses awarded to him in 1871, in recognition of his services, the cross, the ribbon, and the diploma of merit. But, notwithstanding these decorations, we hold that the French nation is still debtor to Captain Carey, although he did not consider it necessary to throw away the life of himself and four more troopers because the heir of Napoleon III. was cut short in his attempt to perfect himself in the art of war.

HOW WILLIAM BERESFORD WON THE V. C.
BY ARCHIBALD FORBES
FROM PEARSON'S MAGAZINE

It was mid-December of 1878 when Sir Sam Browne's column, having occupied Ali Musjid and tramped on up the grim and sullen Khyber Pass, was settling itself down for the winter on the plain of Jellalabad. Lord William Beresford and myself only waited for the Christmas dinner of the headquarter staff, and then we rode down the passes together, blazed at by the Afghan hillmen all the way from Ali Boghan to Khata Khoostia. At Umballa we parted, Beresford to return to duty with the Viceroy at Simla, while I made across the Bay of Bengal for Mandalay, the capital of native Burma, there to study the character and surroundings of King Theebau. While engaged in that somewhat barren operation, there suddenly reached me a telegram informing me of the catastrophe of Isandhlwana, and ordering me to betake myself to South Africa with all speed.

Beresford and I, when parting at Umballa, had trysted to meet next spring for the expected fighting on the way to Cabul; but the startling tidings of misfortune in South Africa disarranged that programme. At Calcutta I found a letter, from Beresford, telling me that he had obtained six months' leave, that he was bound for Zululand, and that I should find him at Aden, waiting for the fortnightly steamer down the east coast of Africa. We duly foregathered in that extinct volcano crater, dodged wearisomely into every little obscure Portuguese Negro port along that coast—stagnant, fever-stricken, half-barbarous holes where, as it seemed, nobody was quite black or quite white.

Finally we reached Port Durban about the middle of April,

1879, to find its roadstead thronged with the transports which had brought the reinforcements out from England, and the hotels of the place crammed with officers of all ranks and all branches of the service. Beresford belonged to the Cavalry arm—he was a Captain in the gallant 9th Lancers—and during the voyage to South Africa he was wishing with all his heart for a position on the staff of his old friend General Frederick Marshall, who was in command of the regular Cavalry brigade which had been sent out.

But yet better fortune was in store for my comrade. That resolute fighting man, Colonel (now General Sir) Redvers Buller, was in command at Kambula, far up in the remote Transvaal, of the irregular Volunteer Cavalry of Evelyn Wood's grand little fighting force, which had just gained a shining victory over .a host of 20,000 Zulus. In one of the recent fights, Buller's staff-officer, Captain the Hon. Ronald Campbell, had been killed.

It was a peculiar and difficult post, which was vacant in consequence of his death, for Campbell was a man whom it was not easy effectively to succeed. The assignment rested mainly with Marshall and on the night of our arrival he, knowing Beresford better than did most men then, obtained Lord Chelmsford's sanction for that fortunate officer's appointment to the post.

Beresford made no delay. Before breakfast on the following morning he had got a kit together, bought his horses, requisitioned an Irish (very Irish) ex-trooper of the Royal Dragoons as groom, cook, and body-servant, and was ready for the long journey. A couple of hours later he was on the road, eager for duty.

Presently I too, joined Wood's force up at Kambula, where I found Beresford too busy to do more than give me a hurried handshake. He was Redvers Buller's sole staff officer, and the force Buller commanded, some 800 strong, was the strangest and most mixed congeries imaginable.

It consisted of broken gentlemen, of runagate sailors, of fugitives from justice, of the scum of the South African towns, of stolid Africanders, of Boers whom the Zulus had driven from their farms. Almost every European nationality was represented; and there were men from the United States, a Greaser, a Chilian,

several Australians, and a couple of Canadian Voyageurs. One and all were volunteers, recruited for the campaign at the pay of five shillings a day.

What added to the complication was that the force comprised some eight or ten subcommands, each originally, and still to some extent, a separate and distinct unit. Beresford had to arrange all details, keep the duty rosters, inspect the daily, parades and the reconnaissance detachments, accompany the latter, lead them if there was any fighting, restrain the foolhardy, hearten the funkers, and be in everything Buller's right-hand man.

Buller was a silent, saturnine, blood-thirsty man, as resolute a fighter as ever drew breath—a born leader of men, who ruled his heterogeneous command with a stern hand.

Beresford, to the full as keen a fighter and as firm in enforcing discipline and obedience, was of a different temperament. He was cheery; with his ready Irish wit he had a vein of genial yet jibing badinage that kept queer-tempered fellows in good humour while it pricked them into obedience. In fine, he disclosed the rare gift of managing men—of evoking without either friction or fuss the best that was in the rough troopers. And, strangest of all wonders, the fellow whom all men had regarded as one of the most harum-scarum of mortals, was found to be possessed of a real genius for order and system.

At length, on June 1st, Lord Chelmsford's army wound down into the valley of the Umvaloosi, and there lay, stretched out beyond the silver sparkle of the river, the broad plain on whose bosom was visible the royal Kraal of Ulundi, encircled by its satellites. Over the green face of the great flat there flitted dark shadows which the field-glass revealed as the impis of Cetewayo practising their martial manoeuvres.

Two days were accorded to the Zulu monarch in which to choose submission or a battle. It was desirable, meanwhile, to gain some acquaintance with the ground in our front, over which a final advance might have to be made. So orders were issued that at noon of the 3rd Buller should make a reconnaissance across the river, without bringing on an engagement, since Cetewayo's "close time" was not yet up.

At the specified hour Buller and Beresford sat on horseback in front of Evelyn Wood's tent, waiting for their fellows to come on the ground. Presently Baker came along at the head of his assortment of miscreants; brave old Raaf brought up his miscellaneous Rangers; Ferreira, leading his particular bandits, was visible in the offing; and then Buller headed the procession of horsemen down towards the ford, Beresford remaining to see the turn-out complete and close up the command. Then he galloped forward to join the scouts; for it was, as ever, his place to lead the advance, Buller bringing on the main body.

There was no delay down by the Umvaloosi bank, where the scattered fire from the Zulus in the Kopjie on the further side whistled over the heads of the horsemen—over whom, too, screamed the shells from the laager, which fell and burst among the crags where the Zulus lurked. The spray of the Umvaloosi dashed from the horse-hoofs as the irregulars forded the stream on the left of the Kopjie, and then, bending to the left, took it in reverse.

The Zulu occupants of the rocks were quick to perceive their risk of being cut off, and hurriedly ran out into the plain through the long grass in front of the riders. Some fell as they headed for the nearest kraal, Delyango, out of which a detachment rattled the fugitives.

Nodwengo was found evacuated; and then the force—Beresford and his scouts still leading, the main body deployed on rather a broad front—galloped on across the open through the long grass in pursuit of the groups of Zulu fugitives. It really seemed a straight run in for Buller and Beresford as they set their horses' heads for Ulundi and galloped on.

Beresford, on his smart chestnut with the white ticks on withers and flanks, was the foremost rider of the force. The Zulu chief bringing up the rear of the fugitives, suddenly turned on the lone horseman who had so outridden his followers. A big man, even for a Zulu, the ring round his head proved him a veteran. The muscles rippled on his shoulders as he compacted himself behind his cowhide shield, marking his distance for the thrust of the gleaming assegai.

It flashed out like the head of a cobra as it strikes; Beresford's cavalry sabre clashed with it; the spear-head was dashed aside; the

horseman gave point with all the vigour of his arm and the impetus of his galloping horse, and lo! in the twinkling of an eye, the sword point was through the shield, and half its length buried in the Zulu's broad chest. The gallant induna was a dead man.

The flight of the groups of Zulus was a calculated snare; the fugitives in front of the irregulars were simply a decoy. Suddenly from out a deep watercourse crossing the plain and from out the adjacent long grass, sprang up a long line of several thousand armed Zulus. At Buller's loud command to fire a volley and then retire, Beresford and his scouts rode back towards the main body, followed by Zulu bullets.

Two men were killed on the spot. A third man's horse slipped up, and his wounded rider came to the ground, the horse running away. Beresford, riding behind his retreating party, looked back and saw that the fallen man was trying to rise into a sitting posture.

The Zulus, darting out in haste, were perilously close to the poor fellow, but Beresford, measuring distance with the eye, believed that he saw a chance of anticipating them. Galloping back to the wounded man, and dismounting, he confronted his adversaries with his revolver, while urging the fallen soldier to get on his (Beresford's) horse.

The wounded man bade Beresford remount and fly. Why, said he, should two die when death was inevitable but to one? The quaint resourceful humour of his race did not fail Beresford in this crisis; he turned on the wounded man and swore with clenched fist that he would punch his head if he did not assist in the saving of his life.

This droll argument prevailed. Still facing his foes with his revolver, Beresford partly lifted, partly hustled the man into the saddle, then scrambled up himself and set the chestnut a-going after the other horsemen. Another moment's delay and both must have been assegaied.

A comrade, the brave Sergeant O'Toole, fortunately came back, shot down Zulu after Zulu with cool courage, and then aided Beresford in keeping the wounded man in the saddle till the laager was reached, where no one could tell whether it was the rescuer or rescued who was the wounded man, so smeared was Beresford with borrowed blood. It had been one of Ireland's good days; if at home she is the "distressful country," wherever gallant deeds are to be done and military honour won, no nation excels it in brilliant valour. Originally Norman, the Waterfords have been Irish for centuries, and Bill Beresford is an Irishman in heart and blood. Sergeant Fitzmaurice, the wounded man whose self-abnegation was so fine, was an Irishman also; and Sergeant O'Toole—well, there is no risk in the assumption that a man bearing that name, in spite of all temptation, remains an Irishman.

Going into Beresford's tent the same afternoon, I found him sound asleep, and roused him with the information which Colonel Wood had given me, that he was to be recommended for the Victoria Cross.

"Get along with your nonsense, you impostor!" was his yawning retort as he threw a boot at me, and then turned over and went to sleep again.

But it was true all the same. As we approached Plymouth on the home-coming, the Prince of Wales, then in the Sound with Bill's elder brother Charles, was the first to forward the news that the Queen had been pleased to give effect to the recommendation. Lord William was commanded to Windsor to receive the reward "For Valour" from the hands of his Sovereign.

But something more may be told. Beresford plainly told Her Majesty that he could not in honour receive recognition of the service it had been his good fortune to perform unless that recognition were shared in by Sergeant O'Toole, who, he persisted in maintaining, deserved infinitely greater credit than any which might attach to him.

Not less than soldierly valour can Queen Victoria appreciate soldierly honesty, generosity, and modesty; and so the next Gazette announced that the proudest reward a British soldier can aspire to had been conferred on Sergeant Edmund O'Toole, of Baker's Horse.

The Battle of Ulundi
& After

The Battle of Ulundi & After

After the news of the massacre at Isandhlwana, and the subsequent indecision and strategical weakness of Lord Chelmsford
had reached England, the opinion was pretty freely expressed that
the time had arrived for superseding that General, and Sir Garnet
Wolseley, K.C.B., was mentioned by the Press as being the fittest
man for the post, owing to his previous experience of native warfare in Ashantee, where he carried the campaign in such a rapid
and decisive manner to a successful termination.

On the 26th May, it was announced by the Government in
both Houses that Sir Garnet Wolseley had been appointed Governor of Natal and the Transvaal, and High Commissioner and
Commander-in-Chief of those colonies and the districts adjacent
to the north and east of the colonies which were the seat of war.
At the same time it was explained that the appointment was not
intended to imply censure on or to supersede Lord Chelmsford,
whose services would still be retained by the country.

THE APPOINTMENT OF SIR GARNET WOLSELEY
BY THE LONDON CORRESPONDENT OF THE
NATAL MERCURY, 7TH JULY, 1879

Sir Garnet Wolseley is to be sent out to Natal as Commander-
in-Chief and Governor, superseding at once Lord Chelmsford, Sir
Bartle Frere, and Sir Henry Bulwer. Sir Bartle will be relegated to
the Cape, but Sir Henry will retain his position as Lieut.-Governor
of Natal. Sir Garnet, who is suffering in health from his residence
in Cyprus, was anxious to stay here a short time to recruit. The intelligence, however, that came from South Africa on Saturday night
was considered very unsatisfactory, and Sir Garnet was requested
by the Cabinet to set out with the least possible delay. This resolution was taken by the Cabinet on Monday.

Sir Garnet had previously had a long interview with Lord Beaconsfield and the Colonial Secretary. Letters received from officers

and influential colonists within the last few weeks, by ministers and their friends, had produced a feeling almost amounting to alarm, and that feeling culminated in a determination to send Sir Garnet Wolseley to Natal, with the fullest powers as Governor and General. Sir Garnet's acquaintance with Natal, the Transvaal, and Zululand, will enable him to arrive at a correct judgment as to what is to be done. He knows Cetywayo and all his military arrangements, having been a visitor at Ulundi.

When he arrived here from Cyprus, he did not hesitate to declare that the war, if carried out as it had been commenced, would cost £20,000,000, and require more than 20,000 troops. Sir Garnet can show a brilliant military record, though only 46 years of age. He was with a storming party in Burmah when but 19; he was also at the storming of the Redan, and brought the Red River expedition to a brilliant close. His services in Ashantee are well known, and since then he has been out in South Africa and Cyprus.

Sir Garnet's instructions are to make peace with Cetywayo, if any sort of acceptable conditions can be obtained from him. Means will be taken to let the Zulu King know that there is no intention to annex his territory, but that in the interests of Natal and the Transvaal his military organisation must be utterly broken up.

Having been preceded by a large reinforcement of Marine Artillery and Engineers, Sir Garnet Wolseley and his staff embarked on board the Edinburgh Castle for the Cape on the 30th May. The staff consisted of Colonel Colley (chief of staff), Lieut.-Colonel O'Neil Brackenbury (military secretary), Major M'Calmont (A.D.C.), Lord Gifford, Captain Braithwaite, Lieutenant Creagh, and other officers on special service.

The Edinburgh Castle arrived at Cape Town on the 23rd June, and Sir Garnet at once telegraphed orders to Natal to collect the native chiefs at Pietermaritzburg with the intention of providing himself, as in Ashantee, with native porterage in order to overcome the transport difficulty, which seemed to have completely paralysed Lord Chelmsford.

Sir Garnet arrived at Durban on the 28th June, and was sworn in at Maritzburg on the afternoon of the same day. In the course of his speech to the assembled chiefs on the subject of porterage, he said: "The Great Queen will go on sending out armies; since the English always do what they say they will do. I shall not leave Africa until the war is finished. This is a war against the King, who has broken his promises, and not against the people, whom the Queen does not wish to deprive of their cattle, their land, or their property. The Queen desires the war to be finished quickly, and I can do so in six or eight weeks if the chiefs provide carriers."

SIR GARNET WOLSELEY'S MARITZBURG SPEECH FROM THE DAILY TELEGRAPH

Such resolute and uncompromising language produced its natural effect upon the Africans who heard it, and Sir Garnet, it appears, can henceforth have as many 'porters' as he pleases.

Sir Garnet sent Captain Stewart with a message to the Headquarters Camp on the Umfolosi on the Sunday, and telegraphed home on 1st July that he expected an answer that afternoon.

The delay in the advance of Sir Garnet Wolseley caused by the storm which prevented his landing at Port Durnford for two days, and which enabled Lord Chelmsford in part to vindicate his reputation as a General, was viewed with much satisfaction by the English Press. It was justly felt that as the latter General had been permitted to make blunder after blunder before Sir Garnet was appointed, some opportunity should have been afforded him of retrieving his mistakes, and such an opportunity was luckily given by the accidental detention of the new Commander-in-Chief off Port Durnford. Mr. A. Forbes, in his telegram to the Daily News gives high praise to Lord Chelmsford's "soldierly coolness and decisive clearheadedness in action," which, he says," go far to redeem the passiveness and peevish vaccillation which are his characteristics when no battle is raging."

A DESPATCH FROM LORD CHELMSFORD TO THE SECRETARY OF STATE FOR WAR PUBLISHED BY THE CAPE PAPERS, JULY 15, 1879

Cetywayo not having complied with my demands by noon yesterday, July 3, and having fired heavily on the troops at the water, I returned the 114 cattle he had sent in, and ordered a reconnoissance to be made by the mounted force under Colonel Buller. This was effectually made, and caused the Zulu army to advance and show itself.

This morning a force under my command, consisting of the 2nd division under Major-General Newdigate, numbering 1870 Europeans, 530 natives, and eight guns, and the flying column under Brigadier-General Wood, numbering 2192 Europeans and 573 natives, four guns, and two Gatlings, crossed the Umfolosi River at 6.15, and marching in a hollow square with the ammunition and entrenching tool-carts and bearer company in its centre, reached an excellent position between Nodwengu and Ulundi about half-past 8 a.m. This had been observed by Colonel Buller the day before. Our fortified camp on the right bank of the Umfolosi River was left with a garrison of about 900 Europeans, 250 natives, and one Gatling gun under Colonel Bellairs. Soon after half-past 7 the Zulu army was seen leaving its bivouacs and advancing on every side.

The engagement was shortly after commenced by the mounted men. By 9 o'clock the attack was fully developed; at half-past 9 the enemy wavered; the 17th Lancers, followed by the remainder of the mounted men, attacked them, and a general rout ensued.

The prisoners stated Cetywayo was personally in command and had made the arrangements himself, and that he witnessed the fight from Lokozi kraal, and that twelve regiments took part in it. If so, 20,000 men attacked us. It is impossible to estimate with any correctness the loss of the enemy, owing to the extent of country over which they attacked and retreated, but it could not have been less, I consider, than 1000 killed.

By noon Ulundi was in flames, and during the day all military kraals of the Zulu army and in the valley of the Umfolosi were destroyed. At 2 p.m. the return march to the camp of the column commenced. The behaviour of the troops under my command was extremely satisfactory. Their steadiness under a complete belt of fire was remarkable. The dash and enterprise of the mounted branches was all that could be wished, and the fire of the Artillery very good.

A portion of the Zulu force approached our fortified camp, and at one time threatened to attack it. The Native Contingent forming a part of the garrison were sent out after the action, and assisted in the pursuit.

As I have fully accomplished the object for which I advanced, I consider I shall now be best carrying out Sir Garnet Wolseley's instructions by removing at once to Entongoneni, and thence towards Kwamagwasa. I shall send back a portion of this force with the empty wagons for supplies, which are now ready at Fort Marshall.

THE BATTLE OF ULUNDI
FROM THE CAPE ARGUS

White Umfolosi, July 4.

After reconnoitering yesterday with mounted men, the cavalry and infantry, with ten guns, crossed the Umfolosi and gave battle to large number of Zulus, who from the surrounding heights had watched their advance, and when the column was well in the open ground, about a mile and a half from Ulundi, closed in on all sides and made a most determined assault. We fought in square with guns at the corners. The mounted men drew on the attack, and then retiring inside the square the infantry poured their fire into the advancing enemy. The guns were splendidly served and repeatedly broke the Zulu attack, the Martini-Henri doing the rest. Once the attack slackened, the Lancers charged them in grand style, and, followed by the irregular horse, put the finishing touches to the battle. They pursued the flying enemy everywhere, killing numbers, until they sought refuge in inaccessible hills. The cavalry of both columns then burnt Ulundi, and all the kraals in the valley, and at half-past 4 the whole column had returned to our camp after as successful a day as we have had in South Africa. Some hundred men were left in camp to defend it, and Lord Chelmsford in person conducted the advance upon Ulundi, and fought the battle. Our loss is inconsiderable, about fifteen killed and thirty wounded, but I cannot speak from official information. The enemy's force could not have been less than 20,000 and their loss was very heavy.

THE BATTLE OF ULUNDI
BY MELTON PRIOR
ARTIST FOR THE ILLUSTRATED LONDON NEWS
FROM THE TIMES OF NATAL

On the day before the battle, viz., Thursday, July 3, Colonel Buller was ordered to reconnoitre the enemy's ground with about

500 men, and crossed the White Umfolosi in two columns, Captain Buller being ordered to cover the retreat.

They had, as our readers are already aware, advanced in pursuit of a few of the enemy, who as it appeared afterwards, were evidently acting as decoys, towards a donga not far from the Umfolosi, when Colonel Buller, at the head of 300 men, chased them; but on approaching the donga Sir Thomas Hesketh, A.D.C., descried a large number of the enemy, and upon this the order was given instantly to wheel about.

On seeing this the Zulus fired a terrific volley into them, bringing four men out of their saddles. It is evident that the old trick which was so successfully played at Zlobane and other places, was again attempted by our wily enemy, and that but for the sharp look-out kept, Colonel Buller would have been entrapped by them. A retreat was then beaten fighting, the enemy firing continuously at them.

This reconnoissance enabled Colonel Buller to choose a good position for the fight on the following day. It is a curious fact in connection with this point that it appears from the statements of the prisoners that it was part of Cetywayo's tactics to get on to the exact spot which was chosen by Colonel Buller. While our natives were at the river getting water, the Zulus used a number of defiant terms to them, saying, 'You are a set of cowards, and are all very well in a laager, but don't dare to meet us in the open; if you do, we will annihilate you.'

This, it seems, was designed to induce us to take the course which we adopted with so much success; and it seems Cetywayo had given orders to attack us at the exact place we took up. The war cry which was going on during the night was of the most diabolical description. Although at a distance of three or four miles, the unearthly yells could be distinctly heard, and some of our natives recognised what they were crying out. The refrain consisted of defiance to the English, and laments over men who had fallen that day.

The ceremony was of much advantage to us, as it enabled us to make every precaution for an attack. The cries began about 11 p.m., and we expected the enemy on at any moment. The order was in consequence given that all horses should be brought in, and in the course of about two hours and a half the camp was in a state of commotion. All that night we enjoyed very little sleep, as we were to move at 5.15 in the following order: To cross the White Umfolosi and as soon as on the other side to form up into a hollow square; the four companies of the 80th to lead, forming the front face, followed by two guns (7-pounders) of Colonel Harness's Battery; the 13th Regiment and the 94th to form the left face; the 90th and the 58th to form the right face; and the two companies of the 21st, numbering about 260 men, to form the rear face—the Lancers forming the rear guard. Buller's Horse was placed as advanced guard and flankers on the front, and two flanks at a distance or about half a mile, to 'touch' the enemy.

As soon as we approached the kraal of Nodwengu the order was given by Lord Chelmsford in person for the whole of the square column to 'half-right, turn,' the result of which was that our right face was towards Nodwengu and our front towards Ulundi. The whole manoeuvre was so creditably performed as to astonish many who were with the column. No sooner had we taken up our position than Lord Wm. Beresford rode in at a hard gallop to inform the General that the enemy was advancing, and very soon after the cavalry was attacked, and drew the enemy on to our position.

The cavalry came into the square, and within five minutes the whole of the four sides were engaged. At a distance of 800 yards the enemy was seen advancing in skirmishing order in the front, and large masses behind them as supports. On they pushed in face of a perfect hailstorm of lead, steadily and unflinchingly, as only a brave and determined soldier can do. But for the coolness which was shown by our troops, from the officers in command down to the bugle boys, it would have been hopeless to stand against the intrepidity which the Zulus displayed. In the course of all the campaigns at which I have been present, I can state without hesitation that I have never come across an enemy which I have felt more pride in seeing beaten. For over half an hour they faced a fire so searching and so deadly that almost any other troops would have flinched before it; and at one moment it was a grave question whether they might not succeed in a rush on one of our faces.

As it was, from 2000 to 3000 formed up about thirty deep, and with a piercing war-cry made a dash for the corner, which was being held by the 58th and 21st, and two guns of Major Le Grice. Lord Chelmsford, who during the action was seen riding first to one point and then to another, on seeing this, rode to the corner threatened, and the words from him, 'Cannot you fire faster' were answered by one continuous rattle from the whole of the infantry in that direction. In a few moments it was evident this had had the desired effect of checking this rush, and almost immediately after they were observed to waver, turn, and finally to fly in all directions. Now was the time for the Lancers; and no sooner was the order given than they sallied forth with cheers from the lines at hard gallop.

We followed the Lancers for a short distance, until the enemy turned and once more showed fight. So courageously was this done that the Lancers had to right-about wheel, but charged again with such effect that the Zulus were soon strewn in all directions under their lances. One of them, while charging, had his horse fall under him, and was immediately attacked by a Zulu, who endeavored to wrench his carbine from him. He called to his sergeant for assistance, and the latter, dashing up, made short work of the Zulu. Another wounded Zulu lying: near was at the same time trying his best to assegai the lancer, whose horse was pinning him to the ground, and a short but sharp engagement took place between sword and assegai.

The sergeant again put an end to the hand-to-hand conflict by passing his lance through shield and body into the ground; and it was with some difficulty that he withdrew it—eventually riding off with the shield still on his lance. At this cavalry charge poor Edgell met his death, together with four lancers and a sergeant. Captain Drury Lowe, who it was reported had been wounded, in answer to my enquiries, informed me he had been hit by a spent bullet on his belt in the back, which had taken 'his breath away,' and he fell from his horse under the impression of being wounded; but in a few seconds, resting on his elbow, he passed his hand over his back, and observing, 'No, no; am I wounded? I don't think so,' he decided the point in the negative, rose up, took to his horse, and joined once more in the conflict. The Zulus, who bolted up a mountain, were soon out of reach of the cavalry, and these were therefore ordered to retire.

While this had been going on, the Basutos and Volunteers were similarly engaged—the former chasing the enemy a mile and a half beyond Ulundi. Over six hundred are put down to the cavalry in the charges. On returning to the square it was apparent that the attack had been pretty severe. I heard that ten men had been killed and about fifty wounded; but the following day it was stated that our casualties amounted to fourteen killed and over eighty wounded.

This number, though to be regretted, is small, considering that the square was opposed to the attack of the enemy on all sides, and the shots which passed over the heads of the infantry came whizzing about us in the centre, and the noise made, as these jagged missiles and pieces of 'pot-leg' came into us, was not exactly encouraging to the non-combatants and surgeons, who nevertheless unflinchingly performed their arduous and painful duties to the wounded, who were being brought in to the centre by native bearers, under Surgeon-Major Stafford and Dr. Busby, from all sides.

The order to cease firing was given as the enemy 'bolted in all directions,' and the soldiers in a few cases actually threw their helmets at their retreating foe. The order was now given to throw a few shells into Ulundi, to discover whether the enemy were there in any force, and Colonel Buller then, with his staff and horsemen, made a dash for it, Lord William Beresford being designated 'Ulundi Beresford,' from the fact of his being the first one to enter it.

As I was pushing on steadily towards the goal, I suddenly heard the well-known voice behind me of Mr. Archibald Forbes, the correspondent of the Daily News, who dashed by me calling, 'Come on, Prior,' and a race for the King's kraal then took place between Art and Literature, the latter winning by a neck. Many of the staff and other officers were in our track, and together we searched the huts. Here I had a very narrow escape, as I did not notice when the others had left, and looking up from a sketch I was making saw the unwelcome face of a skulking Zulu, who appeared to be running away from me. This, however, seemed to me too good to be true, and as I had no doubt he was endeavoring to cut off my retreat, with sketch-book in one hand and pencil in the other, I made for the only means of exit from a perfect maze, rightly judging (as it turned out) that, being only one against any number that might turn up, discretion would be the better part of valor, particularly as there was fire burning on three sides of me. Captain Shepstone later on congratulated me, saying he had seen three or four Zulus after me.

On gaining my horse, which was outside, I galloped off, and on joining the column was informed that the Hon. Mr. Drummond had gone into Ulundi, and from this I conclude he has unfortunately incurred the fate which I so narrowly escaped. From this it was soon determined by Lord Chelmsford to return to our original laager across the White Umfolosi, shields and assegais taking a very prominent part among our men on their return.

Congratulations were freely passing between one and another on their escapes, many being able to show bullet holes through their helmets, belts cut, and other indications of the sharpness of the contest. A ration of rum was ordered all round, and as the day's doings were discussed over it, all agreed that the Zulus had sustained a greater defeat in the open than they had from behind laagers, and that they must then feel that their challenge of the morning to 'fight in the open' had been fairly answered.

THE BATTLE OF ULUNDI
BY ARCHIBALD FORBES
FROM THE DAILY NEWS

Landman's Drift, July 5

The combat at Ulundi was singularly unvaried by striking incident. There was a big hollow square, and men in red coats on the back, rifles in hand. For half an hour this square stood doggedly pouring the sleet of death from every face. Outside this square, mostly at a respectful distance, surged a furious throng of savages, brandishing shields and assegais, and firing heavily but fitfully from their jagged front. Presently these black men wavered; then bolted, sent in flight by the steady administration of canister. The square, still grimly firm, gave one ringing cheer that was heard in the laager behind; the bayonets wavered in the air for a moment; then the business recommenced.

The infantry betook themselves for a few minutes to long shots. A centrifugal whirlwind of horsemen sped from the square as the lightning bursts from the thundercloud, and dashed hot and fierce after the flying foe. Before the cavalry had concluded their innings the infantry were placidly lunching, and the corks were popping off long-hoarded champagne bottles. Inside the square a few dead Britons lay, who had spent their lives for their Queen and country.

The green sward outside was littered thick with dead Zulus, who, not less than our dead, have fallen for their Sovereign. There is nothing more to tell, save of the general fire and smoke that seethed in the bosom of the beautiful valley as we marched from it.

I have no manoeuvring, no elaborate tactics to recount. The affair was simply a struggle, reduced to the first principles of ding-dong fighting, with the natural advantage to the Zulus in numbers to us in the character of the armament. The only manoeuvring done was by Buller's men, whose horse work was superb, clearing the front, masking the division while in the rows of formation in square, stinging the enemy into opportune reprisals, and finally chevying the fugitives many miles. Buller's men had the score of Hlobane to settle with the Zulus and vengeful fury raged in their hearts because of a spectacle which met their gaze yesterday.

In the long grass they found three comrades who had fallen in a reconnoissance the previous day—mangled with fiendish ingenuity; scalped, their noses and right hands cut off, their hearts torn out, and other nameless mutilations.

Strange to say the battle was fought on semi-sacred ground, the soil of a mission station. The ruins of a Norwegian mission and house were a few paces off. They were pulled down to open the range, but before this was done these dead men were brought into the precincts, a grave was dug, and the chaplain, hastily donning his surplice, read the burial service, to which the shell fire gave stern responses, while the bullets whizzed round the mourners.

I never wish to see soldiers steadier. Constant laagering had been threatening demoralisation. Apprehension was unquestionably felt lest the sudden confronting of the men with the fierce Zulu rush should shake their nerves; but the British soldier was true to his manly traditions when he found himself in the open, and saw the enemy face to face in the daylight. Lads of new regiments, who had never seen a shot fired in anger, were as cool as the seasoned veterans of the 13th and 80th. Lord Chelmsford's soldierly coolness and decisive clear-headedness in action go far to redeem the passiveness and peevish vacillation which are his characteristics when no battle is raging. One might wish him a military Rip Van Winkle, only wakening to direct a battle.

Evelyn Wood's face was radiant with the rapture of the fray as he rode up and down behind his regiment, exposed to a storm of missiles. All the officers of the headquarters' staff and Newdigate's staff were unscathed, save Lieutenant Milne, of the 1st, who was slightly wounded, and Captain Cotton, of the 2nd, whose temple was grazed by a bullet.

Owing to the conformation of the ground, the dressing place in the centre of the square was peculiarly exposed. The surgeons worked under a heavy double cross-fire with coolness and skill. The Lancers had their good day at last, and lost several horses. Colonel Lowe was knocked temporarily senseless by a shot in the back, and fell from his horse, but regained consciousness, recovered, and led his regiment in the charge. Lieutenant Jenkins had his lower jaw broken. It was bandaged, and he could not be restrained from accompanying his regiment in the charge. The Zulus squatted thick in the long grass and fired venomously. The Lancers spotted them in a manner reminding one of pig-sticking. Indeed, Keevil Davis killed six *ipsa manu*.

Young James, of the Scots Greys, was blazed at point blank by two men. The two turned on him. They missed. He ran the right-hand man through. The man on the left dropped his musket and inflicted an assegai wound on James's bosom. The latter, extricating his sword, brought it round to the left with a swift swing, and all but severed his antagonist's head. The Dragoons were represented by Brewster, Provost-Marshall, who took out a little detachment and had a good time.

THE BATTLE OF ULUNDI
A FURTHER REPORT BY ARCHIBALD FORBES
FROM THE DAILY NEWS

Yesterday (the 3rd) Lord William Beresford greatly distinguished himself, killing the Zulus with his sabre in single combat, and rescuing a wounded sergeant from under a heavy fire. I understand that Lord William Beresford will be recommended for the Victoria Cross.

The Zulus were much elated by Buller's retreat. The whole force crosses the river to-morrow, intent on penetrating to Ulundi. The 24th Regiment remains to garrison the laager. We shall probably fight our way in and out of Ulundi.

July 4.— At daybreak this morning the whole force was waiting for the order to advance again. Buller's Horse, to the front, crossed above and below the hillock, gained it, and found the country abandoned. The whole force passed the drift and through the bush clear of the Delanyo kraal.

The formation consisted of a great square. The 80th formed the front; the 90th and 94th the left face; the 94th the rear; the 58th and 13th the right face. Inside, ready for action, were the Artillery, the Engineers, the natives, &c. We had passed the Nodwengu kraal, and all was quiet as yet. The enemy was visible in one considerable straggling column moving parallel with us. Another was crowning and descending the eminence on the left rear, towards Nodwengu. Another was visible fitfully in various directions on our left. A fourth great mass was moving down on the right from Ulundi.

It was impossible to tell how many lay in the dongas on and about the direct front. Buller was continually stirring them up, and a brisk fire was exchanged. The Zulus began to close on us on all sides. The guns were moved out on the flanks and into action. Buller's Horse resisted as long as possible, and then galloped back into square. In a short space of time the guns alone were in action; but the Zulus coming on swiftly, the infantry opened fire first, the closest on our right front.

The artillery practice was beautiful, but it failed to daunt the Zulus, who rushed into the Nodwengu kraal, which had not been burned, utilising the cover. Thence men with white shields streamed with great daring against the right and rear of the square, where were two companies of the 21st and two nine-pounders.

The Zulus dashed with great bravery into close quarters amid the deadly hail of the Martini bullets and volleys of canister, and stubbornly assailed us on all four faces of our square, which stood like a rock. The whole affair was in a small compass, which made it seem more animated. The Zulus fired half Martini, and half round and jagged bullets, which rent the air above our soldiers, who observed a stern purposeful silence. At the first shell fired, at 9.30, there rose a mighty cheer from the right flank and rear, the enemy giving way.

A responding cheer came from the left; and then the front square opened to emit the Lancers and Buller's Horsemen, who burst like a torrent upon the broken enemy. The Lancers dashed towards the rear, caught a number of men in the long grass, and cut them down with their sabres and lances. Several officers of the Lancers killed four Zulus each. Two received assegai wounds. Captain Wyatt-Edgell was killed, and two officers were slightly wounded.

The British cavalry effectually vindicated its reputation. The enemy were driven widely distant. Their dead lay thick all around the square, most of them facing the 21st. I estimate that 400 Zulus lay dead. After a slight halt the cavalry moved to the front, and burned Ulundi and the neighboring military kraals. The whole force advanced close to Ulundi, and halted to eat. About 2 o'clock the force marched back to laager. It is estimated that about 10,000 Zulus were engaged. Our loss was ten killed and about fifty wounded, exclusive of natives.

The battle of Ulundi was fought at or near the site of one of the great battles between the Boers and the Zulus, in the early days of Natal and Transvaal settlement.

THE BATTLE OF ULUNDI: A ZULU SPEAKS
BY THE CORRESPONDENT OF THE TIMES OF NATAL
JULY 13, 1879

A prisoner, named Undumwaywaya, son of Umgenene, who was taken by Shepstone's natives, and examined by Capt. Shepstone, said the regiments engaged were the Undi, the Intolobulo, the Udhloko, the Umxapu, the Nodwengu, the Umbonambi, the Nokenke, the Umcityu, the Nkobamakosi, the Ingulute, and the Dukusas. These formed the attacking force.

The Undabakombi and the Uhlantehle regiments were with the King, as his body guard, at the Umlambongwenya kraal, from which the King saw the battle. The King said he wanted to make peace three days ago, and sent 140 of his white cattle as a peace offering to the great chief leading the white army. These cattle were turned back at the White Umfolosi, at Nodwengu, by the Inkandampemvu regiment, who refused to let them pass, saying they wanted to fight, and would not have peace. The King was then at Ulundi, and some of them were killed the day before yesterday, by the King's orders, for the army to eat.

The principal leaders of the army were Tyingwayo, Nydwane, Dabulamanzi, Mundula, headmen of the Nodwengu, Sirayo, and his son, Mehkla; Kayulu was also present. We had no idea that the white force was so strong in numbers till we saw it in the open. We were completely beaten off by the artillery and bullets.

The Zulu army was larger to-day than it was at Kambula; far larger. I was at Kambula fight. All the army was present to-day. We had not much heart in the fight when we saw how strong the white army was. We were startled by the number of horses. We were afraid to attack in the thorns, as we knew you would laager the wagons. We were afraid to cross the river yesterday after mounted men, because of the laager.

We were all by order, up at the Umlambongwenya kraal the day before yesterday, when the King addressed us and said, as the Inkandampemvu regiment would not let the cattle go in as a peace offering, and as we wished to fight, the white army being now at his home, we could fight, but we were to fight the white men in the open, and attack before the Nodwengu and Ulundi kraals, where we were on the day of the fight. The King also told us, when we pursued you not to cross the river, for fear of the guns, which would be left in the laager. The King himself personally placed the different regiments and gave us orders.

We were watching, expecting your army would leave the laager and march for the King's kraal. We saw the force when it started across the river, and we surrounded it as we had been ordered to do. Yesterday we all thought we should have an easy victory if you came in the open.

The two cannon taken at Isandhlwana were at Nodwengu, but are now at the King's other kraal in the thorns. No one knows how to use them.

The white man who writes the King's letters (C. Vijnn) is a trader, who came trading at the beginning of the year, and the King kept him. He is a lame man. A white man was made prisoner at the Zlobane and taken to the King, who sent him back, and said he was to be let go near Kambula.

The army is now thoroughly beaten, and as it was beaten in the open it will not reassemble and fight again. No force is watching the lower column and none has been sent there. How could there be when all were ordered to be here to-day? We mustered here by the King's orders at the beginning of this moon, about ten days ago. We hare not been called out before, and wanted to go over to the white people.

An examination of some wounded Zulus by Mr. Longcast elicited nothing new, except that some of the Tonga tribe had taken part in this fight as well as Kambula.

The Battle of Ulundi
by the Correspondent of the
London Daily Telegraph
from the Natal Witness, July 1879

The British troops marched in hollow square, the 80th Regiment and Gatling battery forming front; 90th Regiment and part of 94th Regiment left flank; 13th and 58th Regiments, right flank; 24th and remainder of 94th Regiments forming rear; a battery of artillery forming each corner. Zulus were seen approaching in force both from the direction of Ulundi and from the bush on the right. At half-past 8 mounted men, under Colonel Buller, were thrown out on rear, left, and front, meeting enemy and keeping them in check. Owing, however, to some mistake, the right was left uncovered by cavalry, and mounted Basutos, under Cochrane, were accordingly sent out on that side to draw the Zulus under fire.

As the Basutos retired before the advancing enemy, the right face of the square came into action, commencing its fire fully five minutes before the remainder of the force was engaged. At about ten minutes to nine the firing became general, all four sides of the square being simultaneously engaged, the Zulus, after their manner, throwing forward horns of their army to surround the British force. They came on steadily, and in complete silence, advancing with the same intrepidity shown at Umgnngunhloyo and Kambula. They continued their advance until they reached a spot not more than seventy yards from the faces of the square.

The British infantry were formed in four ranks, the front rank kneeling and the rear rank reversed, facing inwards, while inside the square were all necessary arrangements for keeping up the supply of ammunition. It was impossible for any force long to face such a deadly storm of lead poured among them at such a short distance. A few now and then made the attempt to advance further, but it was of no use. The main body wavered and paused for a moment—a decisive moment. It was not hail from the Martini-Henry alone; there was artillery continually at work, sending shell after shell through the dark masses, breaking up every, even partial, attempt of the Zulus to concentrate their strength for a rush. Then it became time for the Lancers to be let loose. Riding down with their lances levelled, they came like a whirlwind upon the enemy, and in an instant their lines were broken through. The sabre was at work as well as the lance, and the Zulu ranks were soon torn asunder; their coherency as an army was destroyed, and they were flying before the advancing cavalry.

The Battle of Ulundi
by the Correspondent of the Natal Colonist with General Wood's Column, July, 1879

About 6.45 a.m., the Flying Column, under command of General Wood, and General Newdigate's division following in rear, both under the command of Lord Chelmsford, crossed the White Umfolosi River, the troops marching through the river up to their knees in water.

There were great expectations that we would meet with stiff opposition in crossing the river, as both banks are thickly covered with bush, and more especially on our left front. Where the troops crossed is a low kopjie, which is very rocky, as well as bushy. However, both divisions crossed the river without the least opposition whatever, and marched in columns, keeping very close together, until we got clear of the bush, and passed the first military kraal, which we were told was Nodwengu.

Before the columns reached this point, all mounted troops were sent out in front to see that none of the enemy were concealed there before we should approach it. Having passed and set fire to the Nodwengu kraal, both divisions halted and formed square, the ambulance and ammunition wagons being placed in the centre, field guns, with two Gatling guns, being placed at their respective points of the square. I am beforehand, though, with my story.

While our forces were marching across the White Umfolosi, an impi were forcing their way through the bush on our right front towards the river, apparently with the idea of attacking us while crossing over, but they were too late, as we were about one mile from the White Umfolosi River and close on the Nodwengu kraals.

Colonel Buller and mounted troops went off in the direction of this impi to draw their attention off the fort and laager we left behind on a low kopjie on the opposite side of the river. This being effected, Colonel Buller cleverly drew them (disputing every inch of ground) towards our square until they reached within range of the big guns. At this time we could discern swarms of Zulus coming down from the hills on our left flank. Likewise, from the military kraal, hosts of the savages came pouring forth towards the scene of strife. Being surrounded on all sides, the mounted men retired within the already formed square, the fight commencing now in earnest.

The first salute the Zulus got was from the nine-pounders, which seemed to stagger them for a moment. They, however, rallied with the intention of rushing on us. No sooner had they made this attempt than the order was given to let them have it. Martini-Henris, Gatling guns, and the various field pieces, kept up a most destructive fire.

Scarcely a Zulu managed to come within 40 or 50 yards of the square, every one of them being knocked down as fast as they made their appearance above the long grass. The battle was short and decisive. The last time they rallied it would do one's heart good, and I'm sure it must have been encouraging to all young soldiers, to see what I term the wild but undaunted 13th Regiment, who were waving their hands and beckoning the Zulus to come on, exclaiming, 'come on, you black devils.' This seemed to have great effect in cowing the enemy, who then turned off and fled like deer.

The wing of Lancers were then let loose, as also the brave volunteers, who chased them out of sight. The Lancers were riding pell-mell through the long grass by themselves, the Zulus hiding themselves in dongas, thinking they were the volunteers, so as to entrap them; this was an assegai regiment. On perceiving them to be the Lancers, who were up in a line with the assegai regiment, a portion of the Zulu army armed with rifles let a volley into them, and emptied three saddles—i.e., Captain, Farrier-Sergeant, and a trooper. The Lancers, enraged to see their comrades fall, immediately put their lances into use.

The Zulus put up their shields to parry the thrust of the lances, the latter sticking in the shields, which was a great hindrance to the cavalry using their lances freely; consequently they had to adopt the sword in place of the lance; but the cunning Zulus buried themselves in the ground, rendering the sword now completely useless, as the cavalry horses were going at too great a speed.

The lances were again taken into use, and this time with excellent effect. To use the Lancers' phrase, they said it was just like tent-pegging at Aldershot. I believe the Lancers killed very near a whole assegai regiment, also a great number of others. I scarcely know what destruction would have been effected if all the Lancers and Dragoons had been present.

The Mounted Volunteers did great execution, and are indeed a credit to South Africa; they are a brave lot of fellows, and had some narrow escapes. On our left flank hosts of Zulus were retreating over the hills in black masses, the nine-pounders sending farewell shells after them, the distance being over two miles.

It is said Cetywayo was a spectator of this great defeat of his invincible warriors from the top of those hills. I wonder what he and his retreating army thought of the shells bursting over their heads!

The Zulus being completely routed after one hour's hard fighting, we commenced to burn the military kraals. It was a grand sight to behold the burning kraals sending up their volumes of smoke. Having completed the destruction of Ulundi, both divisions marched homewards to the banks of the White Umfolosi River, the band of the 1-13th L.I., which was the only military band present at the engagement with instruments, played the usual national airs. This enlivened the spirits of the troops after their hard day's work. On the first tap of the drum—(this being the same old drum, I hear, that was captured from the Afghans in 1849 by the 13th Regiment, and which was present on the occasion when the band of that regiment played into Jellalabad the relief for that regiment, which had been penned up so long in that miserable fort, surrounded by hosts of the enemy, and defending it against the assaults which were almost of daily occurrence)—when, I say, the first tap of this haggard-looking old drum was given, all the troops cheered lustily as they marched to the merry tunes of their excellent band.

The The Battle of Ulundi
a Report by Lord Chelmsford
to Sir Garnet Wolseley

The crossing of the river (Umfolosi) by our forces was watched by a large body of Zulus, and when when our column, marching in hollow square, was fairly in the open about one and a half miles from Ulundi, the enemy attacked with great bravery on all four sides. A gun was in position at each angle of the square, and these, with the terrible fire of the Martini-Henris broke the attack in about half an hour. Immediately the wavering commenced the cavalry were let loose, and the rout was complete. So fierce were the repeated onslaughts of the Zulus that at times they approached within sixty yards of our square. Such close quarters and the cavalry charge will readily account for their great loss, estimated by Mr. Archibald Forbes at 800. After a short rest the column advanced upon Ulundi, which they found deserted, and it with several important kraals within a radius of 10 miles was burnt. Our loss during the whole day's fighting amounted to one officer, Captain Edgell, of the 17th Lancers, and 14 rank and file killed; two officers (Colonel Low and Lieutenant Jenkins), and 30 rank and file wounded.

Such are the accounts of the battle of Ulundi, the winning of which by Lord Chelmsford, has undoubtedly been a blow which has materially broken the back of the Zulu war. Cetywayo sometime ago sent a message to Lord Chelmsford asking why (alluding to entrenchments) the latter gentlemen was "like an ant-eater, which when it is attacked, gets underground?" and he said that if

218

the General beat him fairly in the open, he would acknowledge himself beaten. Judging by this message, it might be said that the Zulu war was at an end; but the tradition or early history of the Zulus has shown us that when worsted they have retired northwards into broken country, rather than bow their neck under the yoke of the invader. The Zulu chieftains, Sotyangana and Umziligazi, adopted this course when pressed by Tshaka and Dingaan, and their people are now residing in the direction of the Limpopo.

THE SURRENDER OF DABULAMANZI
BY THE PIETERMARITZBURG CORRESPONDENT
OF THE STANDARD AND MAIL, JULY 19,

The fact that he has given in is of great import, as there is no doubt he was the man upon whom Cetywayo chiefly relied. Sir Garnet Wolseley telegraphs that the chief came into Fort Pearson and is on his road to Fort Durnford. No doubt on his arrival there he will be closely questioned as to the whereabouts and intentions of Cetywayo. The second division under General Newdigate was, on the 10th July, ten miles beyond Fort Evelyn and intended to return to Upolso for wood and grass. It was expected to arrive there about the 16th, but General Newdigate did not contemplate being able to move up again this season owing to the state of wood and grass. Possibly something may be done towards overcoming this difficulty by means of hand carriage by the natives. A general order has been issued containing the conditions under which 2,000 carriers who are not to be used in any other way than that for which they are raised, viz., carriers, are to be organised. They will receive 2s. 6d. a day and be officered by seven European officers and twenty Indunas. Each man is to carry a load not exceeding 56 lb., and will carry assegais. Preparations have been made for covering Cetywayo's retreat to the northwards, which is thought likely in consequence of the defeat he sustained at Ulundi, and the military authorities are keeping a close watch for him at all points. About 7,000 Zulus and their auxiliaries were reported to be gathered about the Intombi. A correspondent of the Mercury writes a significant letter, in which he suggests that Sir Garnet and all under his command be on their guard against Zulu treachery at the present stage of affairs, and adds that no faith ought to be put in any promise Cetywayo may make.

THE CUNNING OF THE ZULUS
BY THE CAPE CORRESPONDENT OF
THE SOUTH AUSTRALIAN ADVERTISER

All the world now admits that the Zulus are brave soldiers; but they are more than this—they are clever diplomatists, and the chances are twenty to one they will yet get to windward of Sir Garnet, and that he in his turn will be only too happy when he is able to pack up his portmanteau and bid farewell to this sunny clime. Our latest advices from the front forbid the hope that a satisfactory settlement of the little bill which Cetywayo has run up will be arrived at as rapidly as the people at home would like, and we begin to think that the British taxpayer will be tempted to bracket Ireland and the Cape of Good Hope together, and to propose that both should be submerged for as long a time as will be required to cure all their grievances.

It is not very long since I forwarded my previous letter to you, and yet it has been long enough to embroil us in another native war. The interesting creatures who have this time taken into their heads to rebel are the Pondos. They occupy a portion of the country whicli separates this colony from Natal. Their country is on the coast line, and it possesses a port which is known as St. John's. A little time ago we annexed the port and possessed ourselves of a portion of the lands which abut upon it. Some of the land was purchased, and some was not, but a magistrate and a custom-house officer were appointed, and just when things were beginning to look business-like a rumpus takes place, and everything is at sixes and sevens. Who the enemy is we have to fight, and what is the strength he may be able to bring into the field, nobody seems to know. The few Government officers who are scattered about in the country affect to treat the outbreak as a very small affair which can be settled without much difficulty; but the mischief is that in these native wars one never can tell who's who, and that your very good friend of to-day will not try his hardest to cut your throat tomorrow. No doubt all the native risings which have been witnessed within the last two years, whether in Gcalekaland, Griqualand, Basutoland, on the northern border, or in Pondoland, have resulted from the intrigue of Cetywayo; and one cannot help feeling sensible that if the movements which have recently been witnessed amongst these different tribes and peoples had taken place simultaneously, the whites would have been sorely pressed to hold their own. Before I leave this subject I may as well say that previous to the departure from the colony of Colonel Wood—who left with Lord Chelmsford—the Colonial Secretary offered him the appointment of Commandant-General of the colonial forces, and it is probable the offer will be accepted. Colonel Wood has gained the good opinion of all who have come into contact with him, and he has proved himself a brave and skilful general. With such a leader our colonial troops would feel no diffidence in entering the field.

Meanwhile the inhabitants of this colony are doing all that in them lies to improve and civilise the natives they have about them. The vacillating and timid policy which has hitherto marked the dealings of the Imperial and the Colonial Governments with respect to the native question is giving place to a healthier state of things. The process of disarming the natives is going on, and they are being taught that the day of power for their chiefs is passing away. The native policy of the present ministry is bitterly opposed by those whom they ousted from office, and by the many more who would be willing to take office, but it commends itself to the judgment of the country, and the bulk of the community feel that while no injustice is done to the natives, and they are amply protected in the enjoyment of their natural rights, they must not be allowed to disturb the public peace or to retard the prosperity of the colony. Time will show whether the plans which are now being worked out by this Government have been wisely adopted, but no one will deny that a change of system was necessary, and that the men who are at the head of affairs have possessed the best opportunities of forming a sound judgment.

Transport Difficulties Hampered
Lord Chelmsford
by the Home Correspondent of
the South Australian Register

To the same vexatious cause—dissensions in high places—much of the discredit which the transport service has incurred is to be attributed. Lord Chelmsford was thwarted by Sir Henry Bulwer in this, as in nearly everything else. Perhaps there was much in Sir Henry's objections which deserved consideration, but when they simply resulted in nothing being done but letter-writing, which will be a monument of shame for both officials, it is impossible to exonerate either side. After the disaster of Isandula Lord Chelmsford, it is said, proposed that the Natal Legislature should proclaim martial law to enable him to seize, subject of course to reasonable compensation, all conveyances and cattle he required. The Natal Government would not make the proposal to the Legislature, and Lord Chelmsford threatened to proclaim martial law at his own hand. It is a pity he had not the pluck to do it, and cut short his correspondence with Sir Henry Bulwer. Between the relief of Ekowe and the starting of General Newdigate's column for Ulundi, a period of fully two months, most of his time seems to have been occupied with letter-writing. The Lord High Commissioner on his return from the Transvaal endeavoured to mediate, but the tone of his subsequent report to the Colonial Office implies that he had not much success. He found it necessary to warn Sir Henry Bulwer that unless all the material resources of Natal were heartily and unreservedly placed at the disposal of the military authorities the Lieutenant-General could not be expected to bring the war to a speedy and satisfactory conclusion. Sir Garnet Wolseley therefore did not arrive in the colony a moment too soon. It is odd to read, in his first telegram to the War Office, that Sir Henry Bulwer was rendering him willing and valuable assistance. But, of course, the relation between the two was different to that of Sir Henry and Lord Chelmsford. Sir Garnet Wolseley was dictator, and made that felt.

From this it would seem that Lord Chelmsford, at least in this matter, was as much sinned against as sinning.

Cetywayo Harbored by Transvaal Boers
by a Correspondent of the Cape Standard
and Mail Utrecht, Friday, August 1

Our correspondent reports: "It has just been reported to the Landrost of this place by native messenger that Cetywayo has been taken from his hiding-place by some Transvaal Boers, who are now harboring him somewhere near Luneberg. The messenger states that the spoor of cart-wheels is perceptible between the Ngomi and the Assegai River, where these Boers have been living during the whole of the war. If such is the case we may look out for a war with the Boers, as they will not easily give him up. I will telegraph again when the report is confirmed."

The report that Cetywayo is being protected by the Boers is extremely serious. Our informant is in a position to have the best possible information on the subject; and it should be remembered that the Transvaal Boers have never shown any hostility to Cetywayo, and ascribe the hostile attitude taken on some occasions against them by the Zulu King to British machinations. It is by no means impossible that our correspondent is right. If so, we feel deeply aggrieved at what is happening; but we cannot but request our readers to judge matters in a fair spirit, and to remember that there are reasons why the Transvaal Boers can feel justified in considering Cetywayo to be a better friend to them than the men who have seized upon their country. We shall not say more for the present, but we trust that Sir Garnet Wolseley will do his utmost to prevent actual war with the people whose country has been annexed, notwithstanding their own wish, to Her Majesty's possessions.

The Battle of Ulundi – New Facts & Theories
by the Derby Correspondent of
the Natal Mercury

New facts and theories about the battle of Ulundi are coming up, and Lord Chelmsford is blamed for not having followed up his victory; perhaps if he had known that the king was not quite half an hour in front he would have sent some one to catch him. It is known now that such was the case, and that in his flight he had no one with him. The night before the battle the English camp was greatly disturbed by the war dance and songs of the Zulus. This is believed to have taken place round a white man who was being tortured by the Zulus. He was one of the Frontier Light Horse, and was taken the day before the battle at Spruit, when the reconnoissance party were attacked when retiring. After the battle the body was found horribly mutilated.'

Cochrane's Basuto's –
the Unsung Heroes of Ulundi
from The Journal

Cochrane's Basutos distinguished themselves at the battle of Ulundi by their dash. They were ordered by Colonel Buller to draw on the Zulus from the right side of the square. Instead of firing a few shots and then falling back upon the square, they made a stand and poured volley after volley into the advancing masses of the enemy. When told to retreat they asked their officers what was now to become of them. They were under the impression that they had to remain outside the square, and wait patiently until they were all killed. As they were retiring the pursuing Zulus tried to afford consolation by shouting after them a few cheerful remarks. 'Gallop on,' sang out Cetywayo's confident warriors, 'but we will overtake you. We are going to kill every one of those red men. Perhaps some of you wild men may escape. But go quick, for we will chase you over the Buffalo'.

The Basutos retreated sullenly. They thought it would be more exciting to die fighting than when flying, but when they drew near the glittering line of bayonets and saw the veteran Thirteenth open a way for them to enter into the square, they saw that they were not to be aimlessly sacrificed. When they had dismounted they asked the soldiers what they had to do. 'Eat your biscuits, Johnny, and lie down,' was the reply, and the Basutos, as they afterwards said, were struck with admiration at the bravery of the British soldiers who could form a laager of their own bodies for the protection of others. They did not think much, of the soldiers before, but then they saw what they could do. A few minutes after the Lancers swept out from the left corner of the rear, the Basutos dashed out at the right corner of the front, and were greeted with ringing cheers from the 13th and 80th as they rushed onwards. It seems incredible, but those one hundred men chased half the Zulu army past Ulundi. When they ceased pursuing they shouted out after the very same regiment that had chased them into the square the ironical words: 'Well, and are you going to the Buffalo now?' The Basutos took three prisoners—the only prisoners taken. During the chase one of the Basutos shot a Zulu in the leg, and then interviewed the wounded man with all the thirst for news which distinguishes a New York reporter. It was a singular time, and a dangerous spot, in which to interview a man, especially a wounded man, but the questioner went to work seriously, and got all the news of the week. Then he gently asked the Zulu if he had got nothing more to tell, and on being assured that there was no more information to be had, he quietly shot the man, mounted his horse, and joined again in the chase. If this was cruel, and deeds which appear cruel in times of peace are regarded in a totally different light in times of war, then there was much cruelty that day, for every wounded man was killed.

The following London telegram, dated September 13th, bringing news from South Africa up to August 22nd, will have to conclude all reference to the present war:

The latest advices from the Cape announce that a second interview has taken place between Sir Garnet Wolseley and the principal Zulu chiefs. In his speech Sir Garnet Wolseley announced that the British Government intended that Zululand should be independent and placed under the rule of an independent chief. He added that the non-capture of Cetywayo was now the only obstacle to the conclusion of a speedy and durable peace.

Capture of Cetywayo and the Close of the Zulu War of 1879
from a Cape Paper

Lord Gifford and his party, consisting of a few mounted infantry, mounted police, Natal guides, and Captain Hayes' troop of Jantze's horse, had for some days followed up Cetywayo's track. Having been misled several times by the Zulus, and even tired upon, Lord Gifford found it necessary to adopt more harsh measures, so he burnt some kraals, took the men, women, and children prisoners, and captured all their cattle and goats.

At last he got some to scout for him and others to bring in real information. They followed so close to the King's heels that the latter gave up riding and gradually left his horses behind until he had none left and had to walk. Even then he managed to keep one day ahead of his pursuers.

On August 27, however, he was so knocked up that he had to rest at a kraal, near the south-west corner of the Ngomi Forest, belonging to the Prime Minister. Two of the enforced spies led them close to it, and then some of their own men went out reconnitering next day and witnessed the people of the kraal kill an ox and go through other performances, which assured our men that the King was there. Lord Gifford then made arrangements to leave the horses, saddles, and other things at the kraal they were at, and proceeded on foot quietly to the place, which was eight miles off, at sundown.

In the meantime, hearing that Major Marter's party of the King's Dragoon Guards and Captain Barton's battalion of the Native Contingent had gone past close by, and were on the north side of the forest, he sent two natives across to them asking for assistance. Major Marter immediately made the two men guide him to the spot, sent all the natives armed, but naked, to go down and surround the kraal, which, when they had done they were to fire a shot as a signal for the rest and the dragoons to come down. The plan succeeded, and Cetywayo was found inside with Umkozana and some petty chiefs with him, also some women.

The King refused to come out for the natives and although there were Zulus in the kraal armed, no resistance was shown, and Major Marter dismounted and entered the kraal himself. Cetywayo came out to him and asked to be shot. He was told that there was no violence intended, for all that he had to do was to come along quietly with them. The rest were all taken prisoners, and these latter with the cattle, over 2,000 in number, are being brought in by Marter, Barrow, and his cavalry. Cetywayo had only a following of twenty with him when he was captured, eleven of whom tried to escape on the road to Ulundi, and five of the eleven were killed. Lord Gifford carries to England the despatches from Sir Garnet announcing the capture of the King.

In Natal the news has been received with great delight. It is perhaps impossible to overrate the effect which the capture of the King will have upon the native mind, and even the sanguine anticipations of Sir Garnet Wolseley that Sekukuni will be brought into a state of submission without fighting is not an impossibility.

Much disappointment was expressed when news was received at Maritzburg to the effect that the Natal Mercury had a telegram from Port Durnford stating that Cetywayo and followers, three wives and one daughter, had all embarked at noon on September 4 per Natal, for the Cape, instead of being sent through Natal to embark at D'Urban. "At a great meeting of Zulu chiefs at Ulundi, on September 1, the anniversary of Cetywayo's coronation six years ago, Sir Garnet Wolseley announced his deposition and banishment from Zululand; at the same time the following chiefs were proclaimed independent in the several territories assigned to them:—Mr. John Dunn, Umgoya, Usibebo, Nucetsobur, Somkella, Gonzi and Sigoeo. The terms upon which they accept chieftainship will be proclaimed later. British Residents will reside in Zululand, who will be eyes and ears of the Government.

The chiefs undertake to respect the boundaries assigned, to abolish the military system, to allow all men to marry, and work as they will, to prohibit all importations of arms and the importations of goods by sea, to take no life without fair trial, to discountenance witchcraft, surrender fugitive criminals from British territory, to make no war without the sanction of the Government, to prevent the sale or alienation of land, and in all cases of dispute with British subjects to appeal to the arbitration of the residents. Succession to chieftainship is to be dependent on the approval of the British Government.

Facing the Zulus
by Harry O'Clery

Buffs, East Kent Regiment

from the Leonaur book
Tommy Atkins' War Stories
Fourteen first hand accounts from the ranks of the
British Army during Queen Victoria's Empire

Facing the Zulus

It was at Canterbury, in July 1877, that I joined Her Majesty's forces. I was led to that step by Recruiting-Sergeant Jack Gavigan, who had the credit, while stationed at St. George's Barracks, of enlisting more men in one year than all the other recruiting-sergeants put together.

I was placed in the Depot M Company of the Buffs.

Having received a fairly good education, I soon afterwards sat for an examination, and having gained a second-class certificate, -- which was thought something of in those days, for men were not then up to the present standard of knowledge, -- I was appointed an assistant schoolmaster to the depot, with the remuneration of fourpence a day. It was my duty to take the two lower classes of the men; and I very frequently found myself in charge of the whole school, as the acting schoolmaster, a sergeant whose name I will not disclose, had frequently to repair to the mess for the purpose of refreshment.

About five months after enlisting, I learned that we were ordered to join the regiment at Pietermaritzburg; and soon afterwards we proceeded to Southampton, where we embarked on the ship *American*, and found ourselves in company with a detachment of the 87th Regiment, known as "The Old Fogs," or the "Faugh-a-Ballagh Boys," from the war-cry of the corps; "Fag-an-Bealoch" meaning "Clear the way."

During the voyage to the Cape we heard this war-cry on several occasions, and the monotony of the voyage was varied by occasional fights between men of the two regiments, who probably considered that, as they were going out to fight, there could be no objection to a little practice beforehand; and I can speak from experience in saying that most of my countrymen enjoy nothing better than a lively argument, and a free fight to wind up with.

We encountered a gale off Cape Finisterre, and had to be battened down below; but at this time I was afflicted with sea-sickness, from which I did not recover for seven days. The rest of the voyage was most pleasant and enjoyable.

We disembarked at Cape Town, and after a few days sailed from thence to East London, where we remained about a week, and then proceeded to Durban on *H.M.S. Himalaya*. Owing to the roll of the sea here, we had to land in surf boats. It was anything but a pleasant experience.

Fifteen or twenty men would go down the ship's side into the boat, and a canvas would be stretched over her to keep out the water. Then, in the dark, we found ourselves jerked and jolted, one against another, for some considerable time, until the boat was hauled to the beach, where we landed more dead than alive, for the rolling and pitching of a whole sea voyage was crammed into that brief trip in a surf boat.

After a short stay at Durban, we marched up the country to Pieterniaritzburg, a distance of upwards of fifty miles, which we accomplished in four days, being cheered towards our journey's end by meeting the band of the regiment, which played us into the town to the tune of a then popular comic song. On joining the regiment I was drafted into the B Company.

While staying in the town we turned out to welcome the 24th Regiment, passing through on their way up the country. They stayed about a week, and I made the acquaintance of two brothers, Fred and George Conboy, both in the band.

Soon we learned that Cetewayo, the Zulu King, had been called upon to pay a fine of a certain number of bullocks, for some filibustering expedition which some of his young warriors had made into Natal; and the date of payment was fixed for the 12th January, which was about twelve months after we had left England.

On and before that particular day we were encamped upon the southern bank of the Tugela River, upon which the Royal Engineers, assisted by the soldiers told off for the work, were busily constructing a floating raft, or bridge, by the aid of which we were, if needful, to cross over into the enemy's country.

We numbered in the camp between two and three thousand men, consisting of the Buffs, the 99th Regiment, Mounted Infantry, Naval Brigade, Royal Artillery, a native contingent, and some mounted volunteers from Stanger and Victoria -- two small towns on the coast of Natal -- who evidently thought they were out for a picnic, and brought with them several waggon-loads of bedding, tinned meats, comforts and luxuries, of which I shall say a word or two in the course of my yarn.

The river was very full, and some half a mile wide, and there were plenty of crocodiles in its waters. Two or three poor fellows, while at work on the raft, were snapped up on falling overboard, and seen no more. One was a friend of mine belonging to *H.M.S. Active*.

It was the day before the final pay-day, and away in the distance we could plainly see a body of natives, who were by many in the camp believed to be the people whose arrival we were awaiting. But the commanding officers, I suppose, thought differently, and sent a shell bursting among them to tell them we were there.

The next day we crossed the river, and then war began. The crossing of the river was accomplished this way -- two companies, of about one hundred men each, marched on to the raft, and it was then hauled across by the Naval Brigade. As soon as the men landed on the opposite side, the empty raft was drawn back again for a fresh freight; and so, as it was a tedious job, the whole day was taken up.

From what I could learn of the plan, the British force was to invade the country in four columns. No. 1, nearest the sea, was under the command of Brigadier-General Pearson, numbered 4200, and was to advance along the coast. No. 2 consisted of 3000 natives, commanded by European officers under Colonel Durnford, R.E., who was to cross the Tugela at Middle Drift and march up the left side of the river to Rorke's Drift. No. 3, commanded by Colonel Glyn, was about 3000 strong, and contained the first and second battalions of the 24th Regiment, numbering about 1000 bayonets. And No. 4, under Colonel Evelyn Wood, also about 3000 strong, was to operate from Utrecht, in conjunction with Colonel Glyn's column.

We, in No. 1 column, learned now and then of the movements of the others, by the native runners, who were sent from one column to another with despatches. Poor chaps, they risked their lives for very slight remuneration, and it was dangerous work to play the spy as they did; for the Zulus, when it became known that we were marching on their capital, determined to make a stand for it.

We were marched up country, and terribly wet weather it was, no mistake, for the first week or so. Not a single shot was fired by any of our skirmishers, who were on in front of us. The natives retired before us, keeping, as they went, a watchful eye upon our movements, but taking care to keep out of range. As a proof of their nearness, however, we found, upon coming to their camping-grounds, that the embers of their fires were still smouldering.

Every night we camped in laager. This consists of drawing the waggons into a circle and digging a slight trench all round it, the earth taken from the trench being thrown up on the outer side to form a breastwork.

Our first laager was formed near the farm of an English settler named John Dunne, who had, I think, married a native woman, and suited himself to the customs of the country. He knew his way about the country, and some little while before we crossed the Tugela he joined our column, bringing with him his family and a large number of followers.

Another stopping-place was upon the banks of a river, and after that at another river. Crossing this at a shallow part, we continued our march, and noticed that traces of the enemy were becoming more and more frequent. This gave us hope of a brush with them.

We were halted to prepare breakfast at a place called Inyezane, when we heard firing in front, and found that our skirmishers were engaged with a Zulu "impi." On pushing forward to the brow of a hill, we found ourselves under fire. Puffs of smoke were appearing in all directions from the bush away in front of us, and we therefore lay down, and fired at every spot from which a puff appeared.

It was my first appearance on a battlefield. We were told by our officers to keep ourselves cool and steady, and fire low; and I tried not to get carried away by the excitement, but it's not so easy, when you know that each puff may mean a dose of death to you or the man next you.

We had with us a naval brigade of two hundred and seventy bluejackets and marines from the *Tenedos* and *Active*, and these had charge of the waggons and two Gatlings. The Zulus came on in fine style, but the steady fire we kept up prevented them coming to close quarters. They, however, attempted a flanking movement; but Colonel Panell led a spirited charge, and cleared the heights, and the enemy were driven off, leaving about nine hundred killed and wounded upon the battlefield. I think we lost in the action seven killed, and about twenty-seven wounded. These we took with us, but left the enemy where they fell.

We had had no breakfast before the fight, and as we had to reach a certain distance each day, we had no refreshment till 9 p.m.

Next day we were overtaken by a native runner, who was taken to the General, and in consequence of the news he brought we were hurried forward with as little delay as possible. These runners are strange individuals; they take to running when they are tired of walking, and I noticed they seemed to get their breath better by so doing.

On the following morning, eleven days after the invasion of the country, we arrived at the village of Eshowe, about forty miles due north of the river Tugela, where there was a mission-station; and here we set to work to build a fort around the church, which was intended to be used as an hospital if required.

We formed a laager, into which we went for safety during the night, the day being occupied in building a fort. Here, upon its completion, we took up our position.

This was how we built the fort. The church tower in the centre was a look-out post for our best marksmen; and around the church, at a considerable distance, we dug a trench, some ten or twelve feet deep, and about twenty feet wide, and into this trench we planted stakes pointed at both ends. The earth from the trench formed a high breastwork, with steps formed on the inner side of the fort; and outside, beyond the trench, we dug small holes, at regular distances apart, into which we drove sharpened stakes, upon which we stretched wire to entangle the legs of the enemy who might venture within the maze.

Our position being considered very secure, the native contingent, with the mounted volunteer picnic-party, were, to the surprise of many of us, sent back, as they could be of no service and would make a considerable difference in our commissariat department.

The mystery of the runner's message was soon cleared up. It turned out that he was the bearer of bad news. A British force had been attacked in camp at Isandlwhana, and literally cut to pieces.

In confirmation of the terrible message we happened to capture about this time a Zulu soldier, belonging to the Kandampemvu Regiment, who was wearing a jacket and carrying a rifle which had belonged to a man of the 24th Regiment.

We questioned him about the battle, and the account he gave was that the soldiers and volunteers retired, fighting all the way, and as they got into the camp the Zulus intermingled with them. One party of soldiers came out from among the tents, and formed up a little above the waggons. They held their ground until their ammunition failed, when they were nearly all assegaied.

As I said before, what a private soldier knows about the plan of campaign is what he picks up from hearsay.

It soon leaked out that our fort was itself surrounded by Zulus, in such numbers that there was no possibility of leaving the place, either to go backward or forward, until reinforcements arrived. We were therefore put on short rations, and the small allowance of meat and flour which was doled out to us we cooked in various ways. For drinking purposes we had a small quantity of either tea, coffee, or lime juice; but we were altogether short of vegetables and tobacco.

I kept a diary while in Eshowe, and took note of the prices realised when the luxuries left behind by the mounted volunteers were put under the hammer, on the 22nd February 1879. Most of the goods were purchased by the officers, as prices were high: --

Item	£	s	d	Item	£	s	d
1½ lbs. tobacco	£1	9	0	1 small bottle of sauce	£1	1	0
1 small bottle of curry	0	14	0	1 pint of ketchup	0	15	6
1 large do.	1	7	0	1 box of sardines	0	11	0
7 cigars	0	9	0	1 bottle of ink	0	7	0
1 tin of condensed milk	0	14	6	1 pot salmon	0	15	6
1 do.	0	15	6	1 pot herrings	0	13	6
1 do.	0	18	0	1 lb. dubbin	0	9	6
1 do.	1	0	0	1 small packet of cocoa	0	11	0
1 tin of lobster .	0	13	6	1 ham (12 lbs.)	6	5	0
1 small bottle of pickles	1	6	0				

The last item, I remember, was knocked down to an officer of the 99th Regiment, who invited the Colonel to dine with him in the evening; but at the appointed time the feast was given up, for some person or persons unknown had stolen the joint!

We were now compelled to keep within the fort, except that occasionally we made raids in search of vegetables. Several times we visited native kraals, from which a few natives would fly on our approach, and here we sometimes found growing maize or pumpkins, which on our return we cooked and ate with much relish. But these raids were not unattended with danger, for frequently the Zulus would fire at us from the bush, and then there would be one or more wounded men to bring back, and place in the hospital tent. Each day, also, some of us were told off to guard the cattle outside the fort, and bring them back in safety at nightfall.

Doleful days were these; the rain used to come down in torrents, and we made our beds beneath the waggons, upon the damp ground, while creeping things crawled and ran over us as we slept. The officers used to sleep inside the waggons, and were, so far, a little more comfortable than the rank and file, but even they were roughing it.

We made the best of our time, now and then having an open-air concert, with choruses by all hands, at which times a few natives might be seen in the distance listening to our melodies; and now and then our marksmen would have a shot at them, for our rifles could reach them while theirs could not carry to us.

Sometimes the tables were turned, and frequently our mounted outposts would be attacked by Zulus, who crept up to them under cover of the long grass. One poor fellow rode back to the fort with more than a dozen wounds. How he managed to keep his seat and fight his way through the enemy I cannot tell. Those who fell into the hands of the Zulus were terribly mutilated, and left on the open ground to be found by their comrades on the following day, and carried back to the fort for burial.

That word "burial" reminds me of the funerals which so frequently took place, for typhoid fever came among us, and, despite the efforts of the doctors, carried off a good number of the men. The Rev. Mr. Ritchie, our chaplain, was a splendid man, and always hopeful and light-hearted. He attended all the funerals, none of which were very ceremonious; we simply wrapped the dead men in their blankets, and laid them in their graves without a parting volley, as ammunition was precious and we had no blank cartridges.

Time dragged wearily on, and there seemed no prospect of relief. Lieutenant Rowden, of the 99th Regiment, made several exploring expeditions, and ascertained the whereabouts of the Zulus; and on two or three occasions we captured from neighbouring kraals a considerable quantity of cattle, which were a welcome addition to our commissariat department.

Several of the Engineers who were with us manufactured a home-made heliograph, and were continually flashing signals to inform Lord Chelmsford of the desperate position we were in. For a long time these signals appeared to be unnoticed, but at last we learned that some reinforcements had arrived from St. Helena in *H.M.S. Shah*; and these, with a number of sailors forming part of the ship's crew, and others from *H.M.S. Boadicea*, together with 3300 whites, 1600 natives, and a small body of cavalry numbering about 160, with rocket tubes and nine-pounders, were marching to our relief under Lord Chelmsford.

To this encouraging information our men replied, cautioning the advancing army that a force of Zulus, estimated at about 35,000, were prepared to bar their progress.

I think it was about the 2nd of April when the relieving column arrived at Ginghilovo, three-quarters of the distance to Eshowe, and here they formed a laager, threw up earthworks, dug shelter pits, and prepared to spend the night. At daybreak the sentries observed the enemy stealing round the camp, apparently making observations; and within an hour or two they were seen advancing, in their usual skirmishing order, with the horns extended on either side, ready to sweep round the camp and attack it upon all points.

The 60th Rifles were prepared for them at the front, and opened a terrific fire, so that the Zulus, notwithstanding their courage and recklessness, did not get within three hundred yards of the camp. Then they changed their front, and attacked the side of the camp held by the 57th and 91st Regiments, making four fierce charges, none of which brought them up to the line of bayonets.

They then made a last attack on the left of the camp, where they came within ten or fifteen feet of the muzzles of the men's rifles, a few bold spirits even rushing forward and catching hold of the latter, and stabbing at the soldiers with their assegais. But the British lines stood firm, and as the enemy retired the handful of cavalry charged out upon them, worrying them as they fled.

We heard later on that the loss of the Zulus was close upon a thousand, while the British lost three killed, and had thirty-seven wounded.

Though we could hear the fighting, we made no sortie, but simply waited until the relief came, and I shall never forget that relief as long as I retain my wits. It *was* good to grasp the hands of men who had risked their lives for us, and how we did enjoy a "square meal" and a smoke. Our friends had brought provisions, but had carefully avoided overloading themselves. Early the next morning we made a successful raid on the kraal of a chief named Dabulamanzi, situated a few miles from Eshowe, and having procured some provisions, with payment in lead, we set out on our return journey to the Tugela.

As we turned our backs upon Eshowe, in which we had spent between seventy and eighty days, the Engineers blew up the fort, so as to leave nothing of which the Zulus could take advantage. We made it a rule to destroy all kraals which we passed on our march, so that our track was marked with smouldering ruins.

These kraals are built something like old-fashioned straw bee-hives. Long thin sticks are stuck into the ground in a circle, and joined together at the top; grass, straw, and twigs are threaded through the sticks, like basket-work, until the whole is weather-tight, almost airtight, I expect, except for the small hole through which one has to crawl. The word kraal stands for either a village or a hut, for the huts are seldom built singly.

We had no adventures on the return march; and camping once more at the Tugela, we waited while Lord Chelmsford continued his march to Durban for the purpose of arranging a general invasion of Zululand on a larger scale, with better organisation. For we had found the people more difficult to deal with than we at first expected.

Besting by the river-side we found time to talk over what had happened, and we then learned further particulars of the massacre at Isandlwhana.

Some of us were fortunate enough to receive papers from home, and I suppose every paper was read and passed on for the benefit of others. No one but a soldier on foreign service has any idea of the full value of a newspaper.

At last Lord Chelmsford fixed the 2nd of June as the day for the second general advance, which was to be made in three columns much strengthened. The first, being that with which I served, was, as on the last occasion, to proceed along the coast-road, with Durban, Fort Pearson, and Ginghilovo as its bases of operation. The second, or central column, was under Lord Chelmsford; and the third, or flying column, was commanded by General Wood.

While on the march, we learned that Sir Garnet Wolseley was to be sent out to take command over Lord Chelmsford, and was on his way on board *H.M.S. Forester*. I happened to be stationed at Port Durnford, assisting in landing stores, when the vessel arrived off the shore, but on account of the heavy sea running she returned to Durban, and disembarked Sir Garnet at that port.

Before he arrived at our camp, we were paraded and ordered to fire a general salute in honour of a victory gained by the second and third columns, and the destruction of the Zulu capital on the 4th of July.

On that day, the two British columns having met, -- whilst No. 1 had not overcome all its difficulties, -- took up a position near Ulundi, forming a large hollow square, with Gatling guns in the centre. Colonel Redvers Buller, who, with his cavalry, had done splendid service in reconnoitring the country, advanced and set the smaller kraals on fire. This opened the ball, and the Zulus at once commenced their attack in such numbers that the cavalry were after a while compelled to retire within the square. All assaults of the enemy were repulsed by steady volleys, and finally, seeing them wavering, Colonel Drury Lowe led a charge by the King's Dragoon Guards and scattered them in all directions.

Nothing then remained to be done but to destroy Cetewayo's kraals, and while this work was in progress, Mr. Archibald Forbes, the special correspondent of the Daily News, set off on an adventurous ride of thirty miles through the enemy's country, to report that the war was practically over.

The enemy's loss was estimated at fifteen thousand, while the English lost under a dozen, which, however, included Captain Wyatt-Edgell, and eighty wounded. The King fled from his capital, attended only by a few faithful followers, and after a wearisome chase he was run to earth on the 29th of August, and escorted to

Cape Town, where, with a few wives to share his captivity, he was allowed to reside as a political prisoner.

The Buffs were sent for two years to the Straits Settlements, and three years in Hong Kong; after which we returned to England, and I quitted the army.

LEONAUR

ALSO FROM LEONAUR
AVAILABLE IN SOFTCOVER OR HARDCOVER WITH DUST JACKET

EW2 EYEWITNESS TO WAR SERIES
CAPTAIN OF THE 95th (Rifles) *by Jonathan Leach*

An officer of Wellington's Sharpshooters during the
Peninsular, South of France and Waterloo Campaigns
of the Napoleonic Wars.

SOFTCOVER : **ISBN 1-84677-001-7**
HARDCOVER : **ISBN 1-84677-016-5**

WFI THE WARFARE FICTION SERIES
NAPOLEONIC WAR STORIES
by Sir Arthur Quiller-Couch

Tales of soldiers, spies, battles & Sieges from the
Peninsular & Waterloo campaigns

SOFTCOVER : **ISBN 1-84677-003-3**
HARDCOVER : **ISBN 1-84677-014-9**

EWI EYEWITNESS TO WAR SERIES
RIFLEMAN COSTELLO *by Edward Costello*

The adventures of a soldier of the 95th (Rifles) in the
Peninsular & Waterloo Campaigns of the Napoleonic wars.

SOFTCOVER : **ISBN 1-84677-000-9**
HARDCOVER : **ISBN 1-84677-018-1**

MCI THE MILITARY COMMANDERS SERIES
JOURNALS OF ROBERT ROGERS OF THE RANGERS *by Robert Rogers*

The exploits of Rogers & the Rangers in his own words
during 1755-1761 in the French & Indian War.

SOFTCOVER : **ISBN 1-84677-002-5**
HARDCOVER : **ISBN 1-84677-010-6**

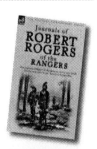

AVAILABLE ONLINE AT
www.leonaur.com
AND OTHER GOOD BOOK STORES

Lightning Source UK Ltd.
Milton Keynes UK
171546UK00001B/192/A